Praise for Astrology: Art and

"Astrology is the language of consciousness. It contains many occult messages about the mysteries of life encoded in its symbols and geometric angles. It takes years to learn the basic astrological language and decades to master this ancient science. But the goal is not its mastery, as not everyone studies astrology to become a professional astrologer. The goal is the path that we take in our efforts to learn and apply these celestial studies to our terrestrial life. This path requires that these profound esoteric truths be communicated in a language that is understandable, sensible, and stimulating. It is not an easy task to be the translator of invisible energies so that they are seen by our eyes and accepted by our minds. In her very user friendly new textbook **Astrology: Art and Science**, Sandy Anastasi does just that and she does it with grace, ease, and erudition. This book deserves to be in the collection of every new student of our cosmic discipline and will add accuracy and simplicity to the reference libraries of all established astrologers and astrology teachers.

—Alan Oken, Astrologer

Sandy's comprehensive yet simple approach to Astrology is a must read for anyone who wants to learn more about themselves and their loved ones. As always, Sandy takes a subject matter that could be considered difficult and makes it easy and enjoyable to learn.

—Jonathan Louis, Psychic Medium

I have known Sandy Anastasi professionally and followed her work for thirty years now. Many people study astrology and then decide to write books or teach. But very few have Sandy's unique, innate awareness of the intimacy of science and art involved in astrology. She is a born teacher. I especially love her diagrams and scientific illustrations in this book. Sandy makes what could be a difficult study, easy. I have recommended this book in its earlier version,

Basic Astrology, *for years and will continue to do so because I also learn something new every time I read her work. Sandy Anastasi is a gifted teacher and metaphysician. All those who stumble upon or are directed to her teachings are fortunate indeed.*

—Joan Kilgan, Vesta Astrological Counseling

I began to study astrology with Sandy Anastasi more than twenty years ago, and in my experience she remains one of the most gifted intuitives and teachers of astrology. Although written in an uncomplicated way, this is not just another book about sun signs, but rather, a book that helps beginning and intermediate students learn about chart synthesis through exercises following each chapter. Sandy's understanding of human psychology and personal relationships helps readers shift away from an old notion of Astrology as "fortune telling," to a more contemporary understanding and use of it as a relevant tool for knowing one's self in relation to the people and events we co-create in our lives. This book is highly recommended for any beginning or intermediate student of astrology.

—Mary Spremulli, MA, CCC-SLP. Voice Aerobics, LLC

Books by Sandy Anastasi

The Anastasi System of Psychic Development Series:

Level 1: The Fundamentals

Level 2: Energy and Auras

Level 3: Tools and Toys

Level 4: An Introduction to Channeling and Spirit Communication

Level 5: Developing the Energy and Skill in Spirit Communication

Level 6: Healing in Spirit Communication (to be released)

Astrology:

Astrology: Art and Science

Intermediate Astrology

Tarot:

Tarot Reader's Workbook: A Comprehensive Guide from Beginner to Master

Kabbala:

Kabbala Pathworking

ASTROLOGY:
Art and Science

Sandy Anastasi

BALBOA.
PRESS
A DIVISION OF HAY HOUSE

Founder of The Anastasi System of Psychic Development and Co-Founder of The Astrological Institute of Integrated Studies

Balboa Press books may be ordered through booksellers or by contacting:

Balboa Press
A Division of Hay House
1663 Liberty Drive
Bloomington, IN 47403
www.balboapress.com
1 (877) 407-4847

Because of the dynamic nature of the Internet, any web addresses or links contained in this book may have changed since publication and may no longer be valid. The views expressed in this work are solely those of the author and do not necessarily reflect the views of the publisher, and the publisher hereby disclaims any responsibility for them.

The author of this book does not dispense medical advice or prescribe the use of any technique as a form of treatment for physical, emotional, or medical problems without the advice of a physician, either directly or indirectly. The intent of the author is only to offer information of a general nature to help you in your quest for emotional and spiritual well-being. In the event you use any of the information in this book for yourself, which is your constitutional right, the author and the publisher assume no responsibility for your actions.

Printed in the United States of America.

ISBN: 978-1-4525-8392-1 (sc)
ISBN: 978-1-4525-8393-8 (e)

Library of Congress Control Number: 2013918206

Balboa Press rev. date: 11/19/2013

Acknowledgments

My deepest thanks to my old friend, Lynn Murgatroyd, who single handedly, dragged me into the amazing world of Astrology more than 30 years ago.

Thanks also to my sister, Pam Boltson, who stimulated my earliest interest in the stars. Thanks to Alan Oken for his leadership and amazing contributions to the field of Astrology. You have been a constant inspiration. And thank you John Edward, my friend, for writing the forward to this book and for helping to introduce people worldwide to this new-old science through your work! Thank you for sharing the journey and lightening the load!

A very special thank you goes to my old partner John Maerz, without whom my journey into the world of Astrology and my years of study, teaching, and writing would have been incomplete. Thank you for the work you did formatting, editing, and creating the graphics for the first edition of this text, *Basic Astrology*.

Thanks to my editors, Emily and Rick Manelius, and Pam Boltson, also to Charles Filius, Rick Manelius, and Trish Vidal for their high resolution graphics.

Heartfelt thanks go, as always, to RonTourville, for his constant support and to my personal assistant Lisa Freeman.

Thanks, too, to all of those students whose need and encouragement helped bring this book to fruition. And a final thanks to every one of you, whose continued interest in Astrology makes all the effort a joy.

Table of Contents

Foreword

by John Edward

Dear Student of the Universe:

Clearly, if you are reading this, you have been searching to unravel and maybe unlock some of the mystery of who you are as a person and to learn about this vast Universe, or playground, that we exist and live within.

Well, I am excited to confirm that you have found one of Earth's best-kept secrets, weapons, and ultimately, KEYS to do just that for you in this lifetime. That is Sandy Anastasi.

Sandy Anastasi has dedicated her entire life to the betterment of mankind and raising awareness. I have stated over and over that she is the only person who can claim to be JOHN EDWARD's teacher, as she was the *most* pivotal instrument in the orchestration of my psychic development. I find her the go-to person for all things metaphysical. Her books, tapes, classes, and webinars are beneficial for the beginner on his journey, or for the professional who has been on his path for decades, but needs to be the student once again. Sandy is "the Teacher's Teacher" regarding metaphysics. This book is just one of the tools, or keys, that Sandy has written to help you on your journey.

In all areas of my work, whether it is a private reading or lecturing to thousands, teaching a workshop or doing radio or television, Sandy's teachings bleed through as the vocabulary and process that I was empowered with. For that, I thank her openly.

I am excited for you that you've discovered this book, and more importantly, are on your journey to discovering and exploring the miracle of YOU through Astrology. Sandy's book will be pivotal for you as well. There is a part of me that feels so excited for what you are about to embark on . . . . Let the discovery begin!

I know Sandy will leave her indelible touch on your life as she has mine.

With gratitude,

John Edward
Psychic, Medium, host of *Crossing Over with John Edward*

Author's Foreword

From my earliest childhood, when my sister, Pam, and I would lie out on the front lawn counting stars and trying to identify the many constellations painted on the velvety black sky above us, astrology has had a very special attraction for me. Pam wished on the brightest star she could find, that I later discovered was Jupiter, for a diamond ring. Sure enough, after a year of wishing, her little diamond ring turned up in the sandbox courtesy of the latest bucket of sand my father brought home from the beach. I was hooked.

Stargazing and star wishing brought me to a place where I felt intimately connected to them, and through them, connected to myself and to the Creator. They were the consistent arrangement of heavenly bodies that said, "You are home." They were the promise of life and travel and existence beyond my small patch of Earth. astrology became my favorite science all the way back then—Astrology, not Astronomy, because Astrology remembered the human qualities that astronomy never embraced.

I read my daily horoscope in the newspaper. I instinctively knew the stars affected us all in unseen ways. I was given a book showing the major constellations and searched for them in the night sky. I was fascinated that each constellation had the name of a Greek or Roman god or goddess, and so I became a young student of mythology. I read the *Iliad* and the *Odyssey* and was more interested in the playful meddling of the gods than the journey it depicted. I watched movies using Greek and Roman mythology as a backdrop. Later, in college, I studied Mythology offside-by-side with my Comparative Religion class. I was, and am, convinced that the character of each god or goddess in classic mythology is a key to understanding the character of the planet or constellation to which it has been assigned. My studies of mythology gave me a brand new appreciation of how the stars and planets affect each of our psyches.

I was 14 years old when Pam gave me my first astrology book. It is now out of print but was titled, *The Coffee Table Book of Astrology*. For the first time, I realized that Astrology was indeed a recognized field, a science in its own right, even if considered a poor and overly imaginative relative of astronomy. I knew better.

I gobbled that book but stumbled over the section dealing with chart construction. Apparently, the author had not discovered the many simple methods of chart construction and so made the business of casting a horoscope almost impossible to do without a college degree in higher mathematics. The effect on me was that I set aside astrology as a potential field of work for many years, still enjoying my horoscope and casual discussions, but knowing I was not up to the mathematical side of it.

Then, in my late twenties, a friend convinced me to enroll in the only actual astrology class I have ever taken. Of course I have attended a myriad of seminars over the years by such greats in the field as Alan Oken, Robert Hand, Karen Hamacher-Zondag, Jeff Greene, and many others too numerous to name. Ivan Martin, sole proprietor of The Society of International Astrologers, taught a 12-session class on the Sun Signs. He was highly entertaining, he re-opened my heart to astrology.

However, when it became obvious that he was not going to teach casting a chart, I dropped out of his classes, disappointed. This was before the age of computers and chart construction had to be by hand. I was desolate. I was foiled again! But help from a higher source intervened. In a local new age bookstore (made famous by its longevity and succession of colorful owners) called *Food For Mind, Body, and Soul* in Huntington, N.Y., a book by Sidney Omar, *My World of Astrology* literally jumped off the shelf and hit me. It landed on the floor open to a two-page section giving simple instructions even I could follow on how to cast a horoscope. I bought the book, and the rest is history.

Later I leveraged Sydney Omar's technique with the simple and easy-to-follow directions Alan Oken gives in his classic, *Alan Oken's Complete Astrology—The Classic Guide To Modern Astrology* to create an easy beginner's way to cast a chart. That technique is described in detail in my *Intermediate Astrology* book, which is currently being updated and is scheduled for release later this year. It focuses on chart construction and planetary aspects, and places emphasis on reading the chart. Like the work you are holding, it is highly interactive and gives lots of opportunity to exercise your own interpretation skills, with built-in feedback.

In this book, *Astrology, Art and Science: A Workbook,* I give you a simple way to construct a solar chart so that armed with only an ephemeris (a book that lists where all the planets are for every single day over a 100-year period), you can quickly plot and eye-up your own and all of your friends' and family's charts. You can understand so much about the people you interact with every day from astrology! The faster I can get a handle on someone's astrological make-up, the happier I am and the more comfortable I am with that person. Even in this age of computers where all you have to do now is press a few buttons and you have a chart, I personally find just opening an ephemeris easier and faster than taking the time to plug in all of the birth data to get a chart out of a computer. These days, I only cast charts for actual clients, and yes, I use a computer to do that. But armed with just your day, month, and year of birth, I can know more things about you, and how you relate to the world around you, than you can imagine.

The book you are holding is your doorway to being able to do the same thing!

It is, in a sense, an astrological primer. The early chapters give a general overview of the field of Astrology so that you will have enough information to move around in the astrological community (and it is a LARGE community). You will not be at a loss for words because you will have the vocabulary required to interact with other people in the field. The real meat of the book, though, is a psychological and energetic look at each of the planets, signs, and houses. I have attempted to give you not only definitions of these, but also insight into the childhood patterning of each sign so that you will have the tools to move beyond the definitions in these pages to create your own interpretations.

I have long felt that astrology should be taught to children starting in elementary school and continuing through high school. If we all grew up with astrology, we would understand that we are all meant to be different. We would understand our differences and that each one of us has particular strengths that fill in the weaknesses of others and vice versa. We would learn to work together from an early age and to accept one another as we are.

What a wonderful world that would be, wouldn't it?

In love and light,

Sandy Anastasi
Astrologer and Psychic Channel

This book is dedicated to my sister, Pam,
who first set me on the path to Astrology.

Introduction

This book was originally written to give my beginning level astrology students a written guide to work with as they proceeded through their classroom studies. It was first published in a far rougher format than this in 1979 under the name *Basic Astrology,* and has moved through many revisions over the years. This latest revision, updated by readers' requests, is the product of thirty years of practicing and teaching the metaphysical science that is my first love—astrology.

This current version is still directed toward beginners, though anyone interested in astrology will benefit from the clear and direct approach and the psychological and spiritual foundations of the signs, planets, and houses in astrology that are given here. My basic premise is that if you know WHY something works a certain way, it is easy to project how it will function under differing conditions. The psychological insights put forth in this book will help you to do just that.

This workbook is particularly helpful for beginners, as it is an excellent introduction to the entire field of astrology and covers the basic tools and knowledge necessary to interpret a simple chart. However, any student of astrology interested in learning interpretation methods will find that it gives a good foundation in the art of astrological interpretation by teaching simple techniques that you can build upon right from the start. I believe that if you integrate interpretation with understanding as you go along, you will develop this skill with ease, as a natural part of your astrological arsenal. And the students I have taught over the years have proven that this approach works. Astrology is a science, but interpreting an astrological chart is an art. To be a good astrologer, you need both abilities. This workbook is designed to help you develop them. If your desire is just to understand more about what astrology is, this book is for you. If you are a complete beginner and want a simple and understandable guide that will quickly have you doing astrology, this is it. If you are an experienced student and have lots of knowledge but experience difficulty with interpretation, this book will be a valuable tool. If you are an experienced astrologer who wants to beef up on your personality types or interpretation skills, you'll find this work helpful as well. This book really is for everyone.

Your journey begins here. Enjoy!

Overview

We'll be covering the following areas:

- What astrology is and how it works
- A brief history of astrology
- What an astrology chart is
- Various approaches to the field of astrology
- Some various types of astrology
- Some different types of charts that may be used, and their purposes
- Detailed characteristics of each Sun sign from a psychological and spiritual perspective
- The characteristics of each planet, focusing on how its energy works
- Detailed descriptions of each house, or life-area, in a chart
- How to cast a solar chart and read it

At the end of each chapter are exercises designed to guide you through beginning interpretation methods. Be easy on yourself. Astrology is a very subjective science, so if your findings do not agree with the offered interpretation, it does not mean you are wrong. Alternative interpretations are possible. Read back through the chapter again to see if you would add anything to your own interpretation or change it in any way.

Your study of astrology should be fun and you should find solid uses for astrology in your life immediately. Those are the two things that will have you quickly loving astrology, thirsting for more knowledge of it, using it, and working with it. So, this book and all the exercises in it are offered in the spirit of opening your mind to the newest—oldest science on the planet.

Chapter 1

What is Astrology?

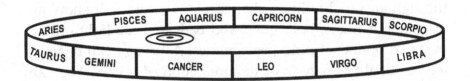

What is Astrology?

Astrology is the study of the movement of the stars and planets through the heavens and how their energies affect us from birth to death. Ancient sources tell us that all the other sciences are outgrowths of astrology, including astronomy. In fact, they tell us that astrology is the oldest science known to man.

Astrology, like psychology, helps us understand our characteristics and abilities and, how the energies of the planets bring about circumstances for change and growth throughout our lifetimes. An astrology chart will show all of your potentials, both good and bad. It sheds light on the past and predicts future probabilities. Astrology can be used for personality analysis or for prediction of events. You can use it as a tool for self-discovery and self-development. You can use it to explore and understand your relationships and your family dynamics or to find your spiritual path. Astrology can be an aid in identifying and repairing actual or potential health problems.

Some astrologers use it as an aid in financial investments or to help find things or people. Some astrologers have successfully used it to predict elections and outcomes of events and to foresee and gain insights into Earth-changing events. Astrology also is one of the means some practitioners use to discover past lives and to gain insight into the soul's journey after death.

Most importantly, perhaps, the artful use of astrology can aid you to make better and wiser life choices.

Every culture on the planet has its own version of astrology. The most common type in the Western world is Earth-centered astrology. But there is a school of astrology used to look at cosmic events that puts the Sun at the center, which is called heliocentric astrology. The Chinese zodiac is lunar based, whereas most Western astrology systems are solar based. Hindu astrology is based on the sidereal zodiac and often uses the moment of conception, whereas Western astrologers use the moment of birth to cast the natal chart. Native American Indians had their own system of astrology, with the Moon and solar cycles being an integral part of most tribal traditions.

All of these systems are effective. They are all different. But they are all worthy of investigation by the curious student of astrology. The one used in this book is an Earth-centered, Western approach to astrology, which is the most commonly taught and used in the Western hemisphere.

Astrology is a metaphysical science that has attracted millions of people worldwide for centuries—because it works.

A Brief History of Astrology

No one has any idea how old astrology really is or even where it originated, though that subject could easily be a matter of hot debate between Eastern and Western astrologers. Every early culture has left indications that some form of astrology was practiced within it, including ancient Egyptians Mesopotamians Greeks Chinese Africans and Mayans.

The earliest astrologers had to not only cast their own astrology charts or star maps, but they had to chart the planets' movements as well! Be glad you are studying this in the twenty-first century, where computers can do these things! I do think it is important to know how an astrological chart is derived, which is why I wrote *Intermediate Astrology* my second astrology book. It teaches a simple method of chart construction and how to identify and interpret the aspects, or energetic connections, among the planets in your chart.

But for students who would rather forego the technical aspects of this science, today there are countless Internet sites, smartphone apps, new age stores, and libraries that are more than happy to employ a computer program to construct your natal chart for you, as well as my own website, www. sandyanastasi.com. All you need to do is to supply your date, place, and time of birth.

Both prior to and during the Middle Ages, astrology was the principal science in Europe. Every king had his astrologer. Nostradamus, the most famous of all psychics, predicted future events that astonish us to this day using astrology, as well as a crystal ball. Astrologers cast birth charts of royal children to foretell the greatness these children would or would not achieve. Children were betrothed based upon whether their natal or birth charts were compatible. astrologer acted in the capacity of both predictors and advisors. Special astrological charts were cast to foretell the outcome of events or of coming disasters.

These early astrologers were primarily interested in using astrology as a tool for prediction, and largely, they were able to do so with astonishing accuracy. One history tells of an astrologer who predicted that a king would die by a lance piercing his helmet, and the prediction not only came true but also at the exact time it was predicted to happen!

Today, unsurprisingly, most people associate astrology with the ability to tell the future, although in this sense, here in the Western world, it is no longer as accurate as it was during the Middle Ages. Experienced astrologers can still make the same kind of potentially accurate predictions, but individual consciousness has changed. Modern man is exerting more freedom of choice than ever before in the history of our planet. As a result, more often than not we are able to alter the circumstances of our lives, thereby averting potential disasters in them. For this reason, modern-day astrologers find themselves more and more often in the role of counselors as opposed to fortune tellers.

Astrology today tends to focus more on what it can tell us about personality and how those personality traits affect someone positively or negatively. In fact, future predictions are usually offered in the form of suggesting several possible ways a person having their chart read could use the energy at work. It is in this way that the twenty-first century astrologer can help his or her client to make more intelligent life choices. The astrologer can tell what energy is coming into the life of the client and how, based upon the positive and negative personality traits in the client's chart, he or she is most likely to react. Then the astrologer can outline other potential ways of dealing with the energy, also based upon the client's positive and negative personality traits. This gives the client something very special. It gives him or her choice and a better grasp on his or her life through choice. What a wonderful gift to give!

The astrologer can also provide the client with the expected duration of time that any energy coming into the client's life will last. What another wonderful gift that is to give. It all starts with understanding the basic meanings of the planets, signs, and houses, which you will be learning about shortly.

Surprisingly, it is easier to make valid and unchanging predictions for large groups, such as nations, than it is for individuals, since these, composed of so many individuals, find it much more difficult to change from a chosen path of action. Hence, individuals have more freedom of choice than nations do.

In the Western world, astrologers have long been aware of the fact that personal choice alters outcome. This is only now becoming more accepted in the Eastern world, where astrologers have traditionally been more fatalistic in their approach.

Astrologers have been employed throughout history by both governments and religious groups. Astrological symbols appear on walls in caves throughout Africa and also in the Great Pyramid in Egypt. The early Roman Catholic Church used astrologers and astrology, which is one of the reasons astrological symbols are prominent in many ancient religious paintings. Many people are unaware that the US government employed the services of an astrologer during World War II. The astrologer was Sidney Omarr, and his services were used largely to keep the US government aware of what Germany's next military moves might be, as he made an effort to second-guess Hitler's astrologer!

And many astrologers believe that Ronald Reagan chose his time to be sworn in as governor of California based on astrological guidance. Why would choosing the time to be sworn in be an asset? Because the time he was sworn in was the birth time of his tenure in office—and by choosing his own time, he could choose a chart that would enhance the characteristics he desired in his governorship! You could use the same concept in choosing a birth date for a business you are forming, a move you are making, or a relationship you are beginning.

It is significant to recognize that governments still use astrologers. Some things *are* worth keeping.

No history of astrology, however brief, would be complete without mentioning Evangeline Adams. Modern-day astrologers owe a great deal to her. She was the personal astrologer of J. P. Morgan, the shipping magnate. During her tenure as his astrologer, the magnate became very successful. Because of J. P. Morgan's enemies, Evangeline was arrested and jailed under a form of the vagrancy laws that originated in England and were brought to the United States.

Unfortunately, these laws are still active today in many states and limit the ability to legally practice many *other sciences* in the metaphysical field. But in all fifty states astrology is legal, thanks to Evangeline Adams. J. P. Morgan supplied an attorney that agreed to represent her if she first proved to him that astrology was real and that it worked. This she did over a period of time, teaching the attorney astrology using her jail cell as a classroom. On the day of her court appearance, Evangeline was asked to use astrology to do a personality analysis of the judge's son, which she did with such accuracy that the judge threw the case against her out of his court. His decision holds to this day.

Astrology Basics

The study of astrology must start with a psychological and energetic understanding of the planets, signs, and houses, which is what this book is about. Such insight gives each individual enormous understanding of the principles underlying every aspect of our world, including, of course, personality.

Armed with such knowledge, you can better understand cause and effect and the inter-relationships between things and people. I am also advocate teaching basic astrology to children so that they might come to understand each other's differences, and learn to cherish them rather than despise them.

Imagine being able to have true insight into why you do or do not like someone. Wouldn't it be easier to work with or live with that person if you knew the cause? Then you could find a way to accept and interact with that person, or with clear conscience to just avoid him or her. And wouldn't it make life a lot easier for couples if they not only knew and understood the things that attracted them to one another, but also could plan for the time when their needs would change and those attractive things might be overshadowed by negative, disruptive ones? Through astrology they might even know when those disruptive events or behaviors would end—or if they would end and how to best deal with them until that time or infinitely, if needed.

Astrology gives us a tremendous advantage in moving through life. I personally believe that astrology's greatest gift to us is self-understanding. Yet its use as a predictive tool that can help us to make better and wiser life choices is indisputable in my opinion.

The natal (or birth) astrology chart, often called the birth chart, gives a wonderful insight into personality and character potential. The well-known psychologist and astrologer Carl Jung was among the first astrologers to utilize a psychological approach to astrology. He found that years could safely be saved in the clinical treatment of his clients by using astrology. Study of the natal chart led him straight to the problem areas. Often patients will cover their major issues by focusing their complaints away from those issues. An understanding of the problem through study of the natal astrology chart prevents that. It allows the psychologist to go straight to the problem, without having to first work through those layers of defense and misdirection that the patient may have erected. Many subsequent astrologers, including me, have had the occasion to work with clients who brought our chart delineations to their psychologist. The psychologists were amazed at the accuracy of the information and were able to help the clients more quickly and directly because of that information. What a wonderful tool, when used properly and integrated with other fields!

It is my sincere hope that in the future astrologers and psychologists may work closely together, or perhaps even integrate the two fields, to better serve the needs of their clients and patients.

The approach used to understand the planets and signs in this book will be a psychological one. This is not because I am trying to make a psychologist out of anyone, but rather because I've discovered that a strong foundation in the psychology of how a planet or sign works will give you the best all around insight into reading charts, regardless of how you intend to eventually use your astrology.

Some Types of Astrology

Psychological or *personality-based astrology* tells about a person's character and personality traits, good and bad. Using this type of astrology, you can gain insight into a person's history, motives, desires, and needs, even their family experiences. This is the most common type of astrology and, this is where the astrological journey begins for most people. Psychological or personality-based astrology is a phenomenal tool for knowing yourself and for improving your relationships with others, as well as every other aspect of your life. This book's primary purpose is to focus on this area. No matter what other forms of astrology attract you, a good foundation in this area of astrology is necessary.

Spiritual astrology can be based upon the factors of the natal chart to better understand the soul's purpose in this life, or can be based upon the mundane, esoteric, and hierarchal rulers of the signs as given by Alice Bailey—but that is an advanced astrology that is beyond the scope of this book.

Predictive astrology uses such things as *transits, progressions, and solar arc progressions* to determine what is coming up in your life. *Transits* are where the planets are right now. When an astrologer looks at where present transiting planets are passing through the natal or birth chart, he or she can see what things in that chart are being activated and worked on. *Progressions* and *solar-arc progressions* are advanced techniques that astrologers use to mathematically move the planets in the birth chart forward a tiny amount each year. This movement shows the gradual growth of the personality. Transits and progressions can be used together to give very accurate predictions. It's like the progression is the archer pulling back the bow string and the transit is the arrow being released. Since these are advanced techniques, they will not be discussed in this book; but if your interest lies in predictive astrology you should definitely plan on studying this facet of astrology.

Relationship astrology explains the positive and negative ways two or more people may interact based upon psychological studies of their birth charts. In relationship astrology it is possible to see not only the problems two people may have, but also their best solutions. By *progressing* the two individual's charts, or analyzing the *transits* to them, predictions and future guidance may also be given.

Medical astrology helps to isolate areas of potential health problems and what means can be used to deal with them as determined by the birth chart and transiting planets.

Horary astrology is used to answer direct questions or to find objects or people.

Financial astrology involves prediction of the stock market and economic patterns and is especially useful in our changing times.

Electoral astrology is most often used for selecting a time or date to hold an event but is sometimes used to help predict the outcome of political elections.

Weather—and *Earth-change astrology,* including the prediction of seismic events, is and area of study for many leading edge astrologers today.

These are just some of the more common types of astrology that you may encounter in your own journey of discovery. All are worth pursuing.

How Astrology Works

Astrology is the study of the movement of the planets and stars, and the effects their movements have on people, animals, governments, cultures, nations, ideas, and things. In essence, that means everything that exists.

No one truly knows exactly how or why astrology works, but one theory is that planets and stars emit rays of energy, which, when absorbed cause us to feel and to behave in certain ways.

There's a well-known vintage saying that astrologers use that says, The stars impel—they do not compel! That is important to remember. The energy of the planets motivates us from within and causes us to choose to act and behave in certain ways. It doesn't apply external force. The planets do not make us do anything. They only motivate us to follow a certain path. As long as we remember that, we also will always know that astrology helps us to make healthy choices. In this manner, it encourages our self-determination.

It's easy to see this relative to the Sun, the life-giver of our own solar system, because we have all had the occasion to have felt our spirits lifted or to have our health and vitality improved, after spending some time out of doors soaking up some rays. Yet, we also have all felt ourselves become overtired, even getting drained of energy after spending too long in the Sun.

It would seem that exposure to planetary energies can have either a positive or a negative effect; depending upon how the energy is experienced and used.

Another theory of how planets might affect us is through their magnetic energy. This is most obvious with those bodies that are somewhat near to the earth, like the moon.

Everyone is familiar with the effects of the Moon. Its gravitational pull creates the ocean's tides, regulates the female reproductive cycle, and even the rise and fall of all fluid production and retention in the body. Doctors are all well aware that surgical procedures done on a full Moon are likely to be accompanied by far more bleeding than those done on a new Moon. And of course, people who work with the mentally ill are aware that additional security and personnel are recommended in dealing with the intensified emotional outbursts of patients around the full Moon each month.

But regardless of how the planetary energies manage to affect us, the fact is that they do. And for many centuries, astrologers from all over the world have been charting and tracking the various planets and constellations and recording events that allowed them to slowly draw conclusions about how each planet acts upon our world and upon us.

Furthermore, by tracking these planets through the astrological signs they moved through, astrologers have been able to discern that the planets do act differently according to each sign. Part of the art of becoming an astrologer is learning to interpret the different ways a planet might act by considering the position it is in.

Astrologers now have a very good idea how each planet, and each sign behaves. The art of astrology is to assemble, integrate, and interpret what the combined effects of the planets will be, as seen in the natal astrology chart, and then use this knowledge to counsel, predict, or advise.

Chapter 2

Astrology Charts and the Art of Reading Them

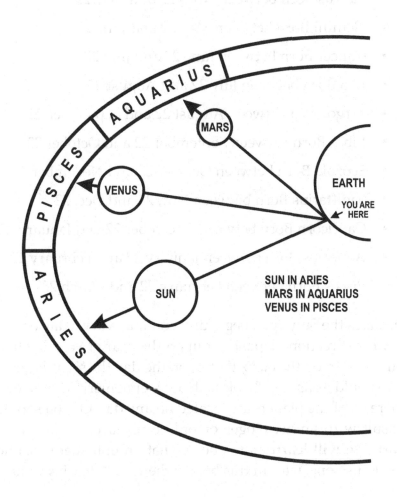

EARTH

YOU ARE HERE

SUN IN ARIES
MARS IN AQUARIUS
VENUS IN PISCES

The Sun Signs

Most people are aware of their Sun sign and some of the qualities it is supposed to represent. For those of you who don't know this, the Sun sign is the sign that the Sun was traveling through on the day of your birth. The following dates are approximate, as calendar dates for the exact beginning and ending of each sign often vary from year to year.

- Aries Born between March 22 and April 22
- Taurus Born between April 22 and May 22
- Gemini Born between May 22 and June 22
- Cancer Born between June 22 and July 22
- Leo Born between July 22 and August 22
- Virgo Born between August 22 and September 22
- Libra Born between September 22 and October 22
- Scorpio Born between October 22 and November 22
- Sagittarius Born between Nov. 22 and Dec. 22
- Capricorn Born between December 22 and January 22
- Aquarius Born between January 22 and February 22
- Pisces Born between February 22 and March 22

The dates the Sun signs begin and end may vary a day or two in either direction, depending upon the year of your birth. If you are born on the cusp, that is, on the day the sign changes, you should consult a book called an ephemeris that shows where all of the planets are located on any day. Or you should consult with an astrologer or online resource to cast your chart. We will learn more about what an ephemeris is, and how to use one, later in this book, when I will teach you how to cast a simple solar chart so that you may use astrology to better understand not only yourself, but also your friends and family.

Most people, once they know and have studied a little bit about their Sun sign, wonder why it doesn't really suit them. They wonder why the daily astrological forecasts offered in most newspapers, and which are based exclusively on the Sun sign, seem to be only partial fits.

The reason is that although the Sun's location when you were born is important, there also are a lot of other factors that need to be considered. There are eight other planets plus the Moon, which all have an effect on you

When an astrologer casts an astrological chart for you, he or she places all of these planets in the chart and weighs all of these factors in evaluating it.

This is one of the primary reasons I will teach you to create a solar chart in this book. Even though there are online services that can have a computer cast charts for you, the hands-on experience of using an ephemeris to locate the planets and then create a chart helps you to learn the art of interpretation more quickly. It is as if it helps your mind to make the connections as your hand is writing!

A natal astrology chart is, in effect, a map of exactly where the Sun, Moon, and planets were at your day, time, and place of birth. This is a sort of blueprint for your personality. As you grow and evolve, you can enhance one part of that blueprint, you can minimize or ignore another part, yet the basic structure that you are forever building upon remains evident throughout your life.

That blueprint shows your potential talents and abilities, as well as your character deficiencies. However, it does not hold them carved in granite. Potentials may be developed. Deficiencies may be overcome. The natal astrology chart shows only the raw material you have to work with.

So, the reason that we generally feel that we are only getting half of the story when we read about our Sun sign is because we are. The Sun is indeed the most important of the planets from an astrological viewpoint, followed closely by the Moon. But remember, those eight other planets also are important. Each gives insight into different areas of you and your life.

And, although we will not be using them throughout this beginner's workbook, there also are a host of other bodies in space—asteroids, planetoids, constellations, and others, that many astrologers consider in their evaluations of clients' charts. These are of less importance, and yet may still have a bearing on certain aspects of a chart.

How a Natal Astrology Chart Begins

Early astrologers plotted the natal chart by drawing a map of the heavens, or cosmos, as viewed from the earth at the time and place a person was born. We still use these maps today, although ours are a bit more detailed. Sometimes the natal chart is referred to as a *birth chart*, a *star chart* or a *star map*.

These first Western astrologers began their map with a simple symbol—the circle with the dot at its center. This circle represents the cosmos about you, while the dot at the center represents the essence of yourself. Interestingly, this is also the symbol used to represent the Sun. (See Figure 1, following.)

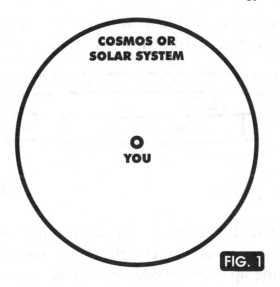

Having drawn this simple symbol, these first astrologers began to create a map of the heavens by placing the various signs of the zodiac around the cosmos or solar system they had drawn, leaving the individual point at the center. The earliest astrologers knew that man and our Earth were not at the center of the universe; but they also knew that each individual man and woman perceived themselves to be at the very center of their own universe, and the forces about them would act upon them.

This type of astrology, which places the earth and each of us at the center of our universe, is called geocentric astrology. Almost all Western astrologers use this type of astrology to cast natal charts.

The signs of the zodiac are not inventions. Each is actually a constellation. The twelve astrological signs we know as the Sun signs lie all around the horizon and they are, of course, visible through a telescope and sometimes on clear nights with the naked eye.

Figure 2 shows the constellations that comprise our present zodiac and where these constellations lie along the horizon.

ARIES | PISCES | AQUARIUS | CAPRICORN | SAGITTARIUS | SCORPIO | TAURUS | GEMINI | CANCER | LEO | VIRGO | LIBRA

FIG. 2

I've often found it interesting that when astronomer friends have tried to point out how well the arrangement of the star group making up each constellation resembles its supposed symbol (for example, the famous bull of Taurus), I fail to be able to see it clearly. Yet in the character of each Sun sign the symbol is apparent to me. The ancient people who named each astrological sign and assigned its symbol surely seemed to have hit upon the character quite beautifully, even if they sometimes left a great deal to the imagination in their tracing of the constellations. An astronomer might tell you this is because the stars are slowly drifting apart over time, or that it is because the ancients used a different number of Sun signs than we use today—and both reasons also would be correct.

Figure 2 has been compressed to show the cosmos and our solar system as a flat disc because this is actually more accurate than the circle shown in Figure 1. Our galaxy, the Milky Way, has been described as a spinning plate. Our solar system, located near the edge of the Milky Way, is also a spinning disc, with most of our planets revolving in a single plane about our Sun. The twelve constellations that make up our zodiac physically can be located along the outer edge, the horizon of this larger disc.

Many people do not realize that our solar system is also moving. Just as the earth we live on and all of the other planets in our solar system revolve about our Sun, our Sun revolves around a point somewhere in the center of the Milky Way, possibly the star known as Alpha Centauri—or at least that is what many astrologers believe. Astronomers are not yet in agreement on this, though most are now accepting that there is a central point that our solar system revolves around. The problem with assessing the exact center of the orbit is that we do not yet have enough points in recorded time to mathematically figure an exact center. This motion of our solar system around a central Sun is so slow that our entire solar system takes more than 2,000 years to move through only one sign! You read that correctly. It takes more than 2,000 years to move through just one sign. Compare that figure to the Sun, which normally spends only one month in a sign, and you will begin to perceive why mankind has some difficulty understanding things on a cosmic or universal scale. One month of our time is the equivalent of 2,000 or more years in cosmic time. What I am describing is known as the precession of the equinoxes and has been popularized in recent years as our solar system slowly moves out of the sign Pisces and into the sign Aquarius. There has been much disagreement among astrologers and the general public as to exactly when this change will happen, but given the slowness of the precession, it is probably safest to say that the entire twentieth century and this first part of the twenty-first century has been the point of change! And as you come to understand the way the signs of the zodiac behave, you will have a fair understanding of what changes in mankind our movement into the Age of Aquarius will bring.

In what we call the natural zodiac, the sign Aries has customarily been placed at the eastern most point of the chart, since Aries is on the horizon in the spring of the year and spring is the time of birth in nature. The natural zodiac is not a birth chart. It is merely a chart that shows us the signs' natural order and position in relation to one another. See Figure 3.

The Natural Zodiac:

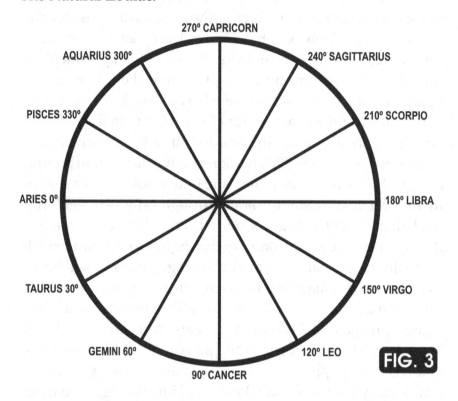

FIG. 3

You will notice that each sign has 30°. This will never vary. The sum total of the number of degrees in a circle is 360. So, 0° of Aries is actually 0° in the natural zodiac. But 0° of Taurus is actually 30° in the natural zodiac, while 0° of Gemini is 60° in the natural zodiac. You will need to know that later on, for the purposes of mathematical calculation. For now, it is just for your greater insight.

The first astrologers took this round wheel of a chart or map and divided it into four sections by drawing a cross within it, through the dot in the center, one line from east to west, and another from north to south. See Figure 4, following.

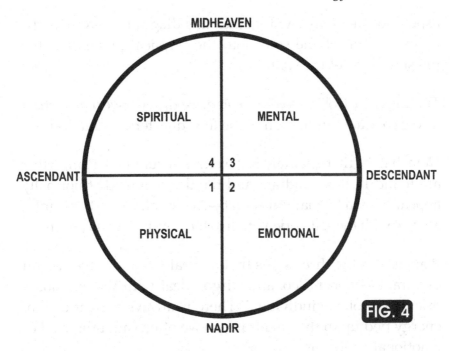

FIG. 4

The spiritual roots of astrology are immediately obvious. The cross within the circle is one of the most ancient symbols, important in most major religions. In astrology, the horizontal line from east to west, which we call the ascendant-descendant line, or the horizon, represents the physical plane of manifestation. The vertical line from north to south, the line of the Midheaven-Nadir, is seen as the line of spirit. The energy of your soul enters life from your last incarnation through the sign on the Nadir, and in its travel, moves upward and crosses the horizontal line of physical manifestation at the central point where the self manifests. It continues its upward movement and eventually out of the wheel through the sign on the Midheaven. Hence, in Figure 1 we saw the symbol for the Sun—the soul awakening, so to speak—and now here in Figure 4 we see it manifesting into physical reality.

The vertical line in Figure 4 could be seen as your soul's journey in this life and, the horizontal line as the physical-material aspects of that journey. Together this diagram represents the manifestation of the soul onto the physical plane. It is the physical birth of the soul.

The ancient astrologers who created, used, and gave us this chart also gave qualities to each of the four quarters, or quadrants.

Note that the first quadrant is the physical quadrant. Planets that are found in this quadrant and the three signs that normally appear here in the natural zodiac—Aries, Taurus and Gemini—all deal with the self's orientation to the physical world around it.

Planets and the three signs that naturally fall into the second quadrant—Cancer, Leo, and Virgo—deal with the emotional orientation of the individual. There is always a great deal of energy tied up in this quadrant, so we often call it the vital or emotional quadrant.

Planets and signs that naturally fall into the third quadrant—Libra, Scorpio, and Sagittarius—deal with the individual's mental and social orientation toward the world around them. This is known as the intellectual quadrant.

Planets and signs that naturally fall into the fourth quadrant—Capricorn, Aquarius, and Pisces—each deal with the individual's spiritual orientation and show us how he or she reaches out in growth-oriented ways. This is the spiritual quadrant.

By now you are asking yourself, "What about the planets? Where do they come in?"

Figure 5 shows a schematic of the planets in our solar system. Note that although not exact, I make an attempt here to show you the relative distance between the planets. By this, you may appreciate that the inner planets, those inside the asteroid belt and closest to the Sun and that are called the personal planets, are all relatively close together. The outer planets, those outside the asteroid belt, are almost as far from one another as the closest in of them (Jupiter) is from the outermost of the personal planets (Mars). This schematic serves to show you the vast distances involved. The sizes also are suggestive of actual scale as is the orientation of the axis of Uranus. It does indeed revolve around the Sun at right angles to the other planets.

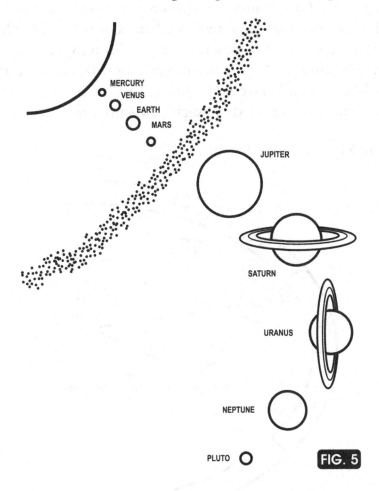

MERCURY
VENUS
EARTH
MARS
JUPITER
SATURN
URANUS
NEPTUNE
PLUTO

FIG. 5

When an astrologer casts your natal chart, he or she "stops the clock" for the exact time and place that you were born and creates a star-map of where the planets were in relation to where and when you were born on the Earth. This map shows the planets relative to the Earth, but against the backdrop of the constellations we know as the Sun signs. By drawing a line-of-sight from your place on the Earth to each planet, and noting which constellation lies behind the planet, the astrologer knows which constellation is filtering its energies through that planet, thereby influencing its action.

This means, for example, that when someone tells you that his Sun sign is Aries, that means when he was born, if a line of sight were drawn from where he was born to the Sun and then to continue on to see what constellation it would point to, that the constellation would be Aries. And, of course, all of the other planets are charted in exactly the same way.

Figure **6** below illustrates this.

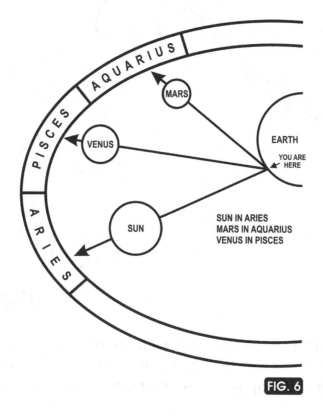

FIG. 6

Now, the first astrologers had to do all of their own mapping and plotting of planets using the first telescopes. But we are much luckier. Instead of using a telescope to plot the planets' positions, we merely look them up in a book (an ephemeris) or we consult a computer, because other astrologers and astronomers have been nice enough to plot the planets' positions for every day for at least a hundred years into the future, and as far back as you would want to look into the past. This book not only tells you the sign each planet is in on any given day, but also its degree of the sign, too. Remember, each sign has only a total of 30°.In this beginner's workbook you will be looking up planets in an ephemeris to chart them in what is called a *solar chart*. You will want to obtain an ephemeris as soon as possible, since later in this chapter you will be learning to create a solar chart. Once you can look up planetary positions and create a simple solar chart, you will be able to create charts for all of your friends and family, on your own, and be able to understand them better.

Ephemerides come in two different versions: those where all of the planets are charted for midnight and those where all of the planets are charted for noon. Midnight ephemerides are easier to use if you decide to learn how to completely cast a chart by hand—not just a solar chart but a complete natal chart using the time and place of birth, as well as the day. They usually cover a period of either 50 or 100 years, so get one for the twentieth century, if you and most of your friends and family were born prior to the year 2000, and one for the twenty-first century if you want to get the planetary positions for people born after that date.

The Astrological Houses

Up until now, I have only discussed the tools that the earliest astrologers used. But modern day astrologers also use houses to aid them in their interpretation of a chart.

Apparently, sometime in the late Middle Ages, some astrologers began to feel that merely dividing the chart into four quadrants and interpreting the planets' meaning by the degree and quadrant in which they were located was inadequate. These astrologers began to use mathematical formulas to hypothetically divide the heavens into twelve pie slices and assigned a specific area of life that each slice would deal with.

There were many astrologers who were involved in deriving the various formulas for dividing the heavens, and as a result, today there are many different variations in use. Among the most popular house systems used today are the Placidus System, the Campanus System, the Koch System, and the Equal House System.

I use the Placidus house system throughout all of my courses is. This is not to say it is the best. I do not feel that any house system is better or worse than any other, although many astrologers argue about the benefits of the system they use. I feel that any system you become comfortable and familiar with using will work the best for you.

Remember also that I emphasized that both planets and signs are real. Houses are not. They are mathematically derived hypothetical structures created by man to aid in chart interpretation; they are not meant to be cast in granite.

Now, let's look at the twelve houses. (See Figure 7, following.)

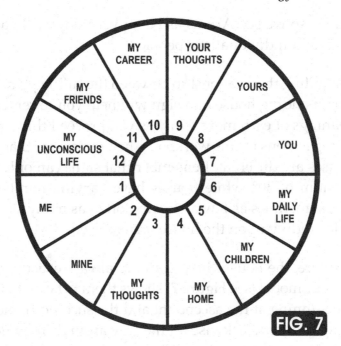

FIG. 7

The meaning of each house is similar in many ways to the meaning of the sign it corresponds to in the natural zodiac and the planet that rules it, as you will see when we begin discussing the astrological signs. The chief difference is that houses deal more with departments of life, while the signs are the actual energy at work.

Let us look more deeply at the astrological houses. You will have noticed that signs and houses have a certain correspondence. The reason that the sign and the corresponding house have similar attributes is that both are ruled by the same planet, so their meanings are actually derived from the planetary energy itself.

For example, the planet Mars is associated with energy, action, and projection. Therefore the 1st house, which it rules, has to do with the area of life describing how you project yourself into the world, and how you act upon it. But Mars also rules the sign Aries, so we see Arians as being very physically active, assertive, and individualistic people.

Understanding the relationship between the ruling planet and the corresponding house and sign will help you to remember the meanings of each more easily as you proceed through the remaining lessons in this workbook. Just remember that signs and houses are different. Remember that signs can only have a maximum of 30°, while houses have varying numbers of degrees, sometimes as few as 15° and often as many as 45° or more, depending upon the house system used.

Furthermore, the houses in a chart are always exactly where those in our model (see Figure 7) shows them to be, with the 1st house beginning at the ascendant and the succeeding houses following counter-clockwise all the way around. They do not ever move.

Signs, on the other hand, can be anywhere in the chart. Yes, I know that since Aries corresponds to the first house, and so on, that you would expect it to always be there, but it is not. This is because as the Earth turns on its axis once every 24 hours, a different sign will appear on the ascendant every two hours. This is the rising sign. Remember, it is not actually the signs that are moving; it is the Earth's rotation that places a different sign on the ascendant every two hours, i.e. as the ascendant turns, it points to a different sign every two hours until all twelve signs have had their chance. The rules to follow here are that signs never have more than 30° in them, and they follow each other in order around the zodiac.

Planets, of course, our third factor, can be anywhere at all in the chart, depending upon what sign the ephemeris tells us that they are in. They do not have to be in either the sign or house that they rule, although they are stronger when they are. They can be anywhere in the natal chart.

When you learn the meanings of each planet and the signs and houses that it rules, it will be best to learn them together, since you will see later, that these meanings strongly inter-relate. Just remember that in an actual chart, only the houses need follow in the expected sequence. Planets and signs can fall anywhere, depending upon the actual day, time, and place of the birth. See Figure 8.

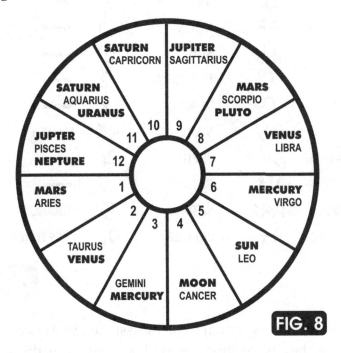

FIG. 8

If any of the above discussion confused you, just read onward and do not be concerned now since, eventually, it will all fall into place. All I am doing here is laying groundwork for you to build upon, and you can refer back to all of this information as often as you like. You should work to understand the material rather than memorize it, which eventually will happen for you.

Now is a good time to introduce you to the glyphs, or symbols, that we use to stand for the various signs and planets. It is a good idea to memorize these, since it saves a great deal of time to use the glyph rather that writing them longhand all of the time. Figure 9 presents the glyph symbols

SIGN		RULING PLANET		CO-RULER	
ARIES	♈	MARS	♂	—	
TAURUS	♉	VENUS	♀	—	
GEMINI	♊	MERCURY	☿	—	
CANCER	♋	MOON	☽	—	
LEO	♌	SUN	☉	—	
VIRGO	♍	MERCURY	☿	—	
LIBRA	♎	VENUS	♀	—	
SCORPIO	♏	MARS	♂	*PLUTO	♇
SAGITTARIUS	♐	JUPITER	♃	—	
CAPRICORN	♑	SATURN	♄	—	
AQUARIUS	♒	SATURN	♄	*URANUS	♅
PISCES	♓	JUPITER	♃	*NEPTUNE	♆

FIG. 9

These planets are secondary rulers, assigned to the signs they rule after they were discovered. The planets in the second column are the old and original rulers of the signs, still recognized by some astrologers as the only rulers. When there are two planets assigned to rule a sign we call them co-rulers.

If you look back to Figure 9, you will note that of the original rulers in the second column, all but the Sun and the Moon rule two signs. This is because each planet unlike the Sun and the

Moon has a generative or masculine side and also receptive or feminine side. Therefore each planet rules one sign that is receptive and one sign that is generative. The Sun and the Moon do not. This is because the Sun is always only generative or masculine, while the Moon is always only feminine or receptive. Therefore, each only rules one sign.

Remembering this difference between the planets and the two luminaries will help you to better understand the relationships between the signs. When the same planet rules two signs, those two signs automatically gravitate toward one another. In a sense, they are two halves of a whole. Figure **10** shows this.

PLANET	POSITIVE RULERSHIP	NEGATIVE RULERSHIP
SUN ☉	LEO ♌	--------
MOON ☽	--------	CANCER ♋
MERCURY ☿	GEMINI ♊	VIRGO ♍
VENUS ♀	LIBRA ♎	TAURUS ♉
MARS ♂	ARIES ♈	SCORPIO ♏
JUPITER ♃	SAGITTARIUS ♐	PISCES ♓
SATURN ♄	AQUARIUS ♒	CAPRICORN ♑

FIG. 10

The signs also alternate polarity as you trace them counter-clockwise around the zodiac, starting with Aries, which is positive. Each sign also is assigned a mode of expression such as cardinal (self-starting), fixed, or mutable (changeable). These also repeat in order around the zodiac beginning with cardinal Aries. Lastly, each sign is assigned an element: Fire, Earth,

Air, or Water. These four elements repeat in order counter-clockwise around the zodiac starting with Aries, the first Fire sign. The chart that follows, Figure 11, shows these qualities that make each sign totally unique. Each sign will have a polarity, element, and mode of expression totally its own:

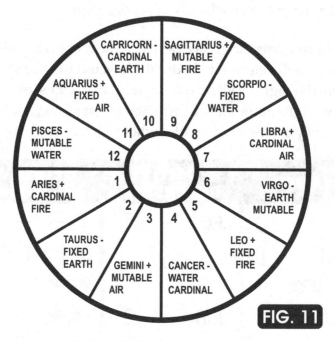

FIG. 11

As you study each sign, in the lessons to come, you will learn to thoroughly understand the elements and modes of expression. For now, just use Figure 11 as a reference tool, one that you will be coming back to many times.

In the following lessons I will discuss many of the things covered in this introductory lesson in much greater depth. I will do this from the point of view of the signs first, tying in the meanings of the houses and the ruling planets. As you progress, you'll also learn how to begin to integrate and interpret all of the factors discussed. You will be studying actual charts.

The Solar Chart

As we close this chapter, I will show you how to construct a solar chart in astrology.

These charts are so simple to create that before long I am sure you will find constructing charts and learning astrology, in general, is fun, since you will be able to see where the signs and planets are in your own, and your friends' charts.

In today's world where it is simple to go online and find a service to cast your natal chart, it is easy to be lazy. But if you learn this simple way to construct a solar chart using only an ephemeris, with a little practice you will find it is far faster than computer services! Of course, this is a solar chart, whereas a computer program will cast the actual natal chart easily. There are many books that will show you how to cast a natal astrology chart by hand. In my *Intermediate Astrology* book, I show you how to construct a natal chart by hand without a computer. Natal chart construction is good to know because it helps you to learn to see and evaluate a chart wheel more deeply as you come to understand how it is derived.

The difference between a solar chart and a natal (birth) chart is that a natal chart is constructed for the exact time, date, and place of birth, and requires either mathematical computations or a computer to construct. A solar chart only uses the date of birth and can be constructed easily using no mathematical computations, directly from an ephemeris.

Now, have your midnight ephemeris for the twentieth century ready, and let's begin with this sample birthday (which happens to be my own!): June 20, 1952.

Steps to Solar Chart Construction

1. Look up the year of birth (1952) in the ephemeris. This is usually located on the upper outer corner of each page.

2. Look up the month of birth in the ephemeris. You will see that the book is composed of tables and that there is a separate table for each month. Find the table for the month of June.

3. Look up the day of birth in the ephemeris by checking the column on the extreme left of the table. The abbreviation for the day of the week is also listed.

4 I am using Michelsen's American Ephemeris for the 20th Century at midnight. The directions given below are for that book. If you're using a different one, the layout may be slightly different, but you should still be able to follow along.

5. The position of each planet is listed to the right of the birthday. You will recognize the symbols for the planets from Figure 9 in Chapter 1, across the top of the table. Place a straight edge across the page right under June 20, 1952. Now you will be able to read the sign and position of each planet for that day, by reading off the number and sign symbol just above your straight edge and then referring to the planet symbol at the top of the column. Please note that sometimes the planet changes signs during the month. In that case, you will find the new sign by looking down the column, closer to the day of birth.

6. Transpose the planetary positions for June 20, 1952 to your own page. When you're done, it should look this way:

(The planets are given in degrees, minutes, and seconds. Degrees are the first column of numbers, minutes are the second, and seconds are the third. For our purposes, we don't need this fine of a breakdown, so I'm going to round any seconds from the third column of numbers that are 30 or over up to an extra minute in the minutes column, and then any minutes 30 or over I will round up to an extra degree in the degrees column.)

Sun = 28°35′59″ = 29° of Gemini Moon = 1°33″00″ = 02° of Gemini

(Two positions are given for the Moon; use the 0 hour position unless you know for a fact the birth was after noon.)

North node = 23°2.0′ = 23° of Leo

Mercury = 11°18.8′ = 11° of Cancer

Venus = 27°14.9′ = 27° of Gemini

Mars = 1°47.6′ = 2° of Scorpio

Jupiter = 11°39.5′ = 12° of Taurus

Saturn = 8°16′ = 8x of Libra

Uranus = 13°13.5′ = 13° of Cancer

Neptune = 18°57.6′ = 19° of Libra

Pluto = 19°39.2′ = 20° of Leo

You should copy out several other sets of planets for other people's birthdays to make sure you have the hang of this.

7. Now, all you have to do is put the planets into the chart. It's easy! First, put the degree, sign, and symbol for the Sun right on the ascendant, as Figure **12** demonstrates.

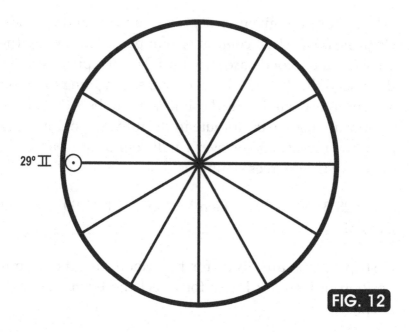

FIG. 12

Next, put the same degree (but not the sign) on each house cusp, as shown in Figure 13.

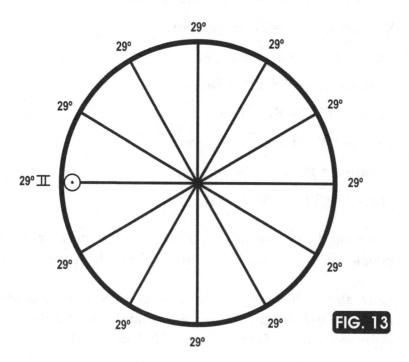

FIG. 13

8. Then, put the sign that would ordinarily follow the sign of the person's Sun in the natural zodiac on the 2nd house cusp. Continue in that manner, placing the proper sign symbols around the wheel counter-clockwise until there is a different sign on each cusp as shown in Figure **14**.

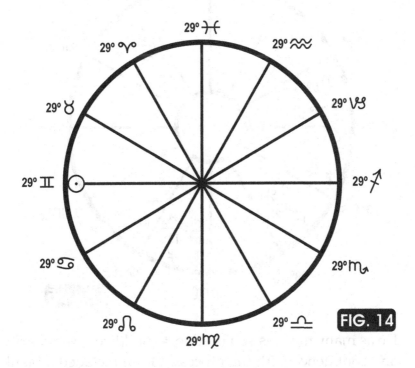

FIG. 14

9. Now, we are ready to put the other planets into the chart. Again, it is easy. The only thing you have to remember is that the numbers in each sign always increase as you move counter-clockwise around the wheel. Just check each planet above and then place them in the wheel by first finding the cusp that holds the sign the planet is in, and then determining if the planet belongs before or after the cusp. If the planet's degree is greater than the degree number on the cusp, place the planet in the house lying counter-clockwise of it. If the planet's degree is less, place it one house clockwise of the cusp.

When you have finished, your chart should look like Figure **15**.

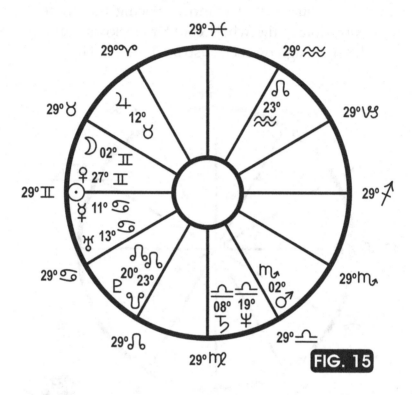

FIG. 15

Do as many more as you need to, to build your familiarity and confidence with the process. I have included a blank wheel for you to make as many copies of as you like, so that you can practice as Figure **16**.

NAME: _____

DATE: _____

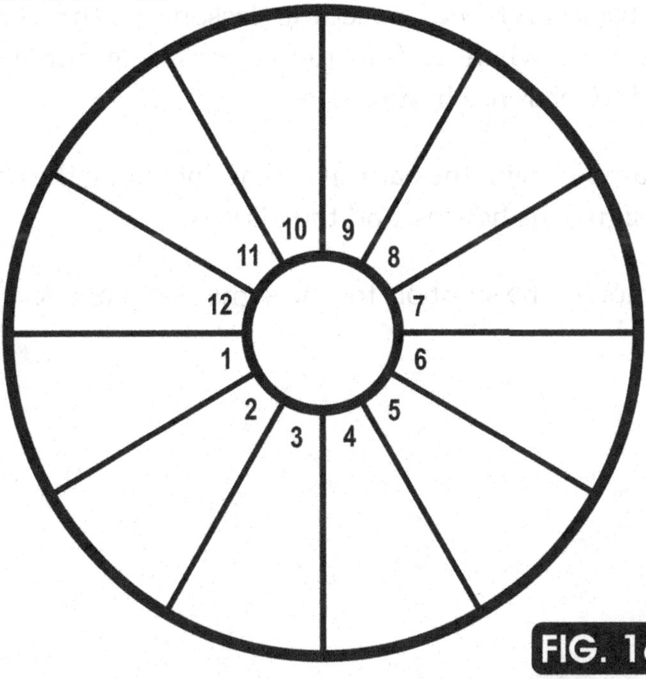

FIG. 16

PLANETARY POSITIONS FROM EPHEMERIS

☉ SUN _____   ♃ JUPITER _____

☽ MOON _____   ♄ SATURN _____

☿ MERCURY _____   ♅ URANUS _____

♀ VENUS _____   ♆ NEPTUNE _____

♂ MARS _____   ♇ PLUTO _____

End of Chapter Exercise

1. Go back over the preceding lesson, so that you will remember where to find the various diagrams you will need to reference in future lessons.

2. Be familiar with the natural zodiac, including the nature of the signs, the houses, and the planets.

3. Memorize the symbols for the signs and planets.

Chapter 3

Introducing Aries and Taurus

Aries—The Intellectual Achiever

Aries is the 1st sign of the zodiac. (See Figure 11.)

Glyph or Symbol—♈—The Ram

Mode—Cardinal

Ruling Planet—♂—Mars

Element—Fire

Corresponding House—1st

Orientation—Masculine

Corresponding Body Part—The Head

As the signs and the houses derive their energy and their meaning from their respective ruling planet, we will begin our discussion of each sign with its ruling planet.

Mars

The planet Mars takes just under two years to complete one full revolution around the Sun.

We all know that at approximately two years old every child goes through a period every parent refers to as the terrible twos. This is the child's first Mars return. That's right. At about two years old, Mars has completed one full revolution of the Sun and has come back to its natal position. The result is an explosion in the child that we adults refer to laughingly as the terrible twos.

Contemplating the terrible twos give us some deep insight into the nature of Mars.

Mars is energy. No matter how many other more intricate descriptions of Mars you may come across, always remember that because it is the most accurate and all of the others derive from it.

Wherever Mars is in your chart shows how you use your energy. If it is in a masculine sign, you will be assertive. If it is in a feminine sign, you will be more reticent, more introspective. To tell if a sign is masculine (positive) or feminine (negative) refer to Figure 11.

When a child has his or her first Mars return, they suddenly have so much energy that they simply don't know what to do with it. Enter, the terrible twos!

You also will discover, as you become accomplished enough at your astrology to begin to study aspects (the relationship between any two or more planets), that when the energy of Mars is backed up or blocked by another planet, the result is always anger.

More parents should know about that. They might deal with those terrible twos a little differently.

Mars has always been associated with war. In fact, Mars was the Greek god of war. But Mars is only warlike when he is blocked. When his energy is free flowing, he is the wellspring of our existence.

Mars enhances our creativity, our ability to recuperate from illness, and our sexuality. Yet when he is blocked, he creates anger, disease and illness, and represses our sexuality.

45

Mars is how we act. He shows how we use our energy. He is assertive and essentially masculine or generative in nature, even though he, like all of the other original planets also rules a sign of the opposite, negative or feminine polarity.

Mars describes the way we perceived our father's action patterns as well. In fact, we copied his methods of acting, or not acting, upon the world.

There are other planets as well that tell us something about Dad's behavior and how it affected us, and we'll be studying them as we go through the signs. When we study how these planets that represent our fathers' behavior patterns interact with one another, we will learn to identify the various conflicts in ourselves that we all have and to see how these patterns are actually handed down through the family.

There are also several planets representing Mom and her patterns of behavior that will allow you to do the same for her. But we'll get to those later.

In summary, you may associate the following meanings with Mars:

- Energy—The way you act
- Anger—The way your father acted
- Aggression—Sex
- Competition—Impatience

Mars rules two signs, Aries and Scorpio, and two houses, the 1st and the 8th. Its action in the 1st house and Aries is totally generative, action oriented. Its action in the 8th house and Scorpio is receptive and inner directed. Since Aries is the sign we are focusing on here, let us see how Mars affects the area of life that the 1st house focuses on.

The First House

The twelve houses that modern-day astrologers use divide the astrology wheel into twelve compartments that effectively break life down into different focuses, or areas.

The 1st house derives its meaning from Mars, just as the sign Aries does.

The actual line of the horizon that falls at the beginning of the 1st house is called the ascendant, and the sign that appears on the ascendant in your actual birth chart (a chart cast for the date, time, and place of birth) is called your rising sign.

In an actual birth or natal chart, the sign that appears on the ascendant may be followed by a second sign that actually occupies the 1st house. Because of this, it is important to understand the meanings of the ascendant and the 1st house as being two different things, although there may be some overlapping in their meanings.

The ascendant is the first thing that the people who meet you see about you. The sign that appears on it describes your bearing, whether you reach out to people when you first meet them or prefer to observe them quietly before introducing yourself. It sets the stage for whether your initial interaction with any new people or situations in life will be aggressive, submissive, reluctant, paranoid, fearful, emotional, assertive, creative, or something else.

When you were a young child, it was the qualities that are part of the sign that appears on your ascendant that your parents and the other grown-ups around you encouraged you to exhibit in public. And even as an adult you fall back on these patterns, reinforced in your childhood, when entering any new situation.

The ascendant or rising sign also has another very important function from a developmental and spiritual point of view. Spiritual astrologers believe that the sign on the ascendant determines the soul's immediate purpose in this current incarnation.

The 1st house is the house of self. This house loudly says to the world, "I AM." You might think of it as the home of the ego, the little self.

Your 1st house and all of the signs and planets in it give rise to the self-oriented, selfish way in which you define yourself relative to the world you live in.

Do you have a good self-image or a poor one? Do you let others impose their will upon you, or do you behave independent of the thoughts and expectations of others?

The 1st house is a fire house (see Figure 11), like its corresponding sign Aries. It is a physical, action-oriented house and its focus is solely upon the self.

Each of the houses that lies first, moving in a counter-clockwise direction following an angle, is also called an angular house. Therefore, each quadrant's 1st house is angular. You will note that the angular houses (1st, 4th, 7th, and 10th) correspond to the cardinal signs in the natural zodiac—Aries, Cancer, Libra, and Capricorn (see Figure 11). All of the angular houses, including the first, are outer directed, action-oriented houses.

Some astrologers feel that the ascendant, signs, and planets in the 1st house define a person's physical appearance as well. I feel that they surely have a strong affect on it, but they are not the sole contributors. Often other factors in a chart can exert an equally strong affect upon physical appearance. Some other factors you might consider would be the house and sign of both the Sun and the Moon, the South Node of the Moon (we will be learning about this later on), and the sign on the Nadir or fourth house cusp.

Associate the following meanings with the Ascendant:

- The way you meet the world
- The way you start new things
- Your soul's purpose in incarnating

Associate the following meanings with the 1st house:

- I AM
- How I define myself to the world
- How I interact with the world

Aries

Cardinal Quadruplicity or Mode

Of the twelve signs of the zodiac, four of them have a cardinal mode. Mode means the manner in which the personality is expressed, the way the individual tackles life, so to speak. The cardinal signs are initiators. They begin things themselves, not needing someone else's steam to get started. The cardinal signs are doers, not watchers. Aries is the first of these, with the other cardinal signs being Cancer, Libra, and Capricorn.

Each of these is a different element from the others, so that each of the elements—fire, earth, air, and water—can be expressed through a cardinal sign. The other modes of expression we will be learning about later are the fixed mode and the mutable mode. Figure 17 shows the mode, the element, and the polarity of each sign.

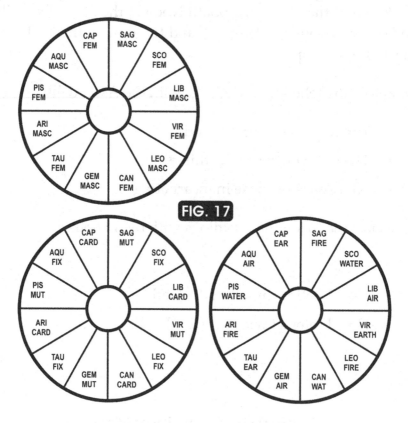

FIG. 17

Fire Triplicity or Element

Three of the twelve zodiac signs are of the element fire. These signs are Aries, Leo, and Sagittarius. Again, Aries is the first of these. The element tells you something about the self-identification tendencies of the individual. All of the fire signs tend to be enormously idealistic, meaning that they identify with their ideals, which to them constitutes a complete value system.

The fire signs are energetic, physically-oriented people. They are sometimes rash; they are always obtuse—that is, they tend to see what is obvious, not what is subtle. In general, they are always emotional and effusive about their own issues, but they may not even notice yours until you almost, literally, hit them over the head with them. However, once they know and understand your issues, they may become as idealistically militant about yours as they are about their own

The mode and the element are both extremely important items in any chart and we will be spending a great deal of time on these, gaining more insight into each as we discuss them from the point of view of each sign. This is so important that in my *Intermediate Astrology book* a whole section is set aside for understanding and working with them. They give you tremendous insight into any individual.

Polarity

The orientation of positive or negative polarity tells you whether the individual was predominately male—or female-influenced in his or her early life (during the first three years or so). In Aries' case, Dad, or some other dominant male figure, was the strongest influence on the child's development during this time, since Aries is a positive sign. Out of the twelve astrological Sun signs, six are masculine oriented, and six are feminine oriented. Figure 11 at the end of Chapter 2 shows the breakdown of positive or masculine and negative or feminine signs, as well as the element and mode of each sign.

The effect of masculine orientation is to make the individual, whether male or female, more comfortable throughout life with men. Positive or masculine sign people tend to be more outwardly directed, more generative, more competitive, more action oriented, and more intellectual.

Women born into the positive—or masculine-oriented signs tend to be somewhat uncomfortable with their femininity, often compensating by becoming overly feminine or just being tomboys. I've often noted that as women born into the masculine sign mature and become more comfortable with themselves, they develop more female friends.

The male born into a masculine-oriented sign also enjoys the company of his male friends and associates and sometimes has difficulty relating to women as friends, since he lacks the softening characteristics we associate with women. Again, as he grows older and matures, he can see the integration of his personality as he develops a new comfort level with women.

Please note here that if you are having trouble relating to this because your positive or masculine Sun sign does not act this way, remember that since you are composed of all twelve signs, you may have many important planets in a feminine or negative sign that throw off this assessment. For example, in a natal chart, constructed for the actual time of birth, having an ascendant in a positive sign could influence the people you are most comfortable with in a very similar way.

All of the factors I will be discussing are characteristics specific to one sign, one planet, one house, or one mode, orientation, or element. Yet you are composed of twelve signs, eight planets plus the two luminaries, and twelve houses. All of these factors in you are integrated, and it is difficult without experience to tell one factor from another. And yet you must learn the specific orientation of each factor in order to eventually be able to integrate them into your reading of a chart. We must break down the whole into its parts to be able to again see it as a whole.

Let's take a look now at the sign Aries.

The Sign Aries

The typical Aries, whether male or female, is born into a family in which Dad may be the power or dominant figure, but Mom is no slouch either.

Poor Aries gets two very strong, very aggressive and assertive, and above all, very expectant parents. That's right. Aries' parents have great expectations—of Aries.

The Aries' parents expect them to be smart, quick, athletic, well liked, and in short, everything they would have liked to become themselves.

Sometimes Aries' parents are out in the open about their expectations, sometimes they are quiet pushers, and sometimes they might use guilt to motivate Aries. But the extremely high expectations are always there.

Somehow Arians come to believe that Mom and Dad's love must be earned by meeting those expectations, by achieving. And that's why achievement and accomplishment are number one issues in Aries' lives.

Arians live with the spirit of competition, with consistently setting and re-evaluating goals. No sooner is one goal achieved than another must be set. For Arians, it is the experience of climbing the ladder and exploring the limits of self that the exploration requires that gives meaning and fullness to life.

Of all the signs, it is Arians who in this current life are supposed to be self-oriented, self-assertive, even self-centered. Arians are supposed to see life from the very personal point of view of self because in this current incarnation they are re-contacting the self, re-learning and re-setting their limitations, and re-defining who they are.

It is not really possible in astrology (unless the astrologer is also a psychic) to determine the evolutionary level at which the individual soul resides. And every sign has many ways that it can manifest depending upon the evolutionary level of the individual.

In an Arian's case, the lesser-evolved Arian will tend to be totally selfish and self-centered, and be very aggressive in his attempts to gain whatever goal he has set for himself. He will be extremely competitive with others and will seem to want everything that anyone else has, whether a job, a house, or a mate.

However, the more evolved Arians will direct their competitive urge inward, seeking any and all methods to develop themselves. They will also appear selfish sometimes, because their Arian nature causes them to approach everything from a self-oriented point of view. And, of course, being a fire sign they often will not even notice your needs until you make your needs obvious to them. However, these more evolved Arians will see even these parts of themselves as challenges, and once they become aware, will seek to overcome anything in themselves that they see as deficient.

Aries also is the sign that we associate with both underachievement and overachievement.

In some cases, Aries' parents really got carried away and set goals and expectations that were simply not possible for young Aries to reach. When this happens you end up either with an overachiever—that is, someone who routinely pushes himself far beyond his abilities and will someday become a prime candidate for either a heart attack or career burnout or Aries' parents have created an underachiever, someone who always does the bare minimum to get by, but refuses to do his best because he knows it will never be good enough anyway.

As long as Arians are measuring themselves against expectations outside of themselves, the tendency toward over or under achievement cannot be overcome. Eventually, Arians must break away from the expectations of their parents and friends, and look into themselves to determine what is important, to set their priorities in life and set out to achieve them.

The Aries who has no goals and no direction in life will be unhappy, unfulfilled, and possibly suicidal. He will attempt to undermine all those around him, in order to make himself feel better about his own lack of success.

The Aries Woman

Like all positive sign women, the Arian female enjoys being with men. She likes to compete with them, as well as to socialize with them. She will tend to see other women as competition for attention. Most, if not all, of her friends will be male and all of her friendships will be based upon common interests, such as career or hobby, whether they are friendships with men or women. Usually, when the interests lag, the friendships end.

The Aries woman usually has a physical nature, enjoying sports and physical activities of all kinds. In her early education she was competitive and she brings that spirit of competition into the workplace. It is not uncommon to find her in a primarily male job, such as fire fighter, police officer, paramedic or soldier. But even when she is not in a male-oriented position, she will tend to associate with the men in the work force, and it is that them she will be most competitive with.

The Aries woman is a born romantic. She tends to idealize her partner, and if she is not careful, may see only her ideal and not the real person that lies beyond it. She is a very sexual being and can readily take on the aggressive role in any romantic or sexual encounter.

It is not unusual to see her vacillate between partners who are much more aggressive and competitive than herself and partners who are weaker. Her ideal partner is someone with whom she can engage in friendly competition, who keeps her on her toes yet does not undermine her goals, but, rather supports and perhaps even participates in their achievement.

Aries makes a good mother, although often she has overly high expectations of her own children. In some cases, Aries may use her children in her competitive contest to be first and best. This is an extremely negative Arian trait, since it puts so much pressure on the children and usually fosters a fear and dislike of all competition.

In some cases, Aries women have children and make the proper raising of those children their goal in life. But I have seen countless Arian women raise happy and well-adjusted children and still have their own very successful careers.

The Aries Man

The Aries man shares many characteristics in common with the Aries woman, including her strongly competitive urges, her idealism, and her physical nature. In fact, most Aries men enjoy competitive sports and physical activities of all kinds.

Aries enjoys the companionship of other men and usually has many male friends whom he competes with strongly in social—and career-oriented ways.

He is often a mental chess player as well, enjoying the planning of his competitive pursuits as much as doing them.

His competitive urge usually has him climbing ladders of all types. He is attracted to anyone or anything that appears just out of reach. And he can be very manipulative and very creative in obtaining whatever goal he has set.

As he gets older, the Aries man generally will find that he also enjoys being in the company of a woman with a strong mind and capabilities to equal his own. But in his younger days the competitive urge translates to a need for sexual conquest. This need attracts him to all kinds of women, from the softly feminine to the hardened player. Some Aries men count the women they have been with the way gunfighters used to count notches on their belts.

Yet, through all of his conquests, he will still be looking for that ideal woman that always appears just out of reach. One of his lessons is to learn to separate his ideals from reality.

It has been well stated that the way to get and hold an Aries man is to keep him following the carrot. Remember, like his female counterpart, he needs to be constantly challenged; he needs to constantly seek success in order to develop and learn about himself. In a marriage he can be faithful, but only if he remains challenged, only if he and his wife still share goals.

The Aries man rises quickly in almost any career pursuit he chooses; he often changes jobs, or even quits upon the brink of success, to begin a new climb. Remember, for him it is the getting there that counts, not hanging on to it once he has obtained it. He is a pioneer at heart.

He cannot accept his own failure, and more often than not, if he fears failure is inevitable, he will not become involved with a situation at all. His lesson here is to create only realistic expectations for himself and others, and to understand that who he is does not depend upon his success or failure, but rather upon how he approaches his goals.

And in whatever situation he finds himself, he will, like his female counterpart, apply himself with single-minded intensity.

As a father, he is concerned with setting a good example for his children, and his expectations of his children will be filled with strong ideals. He will often want sons to follow in his own path. But if he has daughters, he will want to be friends with them and will encourage them to be aggressive and independent.

Associate the following traits with Aries:

- Self-oriented—mental
- Idealistic—physical
- Competitive—goal-oriented

Taurus — First of the Builders

Taurus is the 2nd sign of the zodiac.

Glyph or Symbol—♉—The Bull

Mode—Fixed

Ruling Planet—♀—Venus

Element—Earth

Corresponding House—2nd

Orientation—Feminine

Corresponding Body Part—The Throat

Venus

Venus takes approximately one year to complete a full orbit around the sun. Therefore, in your astrology chart, it always falls fairly close to the position of the Sun, never more than two signs away.

Venus, like all of the original planets, rules two signs and two houses: the signs Taurus and Libra, and the 2nd and 7th houses, respectively.

In the 2nd house and the sign Taurus, its action is negative, or receptive—what we call feminine in astrology, since Taurus' polarity is feminine. In the 7th house and Libra, its action is positive, or generative, as a result of the masculine polarity of the sign Libra. But by its essential nature, Venus is a feminine planet and receptive, just as Mars is essentially a male planet.

Most people who have studied a little mythology tend to associate Venus with love, since in Roman mythology Venus was the Goddess of Love. This is not really too far off, if you just remember that Venus is associated with only the personal forms of love, not the universal. Venus is possessive in her love, as most of the Roman myths surrounding her demonstrate.

In actual practice we see Venus in our astrology charts as the kinds of people and things that we love and are attracted to. Venus describes the type of art and social expression we like to make a part of our lives, the types of things we like to collect, and the types of things we like to do.

Many times Venus forces us to make decisions between those two or more people or things that we want. It teaches us that we cannot have everything and, that some of the things we want are not good for us.

Venus also exerts a softening influence on whatever it touches, since it is a natural opposite to the aggressive influences of Mars. In fact, you will note, if you refer to Figure 8 in Chapter 1, that each of the two signs and houses that Venus rules lies opposite the ones that Mars rules.

Since Venus is essentially a feminine planet, in anyone's chart it represents his or her ideal of womankind as well. This is especially important when you are looking at the chart of a man, because his Venus position tells you what his ideal woman consists of. Interactions between Venus and other planets can then tell you whether his ideal is healthy for him, or whether it will lead him into trouble.

Conversely, in a woman's chart Venus defines the ideal of womanhood that she is living up to. Once again, conflicts between Venus and other planets in the chart will tell the astrologer a great deal about whether the woman is comfortable with herself or not.

For everyone, Venus in the chart also represents self-concept. It describes the way we feel about ourselves when we respond to the external action of the world upon us. When challenged in some way, do you resist, run away, strike out? Think it through. How do you react?

The way that we react to the world around us causes us to define ourselves in relationship to the world. Some of us see ourselves as shy and reticent, some as talkative, some as aggressive and overbearing. For all of us, it is the position that our Venus is in, by sign and house, which defines how we see ourselves.

Venus in Aries is an achiever, a competitor; Venus in Taurus is rock-stable and slow to anger; Venus in Gemini is talkative and mentally agile; Venus in Cancer is retiring, home-loving; Venus in Leo needs approval and respect; Venus in Virgo takes care of everybody else (critically); Venus in Libra is part of a pair; Venus in Scorpio is a behind the scenes operator; Venus in Sagittarius is fun-loving; Venus in Capricorn is responsible for everyone; Venus in Aquarius is different; and Venus in Pisces feels emotionally connected to everyone.

Of course, Venus' meanings are a lot more complex than that, but that gives you some insight into how Venus' placement in our charts can affect the way that we see ourselves.

I should add here that your self-concept has a great deal to do with the way in which your mother perceived herself, too. Since Venus tells the astrologer what role your mother cast herself in during your early childhood years, it is primarily this role that is responsible for your own self-concept, as well as for the way in which you perceive women (even if you are one).

Conflicts between Venus and other planets in your chart can show the astrologer your mother's hang-ups that you may have inherited.

Associate the following concepts with Venus:

- Possessive love

- Desire for acquisition

- Receptivity

- Decision-making

- Self-concept

- Mom's role

- Attitude toward material things

- The perfect woman

The Second House

The 2nd House in the astrology wheel derives its meanings from the planet Venus, just as the 1st house derives its meanings from the planet Mars. Since polarity shifts from positive to negative and back again as we follow the wheel around counter-clockwise, the 2nd house is a negative or receptive house, just like its ruling planet, Venus.

And if you refer to Figure 11 at the end of Chapter 1, you will also see that the 2nd house is an earth house, and that it is fixed. Just like Taurus, the sign that it corresponds to that is also ruled by Venus.

However, when we speak of houses, we don't say "fixed." Instead we say, "succedent." The succedent houses correspond to all of the fixed signs in the natural zodiac. They are the 2nd house, the 5th house, the 8th house, and the 11th house. All of the succedent houses deal with fixed, ongoing, and stabilizing matters.

The earth houses are the 2nd the 6th, and the 10th. All of these houses deal with material matters such as work, money, and things.

The 2nd house is where we create our self-concept through the development of our natural talents and abilities applied toward survival, acquisition, and ability to make money and earn a living.

This is a very personal house. It shows not only how you are likely to make money and earn your living, but also your attitudes and values concerning money and things. You can imagine how important it is that, when two people marry, their 2nd houses are compatible.

I have often noted that when someone has many planets in his 2nd house, he will spend a good portion of his life supporting and taking care of himself, as well as others, and that his ideals and values and ethics will be continually challenged. It is as if his life-lesson is to be challenged to the point where he is forced to develop himself and his own abilities, whether he wants to or not. Often many planets in the 2nd house will show someone who will own his own business, or if not, someone who will be the caretaker of others or the businesses of others.

The sign that appears on the 2nd house cusp in your natal chart will determine your attitudes and approach toward money and things. It will tell you what areas your natural talents and abilities lie in. It will even tell you what kinds of things you like to have and to own, and whether you are any good at handling your charge cards. It will tell you whether you are good at sharing or, whether you are a person who needs to do it all and keep it all for yourself.

The 2nd house, in essence, is where we meet the world in a physical, material sense, and make our mark upon it.

Associate the following concepts with the 2nd house:

- Earning ability
- Natural talent and ability
- Kinds of things you like
- Self-concept
- Attitude toward money

Taurus

Polarity

Taurus is the first negative, or feminine, sign and it is receptive in its expression. As discussed earlier, the signs start with positive Aries, continue on to negative Taurus, and so on around the zodiac from positive to negative to positive traveling in a counter-clockwise direction, ending with six signs of each polarity (See Figure 11).

The person born into a negative polarity Sun sign has usually had the experience of an extremely powerful mother or other female influence during the formative first three years of life. The result is that women born into the negative signs have a good handle on their femininity, and are generally very strong people, no matter how soft and feminine they appear. They often feel that women are the stronger sex and sometimes have a tendency to treat the men in their lives as children, unlike their positive counterparts, who tend to look up to all men as father figures.

However, the man born into a negative sign will be somewhat uncomfortable with his masculinity, much like the woman born into the positive sign is uncomfortable with her femininity. He will exhibit a lot of characteristics that in our society we associate with the feminine—he may be soft hearted, gentle, emotional, and sensitive. When he accepts these qualities in himself, he will become a very well-balanced individual.

Both negative sign men and negative sign women seem to prefer feminine companionship. Often the negative sign man finds himself in competition with other men for the attention of the nearest female, even when he has no real interest in her.

The Fixed Quadruplicity

Taurus is the first of the fixed signs—followed by Leo, Scorpio and Aquarius. Having a fixed modality means that Taurus continues whatever has already been initiated by the cardinal signs. All of the signs in the fixed quadruplicity (see Figure 12) have the qualities of determination, tenacity, stubbornness, and the ability to follow anything through to completion.

The most negative attribute of the fixed signs is that they often do not know when it is time to quit. For instance, it is not unusual to find Taurus holding down the ship long after everyone else has forgotten it ever existed. Generally speaking, the fixed signs need a very large kick in the behind to realize it is time to make a change.

The Earth Triplicty

Taurus also is the first of the earth sign triplicity we will meet. (Again, see Figure 12.) The other earth signs are Virgo and Capricorn. Since Taurus is the first of these, in this sign we see the earth sign traits in their most direct and obvious form.

All of the earth signs find themselves involved in the physical, material world. I've often had earth sign clients who had embarked upon a spiritual path and tried to avoid material goals and pursuits. They were never successful. That is not to say that earth sign people cannot be spiritual. Rather, it is that they were put on this material plane to work with it, to overcome its obstacles, and to realign their values concerning it. In essence, there is no reason for the earth sign person to avoid material concerns to be spiritual, since involvement with the material world is a part of his or her spiritual mission.

Actually, the earth sign people of the zodiac are generally far better equipped to deal with the material issues of our modern world than the other elemental triplicities are.

Earth sign people tend to relate to the world emotionally from the point of view of things, stuff, or money. When earth sign people loan you something, take care of it. They're loaning a part of themselves. Likewise, when they give you something, cherish it because it, too, is a piece of them. If you want to alienate your earth sign friends for all time, borrow something from them and return it in unusable condition. I guarantee your friendship will never be the same!

If you are married to an earth sign person, expect him, or her, to show his love through giving you things or doing services for you. Likewise, if he wants to hurt you, it will be by withholding those same things or services.

The Sign Taurus

No matter what Taurus' socio-economic bracket is, he seems most often to be born into a situation in which his family is better off than most of the others in the community, at least in a material sense. We call Taurus the silver-spoon child.

Taurus' Mom, or some other female figure, is the dominant parenting figure in Taurus' early life. Taurus' mother, in fact, is a real powerhouse. Taurus is one of the three "power" signs in the zodiac, and Taurus learns his use of power from Mom. At some time in every Taurus's life, there is a confrontation, a facing off with Mother. This must occur to set Taurus free from the control of a very strong parent, so that he can come into his own power.

Taureans may be silver-spoon children, yet they are not usually spoiled as children. They may have more material stuff than everybody else, but they do not necessarily have as much nurturance or emotional support. In fact, usually in Taurus' childhood there was a trade-off of material things such as toys or food to replace the nurturance and emotional support that a too-busy parent did not have the time or the ability to give. This is the root of why Tauruses are so possessive of and emotionally connected to their things.

Taurus' father is usually present but does not have a very strong influence upon the child's development. This is the reason why both Taurean men and women copy their strengths from their mother.

Tauruses can be real go-getters, whether male or female. There have been countless generals and presidents throughout history who were Tauruses. We find Taurus just as often in his or her own business as we do at the topmost ranks of corporate structures. Tauruses like power and seek to be around it and to wield it.

Being a fixed sign, Taureans are slow to take action and slow to reach decisions, but once they choose a direction they are unrelenting in their commitment to it.

In my imagination I often equate Taurus to a mountain—enduring, stable, timeless, and with the deepest of roots.

Tauruses will seek to accumulate wealth and position, seeing this as power. Tauruses want to be in charge of the money, of the power and control it confers. And since so many of their life lessons hinge on material values, it is common for Tauruses to have radically fluctuating financial circumstances throughout their lives.

When Taureans feel themselves out of control, that is, poor or lacking in material support, they are selfish and might display a downright miserly character. But when they are wealthy, when they feel in charge of their financial and material well-being, they are generous and thoughtful of others.

Since they are one of the power signs of the zodiac, it is not uncommon to find Taureans in power struggles of some kind with other people in their community. When this happens, it is Tauruses that usually will dig in and wait out the competition, since they are, after all, a fixed sign. It takes a long time for them to even recognize their opposition, let alone become angry. But once they do, their anger is an explosion worthy of notice

Taurus is also statistically the second longest-lived sign in the zodiac. I believe that it is one of Tauruses' lessons to outlive all of the people who were important to them, to teach them that people are more important than things. Tauruses are learning about values. On their evolutionary journey, they are learning to focus their perceptions outward as opposed to inward.

The Taurean Woman

The Taurean woman copies her powerful nature from her mother. As mentioned above, at some time during her life, usually around 28 years old, she confronts or otherwise grows beyond her mother in order to realize her own full potential. As long as she credits her mother with the powerful character that is really her own, she inhibits her own growth and development.

In fact, for some Taurus women, mother remains the shadow they live under until after their own first child is born. If a woman has not yet come into her own power, the birth of her first child usually forces the issue!

The Taurean woman is a go-getter and a doer. She usually has above average organizational skills that can make her a wonderful homemaker and career woman, both at the same time if need be.

She also is well known for being a wonderful mother. I have never quite been able to figure out how a Taurus mother can have dinner cooking, be talking on the phone, planning tomorrow's schedule, and be repairing the can opener while still managing to catch her child just before he falls into the fish tank! I guess we can chalk it up to an extension of that organizational skill.

At work she is a crackerjack secretary, not afraid of work of any kind, no matter how menial, but she rarely stays on the bottom for long, unless it is by choice. She can work for the same place for a long, long time.

She considers herself a simple person with simple needs, and yet she is always the one selected to set up the parties and run the shows because she does it so well.

She usually has lots of hobbies, and if she wants, she can be very creative with her hands. Since Taurus rules the throat, she often also has a pleasant speaking voice and might sometimes even be an excellent singer, as can the Taurus male.

She loves her home and, this is where she is likely to go overboard with decorating, collecting, and spending.

Like her male counterpart, she is slow to anger, yet once she is angry she makes an implacable enemy who will stop at nothing until she obtains retribution. Her only truly negative trait is a tendency toward jealousy.

The Taurean Man

The Taurean male has a more difficult time growing up than his female counterpart. After all, he is faced with an enormously domineering mother and a father who provides him no role model to speak of. Often his mother seeks to foster his dependency on her, and makes it difficult for him to grow up.

He copies the traits of both parents. Like his mom, he develops a powerful personality composed of equal parts of stubbornness and practicality. But from his father he develops a tendency toward laziness, a tendency to seek to get away from the obligations and what he sees as the control mechanisms of the family, and his mom in particular.

The result is that the Taurus man, once he becomes interested in some pursuit, whether it is career or home oriented, will be just as focused and successful as the Taurus woman. But if his interest is not aroused, he will be lazy and will try to get out of whatever work presents itself to him.

Like the Taurus woman, he must have that inevitable confrontation with his mom someday, and for him, it is even more important. If he allows himself to forever live in his mom's shadow, he never grows beyond her limitations to see what he is made of himself.

In some cases, poor Taurus grows up to marry a woman as strong as his mom, and then finds himself in the middle of a battle between his mother and his wife, with himself the prize. The only way for Taurus to avoid this is to claim his own power before the marriage occurs and not let his wife try to do it for him. Sometimes the Taurus man fails entirely to break free from his mom's apron strings, in which case he may never marry or may never leave his mother.

I also have known some homosexual Taurus men who had such a traumatic time breaking the bonds to their mothers that no relationship was possible with the mother afterward. There is no one sign of the zodiac that is associated with homosexuality; yet I have seen many Taurus men whose relationships with their mother hurried them in this direction.

The Taurean man is sensual. Taurus is so strongly connected to the physical nature, and especially to physical perceptions, that a great deal of the Taurus man's life experience is given to sensual experiences of all sorts. It is almost as if in other lives he lacked for physical expression and is making up for that lack in this one through experimentation and experience.

71

If he is an individual who shuns work, as some Taurean men do, he will tend to engage only in what gives him pleasure. But if he has grown beyond the restriction his ties to his mother placed upon him, he will be a strong and dedicated employee, capable and ambitious, who has the capacity to rise to a position of authority or even to own his own business.

He makes a wonderful boss, combining a gentle and yet authoritative approach that makes his employees respect and admire him.

I have found that Taurus men have an interesting growth cycle. Most, as young men, seem to avoid responsibility and typically seem to dedicate themselves mostly to their own self-gratification. They appear easy going and malleable as long as it is their own interests that are being pursued. Cross them and you will find a stubborn and implacable enemy. They are ambitious and want a great deal, so long as the effort required is not great. If they have not yet broken away from their mom, they look for a strong woman who will make it happen for them or a weak one who will give them everything. If they have not yet accepted the softness within themselves, they sometimes adopt very aggressive and reckless physical behavior as a cover up.

Yet as the Taurean man grows older an amazing metamorphosis usually occurs. His values, such that they are, begin to change. People become more important. Selfishness diminishes. The stubbornness of his youth becomes tenacity and willpower. He becomes self-responsible. He becomes concerned for others. The gentleness he denied in his youth asserts itself. His sensuous nature changes from a need to experience every physical thing to a joy in the simple pleasures of life.

Taurus generally does not take joy in having children, but if he has them when he is older, he will make a good and caring parent, although he usually does not take a very active role in their upbringing. If he has them too young, he is liable to see them, especially the boys, as competition for his wife's attention. This is especially true if he relates to his wife in a motherly way—an expression of the undeveloped Taurus.

Associate the following characteristics with Taurus:

- Slow and methodical
- Tenacious
- Stubborn
- Organizational ability
- Endurance
- Physical perceptions
- Materialistic
- Learning values

End of Chapter Exercise

1. Be familiar with the Sun sign qualities of Aries and Taurus.

2. Know what Mars and Venus, the 1st and 2nd houses represent.

3. Know what the general qualities of fire and earth signs are.

4. Understand what cardinal and fixed modes of expression are.

5. Understand the difference between positive and negative polarity and how it affects men and women differently.

6. Using the information in this chapter, analyze the natal chart below, assuming the person is a man. Considering the questions below Figure 18 will help you with your analysis:

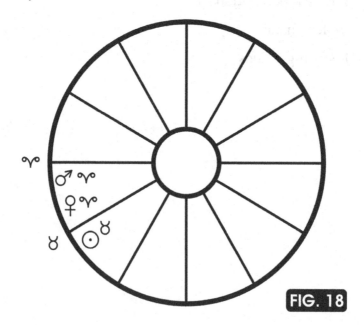

FIG. 18

a) What are the basic characteristics of a man who has his Sun in Taurus?

b) What are the basic characteristics of the Sun in the 2nd house?

c) How will this gentleman come across to the world with Aries on his ascendant? Do you think a Taurus would be comfortable coming across like an Aries?

d) What characteristics do you associate with Mars?

e) How will Mars in Aries affect the ascendant in Aries?

f) How will Mars being in his 1st house affect him?

g) What effect do you think that Venus also being in the 1st house, and in Aries, will have on Mars' action?

h) How do you think Venus in Aries in the 1st house will behave?

CONGRATULATIONS! YOU HAVE JUST ANALYZED YOUR FIRST CHART!

The key for this End of Chapter Exercise can be found on page 309.

Chapter 4

Introducing Gemini and Cancer

Gemini—I Think and I Communicate

Gemini is the 3rd sign of the zodiac.

Glyph or Symbol—♊—The Twins

Mode—Mutable

Ruling planet—☿—Mercury

Element—Air

Corresponding House—3rd

Orientation—Masculine

Corresponding Body Part—The Extremities

Mercury

Mercury takes approximately one year to move completely around the sun. Therefore, like Venus, it always falls close to the Sun, never more than 28° (one sign) away.

The two signs that Mercury rules are Gemini and Virgo, and the two houses it rules are those that correspond to these signs, the 3rd and the 6th respectively.

I've always been fascinated by the attraction between Geminis and Virgos, which is based upon their common Mercury rulership. Mercury rules the mind, so essentially Geminis and Virgos are fascinated with each others' thinking. Yet no matter how fascinated they may be with each other, they cannot ever truly understand the other's way of thinking because, in

Gemini's case, the thought processes are generative, while in Virgo they are receptive.

Since Gemini is a positive sign, Mercury acts through it in a generative manner, keeping Gemini's thoughts bouncing from thing to thing, issue to issue, talking and reaching out to learn and communicate all the while.

In negative-polarity Virgo, on the other hand, Mercury can be silent, thoughtful, secretive, and inner-directed, even though it's just as mentally active.

The planet Mercury in Roman mythology was the messenger of the Gods, usually shown as a hermaphrodite, being both male and female. Consider this representation well, as it gives away more of Mercury's true meaning than you may think.

First of all, since Mercury's primary involvement is with the mind and thought processes, it is essentially sexless. Hence, it is represented as a hermaphrodite.

This does not mean at all that Geminis and Virgos are sexless— it only means that their ruling planet is. The sexuality displayed by Geminis and Virgos has to come from some other source than their ruling planet.

Of greater interest is the concept of Mercury being the messenger of the Gods. In Esoteric (Spiritual) astrology, Mercury is known as one of the sacred planets. Could it be that Mercury's messages go beyond thought and mere interpersonal communication to include communication with the higher self?

As a practicing psychic, as well as an astrologer, I have come to associate Mercury with all forms of psychic disciplines, such as telepathy and channeling. And yet mental disciplines such as meditation and self-hypnosis also are Mercury ruled.

On a more mundane level, the planet Mercury is involved in every conversation you have. Where your Mercury is located, by its house and sign, determines how you communicate, what you like to communicate about, as well as how you think and what things you tend to think about.

Mercury rules the art of communication, which means listening as well as speaking.

Interactions between Mercury and other planets in your chart determine whether communication is easy or difficult for you. By looking at the position of a child's Mercury, it is even possible to determine how he or she will do in school and whether a public school education is the right one for the child.

In fact, Mercury rules early or foundation education of all kinds, since this is one place where thought processes are developed. Mercury can be very creative and is usually prominent in the charts of writers, teachers, inventors, counselors and politicians.

Mercury also rules less obvious forms of communication, such as letters, telephones, telegraphs, television, and so on. And even short-distance travel is considered to be a function of Mercury. That means that by considering the position of your Mercury, I would be able to tell if you like to stay home all day on your day off or if you're a person that's hard to catch at home because you like to make many short jaunts around town on those days off

We also associate Mercury with your siblings (your sisters and brothers) and very close friends for whom you have a brotherly or sisterly feeling. Again, these are the people with whom you primarily communicated as a child. Your interaction with them is responsible not only for much of the way that you communicate, but also for the way that you look at a lot of the personal things in your life that you have talked to them about.

We also can gain a great deal of insight into Mercury, the planet, by studying the metal mercury. At normal temperatures mercury acts like a liquid, which enables it to be used in thermometers. But even though mercury acts like a liquid, it is not. Break the thermometer and mercury runs out of it like a liquid, but then forms into a myriad of tiny metal balls that appear solid. Then brush those tiny balls into any holding vessel, and mercury will take the shape of the vessel, like a liquid would.

Applying these insights to the planet Mercury gives you insight into the extreme flexibility of this planet. It can take on the shape and form of anything it touches or is exposed to. And yet it does not hold that form permanently

Associate the following concepts with Mercury:

- How you communicate—How you think
- Telepathy and psychic skills—Foundation education
- Communication services; Communication equipment
- Flexibility—Short distance travel
- Siblings, especially the oldest

The Third House

The 3rd house derives its meanings from the planet Mercury.

By referring to Figure 11 in Chapter 1, you will see the polarity, element, and modality of the sign Gemini, as well as the 3rd house that it corresponds to.

The 3rd house is positive in polarity, so you can expect all of the concepts associated with it to be generative in nature.

Its element is air. The air element is considered masculine, or positive, yet, like the planet Mercury, the air element deals with mental things. Therefore, it is hard to really see air as masculine or feminine. But it is easy to see it as generative, since all things begin with ideas. It is from this mentally generative quality that all of the air signs (Gemini, Libra, and Aquarius) and all of the air houses (3rd, 7th, and 11th) get their positive polarity. All of the air signs, as well as the three air houses, deal with social and mental issues.

The 3rd house is what we call a cadent house. By referring to Figure 11 in Chapter 1, you can see that the cadent (mutable) houses are the 3rd, 9th, and 12th houses and they correspond to the mutable signs of Gemini, Virgo, Sagittarius, and Pisces, respectively. The cadent houses are the last houses in each quadrant. They have essentially the same quality of mutability, or changeability, that the signs they correspond to in the natural zodiac do. But remember that cadent houses are also very internally directed houses.

The individual with a lot of planets in cadent houses in his or her natal astrology chart will, of a necessity, go through many changes in life. Yet those changes will generally be massive, internal changes of attitudes and ideology with just enough outward changes to make the internal ones necessary.

You might see these cadent houses as setting the stage internally for the next outer developments, which will take place as we cross the angle into the next quadrant and enter the next angular house.

The 3rd house is, like the 1st and 2nd houses, a very personal house. It sets the stage for our social development and our thinking processes.

The young child develops his socialization skills through his interaction with siblings, with neighbors' children, and with classmates. As these socialization skills develop, he creates patterns of thought and communication that encourage the type of socialization he is most comfortable with.

The sign that appears on the 3rd house cusp in your natal horoscope reveals what type of socialization you are most comfortable with and, how you think, communicate, and interact with your peer group. The sign on the 3rd house cusp tells how you approached your early childhood education, as well as how you got along with the other students in your class.

With Aries on the 3rd house cusp, you competed for first place in grades and social position. With Taurus here, you hung back, took your time and learned slowly, but developed some long-term friendships. Gemini on the 3rd was talkative and well liked, maybe even teacher's pet. Cancer didn't belong, felt pushed out and insecure or incapable. Leo needed to be the leader or did not want to play. Virgo had lots of friends and was a good student. Libra was more concerned with his friends than his grades. Scorpio tried to be invisible but had one close friend. Sagittarius was rowdy and talkative, and got good grades because of his smile. Capricorn took it all too seriously and had few friends. Aquarius was the socialite but was too out of step to get good grades. Finally, Pisces formed long lasting friendships but only did well if he liked the teacher.

This early pattern of how we relate socially, as well as how we think and learn, follows us throughout our lives. Whether a person is open or close-minded will show up in his 3rd house, as well as what learning techniques work best for him.

The 3rd house is concerned with communication and with language, both written and spoken. People who are writers, public speakers, or radio or television personalities often have a lot of planets in their third house. Conversely, I've seen people with planets here who are speech therapists or who have major problems with language.

The 3rd house also rules short-distance travel and again, the sign on the cusp tells whether you do or do not do a lot of travel around town. Gemini, Virgo, Sagittarius, and Pisces (the mutable signs) are usually the ones who do the most running around, spending a good part of their whole day out if they can. Conversely, Taurus, Leo, Scorpio, and Aquarius (the fixed signs) are perfectly happy for the world to come to them, only going out for specific purposes. Aries, Cancer, Libra and Capricorn (the cardinal signs) like to go out, but once a day is enough. Interestingly, Sagittarians (ruler of long-distance travel) often view jaunts that take them hundreds of miles as short trips when that sign appears on the 3rd house!

The sign on the 3rd house cusp also gives some insight into whether you will have siblings, and if so, what your relationship with them (especially the oldest, who shows up most strongly here) will be like.

Associate the 3rd house with the following concepts:

- Thought processes
- Learning ability
- Communication
- Socialization
- Beginning education
- Teaching ability
- Short-distance travel
- Siblings

Gemini

Polarity

In the sign Gemini, we return to the masculine, positive polarity. Gemini is generative. Since it is an air sign, the positive polarity makes it mentally creative, outgoing, social, and talkative.

As with all women born into a positive Sun sign, the Gemini female will be somewhat uncomfortable with her femininity, preferring the companionship of men until she begins to fully accept herself. Then you see her developing close female friends as well.

Sometimes she, like the Virgo woman (negative polarity but also Mercury ruled), can develop an outer demeanor that is essentially sexless. This is common, especially when she works in a primarily male field in which she seeks to keep her relationships professional.

The Mutable Quadruplicity

Gemini is the first of the mutable quadruplicity, and hence this quality is the most apparent in it. The other mutable signs are Sagittarius and Pisces (See Figure 12.). The quality of mutability makes Gemini changeable and flexible, a sort of mental chameleon.

If the mutable signs share one fault, it is that they sometimes tend to want to change things that don't need changing. It is as if they have an insatiable urge to upset the balance of every situation they walk into, just a little.

In Geminis' instance, you can even detect their mutable nature in a simple conversation—just note how many times they change their minds or their points of view during your talk. Often they will be contrary, just to lend opposition to whatever the current view of a situation is, and perhaps assist in changing it.

As a Gemini myself, I am highly aware of this tendency we mutable people have that causes us to want to make changes in whatever we encounter in life. I have tried to counter the negative side of this in myself by not seeking to bring about change unless I can think of something new and better to replace the old with.

In dealing with mutable sign people, it is important to remember that though their desire to stir up everything around them is sometimes frustrating, they do serve an important purpose.

It is the mutable signs that show the need for change in whatever the fixed signs have been preserving. Once the areas that need change are evident, it is the purpose of the cardinal signs to begin to initiate them. All three modalities must work together in order for evolution, in the individual or the species, to occur.

The Air Triplicity

Gemini is the first sign of the air sign triplicity we will meet (See Figure 12.). The other air signs are Libra and Aquarius. Since Gemini is the first, the air quality is easiest to see in it.

All of the air signs are concerned with thoughts, ideas, communication, and socialization. In fact, ungrounded air sign people can become so wrapped up in the world of ideas that they sometimes see the idea as an end in itself, rather than the means to the end.

Communication of ideas is incredibly important to all air sign people. They show their love by communicating their ideas, and in return, listening to yours. They send cards and poetry (sometimes they even wrote it) to you to express their deepest feelings.

Often, they have no other means of expression, fearing open displays of emotion and shying away from overt physical expression.

The way you can show them that you care is to listen to them. They often have very big telephone bills. If you want to hurt or insult them, just refuse to listen to them, or interrupt them. Or, in the middle of a conversation with them, turn and walk away without a word. Also, throw their latest poem in the garbage for them to find. Communication of their ideas is so important to them that this form of rejection is the worst thing you can do to them.

Air sign people need people and seek out social situations. And yet, as if they are processing their experiences, they also need enormous amounts of time alone, at these times appearing almost anti-social.

The Sign Gemini

Geminis begin their early lives with two strong parental figures who are in a constant verbal battle with each other. Very quickly, Geminis learn the power of words as they see both parents physically, and often violently, reacting to the words of the other. When the verbal battle is not between the parents, it is between mother and grandmother or sister and mother. It does not matter who the individuals are; they are in a verbal war, and Geminis are psychologically influenced by it.

By the time Geminis are three or four years old, they have already learned to fear and respect the power of words. The verbal warfare Geminis are witness to produces various effects depending on the individual response of the Gemini.

Some Geminis copy the aggressive verbal skills of their parents and become adept at using language skillfully and using language to manipulate or hurt others.

Other Geminis run away from the verbal warfare they experienced in childhood and fear to express their feelings, values, or needs. These Geminis may be so afraid of hurting someone with their own speech, or of being hurt themselves, that they do not communicate at all.

These latter types will first respond to your yelling at them or reprimanding them for something by bursting into tears. For them, the burst of angry words is the equivalent of the lash of a whip. When Geminis are forced to speak up to say those angry words themselves, they often have to do it through their tears, with their anger being so intense it provokes a physical response.

After many years of observation and research, I have concluded that this super sensitivity to angry words is due to the fact that Gemini is both a telepathic and empathic sign, causing Gemini to hear the words physically and as an energetic attack. Since Gemini is the ruler of communication, there is a major key to understanding autism here.

In the extreme, the verbally unexpressive Gemini can become violent given the correct circumstances in which he or she has been verbally backed against a wall and can see no escape. Be careful of pushing this type too far.

By now you realize that all Geminis deal with communication. But that does not necessarily make them good communicators. In fact, I believe that all Geminis are born with communication problems of some kind that must be overcome and worked through. And in working through them, Geminis become truly good and responsible communicators who are able to see, understand, and present the various faces of any issue. People who have worked through their Gemini communication problems become wonderful writers, teachers, counselors, diplomats, scientific investigators, politicians, newsmen and women, and lawyers, and can shine in any field or calling wherein strong communication skills are an asset.

Some of the communication problems exhibited by undeveloped Geminis throughout life include the following: not listening, not speaking, interrupting others, trouble keeping their minds on the subject at hand because they have already decided what they want to say or do next, poor memory retention, and limited powers of observation, because their minds are focused on the verbal interaction at hand and not the world without. And these examples are only a few. In essence, any problem that you perceive someone to have with communication is a Gemini problem.

Geminis can experience physical communication disorders as well: dyslexia (reading words, numbers, or letters backward or out of sequence), autism, speech impediments, and hearing disorders are all a part of the Gemini experience.

Geminis are rarely close to their mothers during their growing up years, since this sign is masculine and is usually father dominated. But that does not mean that Geminis cannot have relationships with Mom, and that sometimes the relationship is even a good one. However, most Geminis will remain a bit reticent with Mom because of an innate distrust of women. That's right; both male and female Geminis do have an innate distrust of women. In some cases, Geminis even compete with Mom for Dad's affections.

For most Geminis, the relationship with their father is the one that carries the most important impact as they are growing up. Since Gemini is a positive air sign, the tendency is to put Dad on a pedestal. The children you have overheard comparing how great their dads are probably are a mixture of Gemini and Aries.

Geminis may copy their personality traits from either Mom or Dad, but they mostly look to Dad for affection. Geminis want to impress Dad, they want to be with Dad, and they want to be like Dad. And yet, as all Geminis grow up, it is inevitable that at some time during those early years they will suffer a rejection from Dad.

This rejection takes many forms. Today, with divorce so common, a Gemini may view his or her mom and dad's divorce as Dad's rejection of him. But that rejection may be far subtler, something no one is aware of but Gemini. The Gemini girl may reach puberty and her relationship with her father naturally alters; she may see that alteration as a rejection. Dad may promise his Gemini son that he will take him skiing this winter, and then forget his promise. Gemini sees this as a rejection; if Dad cannot remember something so important to him, he must not be important to Dad.

It is not necessarily an actual rejection that is taking place here, but Geminis' perceptions that Dad has rejected them. And this perception of rejection sets the stage for much of the way that Geminis will relate to people for the rest of their lives.

Gemini had formed no bond of trust with his mother, and now the bond with his dad is severed. Of course, Gemini continues to interact with his dad and the rest of the family. But something has changed. Gemini has learned to place emotional distance between himself and the people he cares the most about. Geminis are the true loners of the zodiac, giving real trust to no one. Geminis can be, and often are, alone in a crowd.

Mercurial Geminis learn to show people what they want to see. They develop a talent for acting and hiding true values, feelings, and sometimes ideas beneath a veneer of friendliness and openness. Unsure of their own social graces and ability to be accepted, Geminis imitate the facial expressions and mannerisms of those they admire. The intense need to show someone their true selves diminishes with time. They satisfy this need by showing a lot of different people a little bit of the truth. That way they cannot be hurt.

Often others see the mature Gemini as a jack-of-all-trades, yet, master of none, since he rarely stays with one interest long enough to become a true master of it. I have heard Gemini described as a socialite, flake, fickle, and undependable. All of this name-calling is true for most Geminis at some time in their lives, but most Geminis outgrow these most negative traits as they find people who trust them, admire them, respect them and finally allow them to feel accepted once again.

The Gemini Woman

The Gemini woman was usually something of a tomboy while she was growing up, shunning the cooking and dolls and opting for the baseball mitts and cars. Usually, she was an athletic youngster and climbing trees may have been a specialty. But even if she was not an athlete or a tomboy, she was hard to keep up with because she was always exploring something new, with that quick, curious mind of hers. Unquestionably, she led her peers and friends into more fun and more trouble than they had ever expected.

Like the first positive sign woman we discussed, the Aries, the Gemini woman enjoys being with men. As a youngster, most of her best friends were male, until they grew up and wouldn't be her friend any more, preferring to impress her and flirt with her. As an adult, she still enjoys the friendship and companionship of men, and if the only way she can get it is to flirt, she will be an outrageous one. But in her true self, she wants to be liked and respected for who she is, for her fine mind, not for her body (although she usually puts a lot of care and attention into looking good, too).

She will compete for the attention, if not the affections, of the men around her. In childhood, this competition may have been for Dad's attention, but later on she competed with her girlfriends at school for the attention of the most attractive young men. With her ability to mimic, act, and play whatever role was required to the hilt, she generally ended up with the best of them.

But she does not just want to play the socialite either. She wants to go fishing with her man, to help him work on the car and run his business; she wants to be his equal. And she will belong to at least four or five clubs, too.

She does not need to be entertained. With her active involvement in just about everything that comes along, she will entertain you. In fact, she can probably talk enough for you both. She tends to scatter her efforts so that she rarely has the time to complete all that she has set out to do.

At work, she is a powerhouse who can do a little bit of everything. She is great with people, too. But don't ask her to file. Any job that doesn't fully occupy her attention is dangerous because she is so easily distracted.

She is not necessarily an ambitious woman, but when she is, her versatility and verbal and mental skills can make her very successful. The best jobs for her are those that utilize her people and acting skills. She's good in sales, personnel, theater, drama and any position that requires the ability of thinking on her feet. She's not necessarily a liar, but when she is, her creativity and verbal skills make her a good one.

She is not known for her abilities as a mother. The Gemini woman, being an air sign, is more effective nurturing minds (for example, as a teacher) than bodies. Many Gemini women never have children. But when they do, they will have to have a carryall to bring the child along as they jump from place to place and interest to interest. Otherwise, they are liable to put the child into daycare while they continue their wild schedule.

Gemini loves to cuddle and hold the little ones but is often too involved in her latest book or project (which may never be finished) to notice the child's needs. She does a better job with the older ones with whom she can talk. She loves to nurture those minds.

The Gemini Man

The Gemini man shares many of the same characteristics of versatility and flexibility as the Gemini woman, as well as her physical nature, her active mind, and her ability to role play. Like her, he is social and enjoys interactions with others, making a good salesman, politician, or businessman. And like her, too, he needs a lot of alone time when he is not turned-on to activities, when he is only in his own space.

As a child, he suffers the same rejection from Dad that she did, but in him this does not just create a simple lack of trust; it causes him to distance himself from those around him emotionally, so that as an adult he tends to form few real emotional bonds. Many women complain that their Gemini mate was more open and affectionate before they married than after. This is because he uses his naturally mental nature to create distance between himself and anyone that he thinks is close enough to hurt him.

Watch him carefully, and you will see that the more emotional you become, the more calculating and distant he becomes. All Geminis are uncomfortable with real uncontrolled emotional outbursts, but the Gemini man will put up thicker and thicker walls to protect himself from them.

All air signs (Gemini, Libra, and Aquarius) behave this way to some degree, but we see it most clearly in Gemini, and in the male especially, since he is less comfortable with emotions.

Remembering that his primary role model was Dad, we know that it is from his father that the Gemini man will copy most of his personality traits. He tends naturally to see our world as a masculine place, and may, as a result, be somewhat macho in his philosophy and his way of treating women. And, of course, there are always women who are looking for just this strong, masculine image that some Gemini men project.

His active mind and quick wit make him a success with the ladies, as well as particularly good in advertising, merchandising, and in the entertainment field. He is not really a good candidate for the role of counselor or diplomat because, although he is wonderfully entertaining and exciting, his witticisms often have a sharp edge. When angered, his wit and sarcasm can be a potent weapon.

He is capable of following one career path throughout life, yet if he doesn't have enough flexibility in what he is doing, he usually loses interest and moves on to another job or field.

Likewise, many Gemini men have been married to the same woman all of their lives, but since flexibility and change are such an integral need of Gemini, he is apt to have several marriages or to have one very flexible marriage partner.

He is also likely to have many friends, although rarely are those friendships based upon exchanges of confidences.

I have often noted that there are differences in the way people use the characteristics of their sign depending on whether they are born toward the beginning, the end, or the middle of the sign. This is especially true of Mercury-ruled Gemini, with its flexibility. And we see this even more strongly in the Gemini man than the Gemini woman.

If the Gemini man is born toward the beginning of the sign, he will exhibit some Taurus traits, such as stubbornness, rigidity, and materialism. If he is in the middle of the sign, he will be the typical Gemini. But if he is born toward the end of the sign, he will have some apparently Cancer traits and may be more emotional than the average Gemini man.

Like his female counterpart, having children is generally not his major focus in life. But if his partner wants them, he will agree to have them so long as she bears the brunt of rearing them. He will see fathering as setting an example for his children rather than nurturing them, and may have trouble establishing bonds with them.

Associate the following traits with Gemini:

- Talkative
- Problems communicating
- Mentally agile
- Changeable
- Quick moving
- Versatile
- Mimicry
- The loner

Cancer—Born to Nurture

Cancer is the 4ᵗʰ sign of the zodiac.

Glyph or Symbol—♋—The Crab

Mode—Cardinal

Ruling Planet—☽—The Moon

Element—Water

Corresponding House—4ᵗʰ

Orientation—Feminine

Corresponding Body Parts—The Stomach and Breasts

The Moon

The Moon completes its cycle around the Earth in twenty-eight days, which means that it goes through all of the signs of the zodiac each month, spending about two and a half days in each.

Unlike the other original planets, the Moon rules only one sign of the zodiac, Cancer. And like Cancer, its polarity is wholly feminine.

After the Sun, the Moon is the most important factor in considering an astrology chart. In fact, if you know a person's Sun sign, Moon sign, and Ascendant, these three factors alone will tell you a great deal about a person.

In astrology, the Moon represents the *lower* personality traits and especially the emotional patterns you are likely to follow.

The Aries Moon person is self-indulgent, competitive, and emotionally impetuous, whereas the person with a Taurus Moon is slow to anger and emotionally very stable. The person with a Moon in Gemini, on the other hand, is flighty and may be emotionally unpredictable. The person with Moon in Cancer has a tendency to be insecure, and makes a nest out of their home. The person with a Leo Moon is dependable, and it's important for them to be good at what they do, and respected and admired for it. The person with Moon in Virgo is critical of themselves and others, but needs you to evaluate them to show you love them. Someone with a Moon in Libra tends to create an emotional interdependency with a mate, and someone with a Scorpio Moon sees danger and intrigue in every shadow. The Sagittarian Moon person needs to be like Dad, or to marry him, and the Capricorn Moon person will take everything too seriously. Lastly, the person with their Moon in Aquarius is emotionally distant, whereas the person with their Moon in Pisces feels guilty for almost everything.

Of course, this is just a quick synopsis, and you already realize that the qualities displayed by each zodiacal sign are much more complex than this. But it gives you a little bit of an idea of just how important the Moon can be.

In children up to age 7, you will often see the characteristics of the sign the Moon is in as being more predominant than their actual Sun sign. Children up to age 7 are ruled by their emotions and the lower personality. But as the child grows and the intellect and higher personality begin to develop, the Sun sign characteristics begin to predominate over the Moon.

The only occasional exception to this is in people who are Cancerians. The sign Cancer, being Lunar ruled itself, is particularly sensitive to the Moon's position—so much so that many Cancers display very strong personality traits indicative of their Moon's position all of their lives. Cancers also are particularly sensitive to the influence of the transiting Moon. (Transiting means where the Moon is right now.) Cancers, and people with Moon in the sign Cancer, generally know exactly when the moon is either new or full because it affects them so strongly.

Animals are also particularly strongly affected by the Moon. If you are doing the chart of your dog or cat, plan to consider the Moon sign to be equal to or more important than the Sun sign.

But even though we might tend to give the Moon a bit more importance if we are doing the chart of a Cancer, a child, or a pet, the Moon is of great importance to us all, representing, as it does, our emotional patterns.

All of us have emotional patterns that are our first instinctive response to any situation that we have not planned or in which we feel out of control. Most astrologers feel that these patterns are learned in childhood from our mother or some other female figure. I feel that in many cases these patterns were also learned in a life previous to this one and may be partially responsible for why we were drawn to the particular parentage and circumstances that we chose to be born into.

But no matter how you prefer to look at it, the Moon in the chart represents the automatic emotional response patterns that the individual will have throughout his life, until he begins to recognize them and take responsibility for them.

Some of these patterns will be good patterns, and some of them will be bad. Naturally, we would all like to make the best use of the good ones and eliminate the bad ones. But since they are all automatic, it does not work quite like that. A good part of our personal evolution as we proceed through life has to do with our recognizing and overcoming the negative side of our Moon sign traits.

As we learn to embrace the solar qualities of the Sun sign into which we were born, a natural conflict between emotional needs (the Moon) and personal growth needs (the Sun) is usually set up. And as we, little by little, bring our childhood emotional patterns into alignment with our need to grow and develop, we overcome those negative patterns that are holding us back.

It is for that reason that when the astrologer sees a conflict between the Sun and the Moon in a person's chart, it is the needs of the Sun that the astrologer should first help his or her client to meet. The Moon's needs cannot be neglected either, but if the needs of either planet are to be re-directed, it should be the Moon.

Since the Moon rules the emotions, it is also strongly linked to intuition and psychic ability. Indeed, everyone has the ability to be psychic, and the Moon's position by sign and house often tells the natural way your psychic ability will manifest.

When the Moon is in a fire house or sign, the psychic ability will be strongly linked to gut feelings and direct intuition. When it is in an earth sign or house, it will manifest by the person always seeming to be in the right place at the right time. When it is in an air sign or house it will manifest as telepathy or the ability to link in to ideas. When it is in a water sign or house it will manifest as strong, emotional feelings that usually need to be interpreted to determine if they come from another individual or are your own.

Also, since our emotional state is so strongly connected to how we feel physically, the Moon is also considered to represent the physical body. That means that the location of your Moon by sign and house has something to do with the way you look, as well as the types of ailments and illnesses you may be prone to.

There are two points, called the Moon's Nodes, where the Moon's orbit crosses the elliptic (see Figure 9). The North Node is shown in the ephemeris by this symbol ☊. The South Node, shown as this symbol ☋, is understood to be directly opposite of the North Node. Essentially, the Moon's Nodes represent our direction in life. Since they do not rule any sign or house, we will not be discussing or working with them in this book.

Associate the following concepts with the Moon:

- Your emotional patterns
- Your physical mother
- Your intuitive ability
- Your physical body
- Your "lower" personality traits

The Fourth House and the Nadir

The 4th house in astrology derives its meaning from the Moon, just as the Nadir or 4th house cusp and the sign Cancer does.

The 4th house has a negative, feminine polarity since it follows the positive polarity of the 3rd house. The polarities alternate as we follow the wheel around.

The Nadir (cusp or line that marks the beginning of the 4th house) is always considered the same polarity as the sign that appears on it. The polarity of the sign that appears here usually indicates which parent, male or female, was the nurturing parent. Occasionally, we find that the dominant parent was actually the sign on the Nadir.

Additionally, the sign that appears on the Nadir shows strongly developed personality traits that we have brought into life with us. Often, I find people have difficulty or lack patience in dealing with other people whose Sun sign is the same as their Nadir sign; since they have already overcome most of the problems those individuals are now dealing with, they tend to see them as incompetent or immature.

As we move through this workbook we will use the natural zodiac for our sample charts, so these charts will always have Cancer on the Nadir, giving it negative sign qualities. Yet in your solar charts you may find a positive sign here. If so, the Nadir or Inum Coeli (IC), as it is sometimes called, would exhibit positive sign traits, even though the 4th house itself is still a receptive or negative house, which by its nature, deals with emotional issues.

The 4th house is cardinal, or angular. The other angular houses, remember, are the 1st, the 7th, and the 10th. All of the angular houses are action oriented and mark the flavor of the quadrant into which they lead.

The second quadrant is emotional, so the 4th house sets the emotional tone for the way things are related to throughout the entire second quadrant!

The 4th house is also the first water house we are seeing. The other water houses are the 8th and the 12th. All of the water houses deal with emotional issues.

The 4th house, like the three houses of the first quadrant, is a very personal house. It deals with the issues of mother (or the nurturing parent), home, and family. It shows not only the type of home environment you grew up in, but also the sort of home you create for yourself over and over again as you go through life. It even shows the conditions that will prevail at the end of your life. All you have to do is look at the sign on the 4th house cusp (the Nadir) in your chart, at any other sign that might also be in the house, and at any planets that are in the 4th house.

Let's look at an example:

Take someone with Taurus on the 4th house cusp, and no other signs in the house. Say he has Venus in the 4th house, in Taurus.

Since Taurus is on the Nadir or 4th house cusp itself, the nurturing parent was probably the mother (Taurus is feminine, remember). Since the entire 4th house is also Taurus, the mother probably set the stage for the home environment as well. The home environment she created was ordered, solid, disciplined, and well cared for. The family was important and very stable. When the person grew up, he either re-created that environment for himself, or, if he reacted to Mom, he might have created the reverse environment. He might even flip back and forth at various stages of his life. Since Taurus is long lived, this person will have a long life and will probably have female care at his end, which is well organized and stable.

When we add in the influence of feminine Venus, the motherly involvement of a strong female presence in the home throughout life is emphasized. Venus also brings in a love of beauty and harmony that will persist, no matter where the person lives.

Look at your own solar chart now and see what your 4th house cusp tells you about your own home and early environment.

Even though the solar chart is not an actual natal chart, it will still accurately give you this information, as seen from the point of view of your Sun, which appears on the Ascendant in the solar chart.

Associate the following concepts with the 4th house:

- Early home environment

- Family roots

- The home you make yourself

- End of life

- The parent who was active in the home

Associate the following concepts with the Nadir or 4th house cusp:

- Well-developed character traits you have brought in to life with you

- Polarity shows whether the nurturing parent was mom or dad

Cancer

Polarity

Cancer, like Taurus, is a negative, feminine-oriented sign. You now know that this means that it is receptive in its nature and that the dominant parental figure in early childhood was female.

In Cancerians, this receptive nature results in strong intuition, a gentleness of character, artistic ability, and susceptibility to the emotional projections of those around them. Cancers' intensely receptive nature makes them so aware of others' attitudes and feelings that they become extremely insecure, always waiting for rejection.

Like all of the negative signs, Cancers of both sexes tend to be more comfortable with women than men. It is typical for male Cancers to have female friends, as well as male. I have also noted that the male Cancers' male friends are usually positive-signed men.

Cancer is the only sign ruled by a planet that is wholly feminine. Remember, the Moon has no positive polarity sign that it also rules, as do most of the other planets (See Figure 10). This means that women born into this sign partake of a wholly feminine nature, while men born into it are at quite a deficit, having to cope with a softness and sensitivity within themselves that our particular society encourages them to shun.

As a result of this extremely feminine polarity that we see in Cancer, the Cancerian woman often becomes Mommy to everything and everyone around her, while the Cancerian man who accepts the feminine, nurturing side of his character also makes a better Mommy than most women do.

Quadruplicity

Cancer is the second of the cardinal signs, the first having been Aries.

Cancerians, like all cardinal signs, are self-starters. In fact, Cancers are so good at getting things moving that you will find that most new projects and new businesses have at least one person involved who is a Cancer or has a strong Cancer influence in his or her chart.

Cancer is the nurturer of the zodiac, but it is not always children we find them nurturing. Often Cancers' children are the businesses they gave birth to and are now nurturing, or the projects or endeavors they are now involved in. Be careful not to cross them or to threaten their children in any way— remember, they are the protective mothers, as long as they perceive themselves to be needed

But once Cancers' children have outgrown the need for constant nurturance, Cancerians are off to new horizons, looking for the next enterprise to be involved in. Remember though, their emotional attachments are deep, and though they may appear to have forgotten that child, they have not. They never let go until forced to do so by circumstance.

Many people associate Cancers as being the homebodies of the zodiac. Sorry to disappoint you if you are one of them, but if you are waiting to find Cancers at home, you may have a long wait. Cancers are far too cardinal in their nature to hang around at home. They are home when there is a project to be done there or when they have stopped to pick up a few things they need for their next activity. Cancerians love their homes and are attached to them, treating the home as a nest. But remember, the nest is a place to sleep, to be safe in, and to retreat to when you need a rest; it's not where most of the action in your life happens!

The Water Triplicity

Cancer is the first of the water signs we will meet. The other water signs are Scorpio and Pisces (See Figure 11.).

The hallmark of the water signs is emotion. All of the water signs see life from the point of view of emotion. Everything they do, experience, think, and have is either motivated by emotion or affects them emotionally. Since they are so emotional, all of the water signs are highly intuitive, although sometimes they cannot separate their emotions from their intuitions.

And, since they are so emotional, they are subject to extreme ranges of emotion that can push away the positive signs of the zodiac. The positive signs consist of all of the fire signs and all of the air signs. The air signs run from these emotional displays, whereas the fire signs stimulate them so they can watch.

Water signs get along best with each other, or with the earth signs. Earth signs get along best with each other, or with the water signs. Air signs get along best with each other, or with the fire signs. Fire signs get along best with each other, or with the air signs. In Cancerians, we see the water element the most clearly since Cancer is the first of the water signs.

The Sign Cancer

Cancer is usually born into a situation where material wants and needs are not easily met, and where the dominant role model for the first three years of life is female. It is from this woman, whoever she is, that Cancer develops his strength of character, which is considerable!

Additionally, Cancer is born into a situation where either one or both parents are missing or gone a good deal of the time. Cancer is the orphan child of the zodiac.

Sometimes, in actuality, Cancer is an orphan, but other times the feeling of being orphaned comes because a father is away on business or in the service, or a mother spends an extended time in the hospital, or perhaps the parents are divorced and the Cancer child experienced the loss of one of them almost as a death. Sometimes both parents are present, but yet the Cancer child still feels that he is an orphan, having no one to turn to in a time of need. Perhaps the real nurturer in his early environment was a caretaker or elderly grandparent who is no longer present.

Whatever the reason, on some deep, inner level, Cancers perceive themselves to be orphans, alone and in need, with no one to turn to.

This causes Cancers to turn inward. Many Cancers are shy and withdrawn until you get to know them well. It is also the reason why Cancers are so intensely creative and imaginative, often in childhood having no one but themselves to play with. And they are intensely emotional, wearing their hearts on their sleeves for all to see.

Wherever the sign Cancer, or its ruling planet, the Moon, appear in your own chart, you, too, will have the insecurity of the orphan, along with the emotionalism and creativity of Cancer.

Both the material sparseness of Cancerians' early beginnings and their emotional experience of being orphaned create in Cancers an insecurity that gives them an insatiable need to strive for security in material circumstances and in relationships.

You can find them as adults in their own business, as well as in large corporations, but always where they feel they can build security.

Since many Cancers felt their early home life lacked security and closeness, they will strive as adults to create a warm, close, and secure family environment. They will seek to re-create the happy remembrances of their own childhoods, but unfortunately will re-create many of the bad ones, too. Family and children are of great importance to Cancers, even though these can also sometimes be the source of greatest insecurity.

Because of their inauspicious beginnings, Cancers will be frugal with money and will quite naturally be good savers. Since financial security is so important, Cancers like to have their money in a bank where they know it's there just in case.

The *I might need it syndrome* extends to things as well. Cancerians have an emotional attachment to many things and tend to save them, just in case. Cancers are packrats who might have stored anything from Grandma's first booties to old Fido's last bone (never can tell if you might not want to give it to the next dog).

Cancers have enormous reservoirs of energy and always seem to be on the go. They love to complain to you about their problems, but usually do not have a whole lot of time to listen to yours. However, when they see you are truly in need of their nurturance, their heart goes out to you and everything else is set aside. Their mothering instinct takes over. For somewhere in their own childhood they did experience nurturance of high quality. And when it was lost, they also experienced the extreme pain and insecurity that resulted. And because of that, once they have achieved their own security, they are the greatest nurturers in the zodiac.

Wherever Cancer and the Moon appear in your chart is where you will have a particular skill at nurturance—that is, taking care of others and helping them to develop and grow.

The Cancer Woman

The Cancer woman is a born mother. Even as a child, her dolls received the most careful care, and if she had a little baby brother or sister she was in her glory playing Mommy.

Of course, once she was done playing with the dolls, they gathered dust on the shelf. And as soon as she was done with her role playing of Mommy to brother or sister, she promptly dropped the role and went on to her next game, leaving them to wonder whether her nurturing of them was real or not.

You see, she is learning about nurturance. And in her learning she role-plays. Sometimes she is the child herself, and sometimes she is the Mommy. She has to be careful not to let her role-playing stop her from being a real person or from seeing others as they really are.

As an adult, her assumption of these roles continues. In her relationships with men, she alternates between acting as their mother and relating to them as their father.

Likewise, with her children she role-plays. When she is their mother, she is the best of all mothers. But then she reverses the role and the child finds himself or herself in the role of being the nurturer, the Mommy to her. In this way she is teaching the art of nurturing, as well as constantly improving her own grasp of it.

She feels a deep need to be in control of all of her relationships because inwardly she is always afraid of being orphaned again. Much of her role-playing is an effort to control through manipulation, an art she learned from her own mother in her early childhood. For Cancer's mother was manipulative, and Cancer learned her emotional pattern from Mom.

She often marries an older man or a strong man that she can lean on in her search for security. But Cancer comes into her own after age 28 (the first progressed Lunar return—you'll be learning about that in advanced astrology) and will usually begin to dominate the relationship after that.

She has a strong need to accumulate things as a hedge against poverty and insecurity, yet soon discovers that no amount of money or things can create the security she needs.

The saying, *My home is clean enough to be healthy, but messy enough to be happy* suits Cancer to a T. But some Cancers (male or female) who are particularly insecure carry the accumulation of things to pad their nest with to the extreme. In these cases, the clutter and mess can be amazing.

Cancer needs a lot of overt affection, but may have trouble giving it in return, at least until after her security needs are met.

She continually strives to place herself in a position of security, but must eventually realize that she is the one who must create that security herself. When she finally stops looking outward for her security and instead finds it within herself, she has found her own strength. From that time onward, she will be a powerhouse of a woman who is capable of any success.

She makes a wonderful mother, but she must take care that she does not fall into the trap of placing children before spouse, as many Cancers do. If she does, her marriage will not fair well.

She has no trouble raising a family and working, too. We find the Cancerian woman in many fields, but she is particularly fond of working for large secure corporations such as insurance companies and banks, or government. She makes a wonderful waitress or cook since Cancer rules food. And, of course, she is a good homemaker—just do not expect to find her there all the time.

The Cancer Man

The Cancer man has a much more difficult time of it than the Cancer female, since he is a man in a totally feminine sign.

I believe that one of the reasons a man is born into the sign of Cancer is to bring out his feminine, emotional, and intuitive side in a thoroughly masculine way. For in the mature Cancerian male who has accepted his feminine side, we see a truly creative, gentle, understanding, and nurturing man who has no trouble reaching out to comfort and give succor to those in need. But he seems to have a hard road to reach that maturity. Some Cancer men never do.

His mother (or some other equally powerful female in early childhood) was strongly protective and yet erratic in her nurturing. His bond to her was often unusually close, so much so that he copied not only his strength of character from her (which is typical of all negative signed men), but also his emotional disposition. He often has great difficulty breaking away from her, even in adulthood.

Like other negative signed men of the zodiac he enjoys the companionship of women to that of men and will often compete with other men for the attention of the available female. He is intensely emotional and like his female counterpart, he may tend toward selfishness until his security needs are met.

He is moody. And his moods swing readily from one extreme to the other. Indeed, he used these mood swings in childhood to manipulate Mom, just as she used hers to manipulate him. In his adult relationships, he needs to experience constant intense emotion in order to be sure his mate cares about him. In this undeveloped state, he is often unhappy, never understanding that his intense emotional fluctuations serve to drive many of those he loves away. He is constantly fearful of being deserted and so often realizes his fear.

This fear of desertion is the result of Mom's fluctuating interest in him as a child. And many Cancer men have learned that the best way to keep Mom's attention (attention = love) is to do something wrong whenever her interest strays.

As adults, many Cancers continue the role-playing game just like their female counterpart does. And in the role of child, he is liable to act out in the same ways he did as a child in order to regain his wife's attention. In extreme cases, Cancer has even been known to cheat on his wife just to secure her jealous attention. To this end, he usually sets himself up to be caught. Likewise, it is a Cancerian trick to play two women against each other, and thereby retain the interest (remember, attention = love) of both.

In Cancer's other role, he is the caretaker, and in this role he makes a wonderful father and husband. It is the playing of the parental role that ultimately leads him to an acceptance of himself, provided he develops the soft and feminine side of himself as well.

In addition to being known as the small businessman of the zodiac, Cancer makes a wonderful restaurateur. When he is in his insecure mode, he, like his female counterpart, is attracted to those secure jobs like banking and insurance. And when he is in the mode to develop his male caretaking abilities, we find him in the police force or the military or even as a priest or missionary.

Associate the following characteristics with Cancer:

- Emotional
- Manipulative
- Nurturing
- Difficulty giving
- Creative
- Insecure

End of Chapter Exercise

1. Be familiar with the Sun sign qualities of Gemini and Cancer.

2. Know the general qualities of the elements air and water.

3. Understand the mutable mode of expression and its relationship to cardinal and fixed modes.

4. Know what qualities to associate with Mercury and the Moon.

5. Know what areas of life to associate with the 3rd and 4th houses.

6. Referring back to the chapter as much as you need to, continue your analysis of the chart we are working on by adding in the new signs, planets, and houses you have learned. Answering these questions will guide you through your analysis:

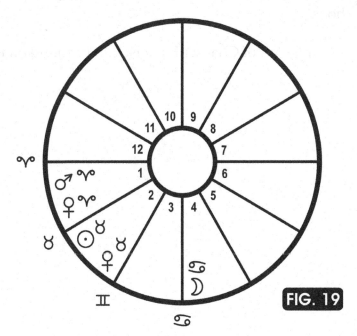

FIG. 19

a) What does the sign Gemini on the 3rd house tell you about how this person will deal with the issues of the 3rd house?

b) Since the sign Cancer is on the Nadir, what can you deduce about who the nurturing parent was and what kind of well-defined characteristics this person may have come into life with?

c) Since Cancer is the sign of the 4th house, what kind of home life is indicated?

d) The Moon is in Cancer in the 4th house. What do you think that means? How will the Moon here affect the affairs of the 4th house?

e) Mercury is in Taurus in the 2nd house. How will Mercury act in Taurus? How will that affect the affairs of the 2nd house?

The key to this End of Chapter Exercise can be found on page 311.

Chapter 5

Introducing Leo and Virgo

Introducing Leo and Virgo

The first four signs we have studied—Aries, Taurus, Gemini and Cancer—are called the personal signs of the zodiac. They tend to be more self-centered than the other signs of the zodiac, seeing life from their own personal viewpoint. Because of their orientation, they see everything in life relative to themselves. They cannot truly understand something they have not directly experienced or been exposed to.

The next group of four signs begins with Leo and Virgo, the signs we will cover in this chapter. These are called the socio-intellectual signs. I prefer to think of them as the *we* signs. The we signs consist of Leo, Virgo, Libra, and Scorpio.

All of the *we* signs look at life from a less personally oriented point of view than the personal signs did, and as a result, they appear to be less selfish and self-motivated. In fact, they perceive themselves in terms of the group, and they can be just as narrow and self-oriented as the personal signs, but in reference to the group they belong to as opposed to their individual selves.

They see themselves as a part of their group, or the group mind, relative to the rest of the world. Their group may be the family they belong to, their peer group in school, their co-workers, their club-mates, or even the religious or national group they perceive themselves to be a part of.

There is one sign representing each element that together make up the socio-intellectual group of signs. The Leos (fire) will base their ideology and their belief system upon the group belief; the Virgos (earth) will work for and serve the group cause; the Libras (air) will depend upon the group for socialization and the development of their self-concept; and the Scorpios (water) will derive their emotional support system from the group and will work to enable individuals within the group to manifest their potential.

Leo—I Shine In The Light of Love

Leo is the 5th sign of the zodiac

Glyph or Symbol—♌—The Lion

Mode—Fixed

Ruling Planet—☉—The Sun

Element—Fire

Corresponding House—5th

Orientation—Masculine

Corresponding Body Part—The Heart

The Sun

The Sun completes its cycle around the astrology chart in one year.

We know that our solar system is moving through space, but this occurs at a very slow speed, and all of the planets move at the same speed as the Sun through its orbit around that central Sun (Refer to Precession of the Equinoxes, Chapter 2) so that this motion is barely perceptible to us. When I say that the Sun completes its cycle in one year, I am not talking about this motion at all. Rather, the earth takes one year to complete its

119

orbit around the sun. Relative to your position here on Earth, it appears that the Sun is moving through the twelve zodiacal signs in succession, completing the cycle of the zodiac in one year.

This also lets you in on an interesting fact: since the position of the Sun is determined by the Earth's position relative to it, your Earth would be located directly opposite of the location the Sun appears in your natal chart, by sign and degree. For example, if you are a Leo with your Sun located at 12° of Leo, your Earth would be in the sign that opposes Leo—at 12° Aquarius.

Most astrologers do not do much with the Earth in their readings, so in your ephemeris, the Earth's position is not noted. But among astrologers who work with it, they see it as the arena in which the events, actions, and emotions of your life occur.

The Sun is the life-giver of our solar system. Without it there would be no life on earth. Likewise, the Sun in your chart is the life-giver. It is the single most important factor in the astrology chart. Whenever you read a chart, you should thoroughly understand the position of the Sun in the chart before you move on to a discussion of any other part of the chart.

The Sun shows your vitality level. When the Sun is well-aspected and strong in a chart, the individual's energy level is high and he is rarely, if ever, ill. When the Sun is poorly aspected or weak in the chart, the individual will exhibit low energy in general and will be more prone to illness.

In a sense, we can say that the sign the Sun is in in your natal chart is the sign you have been born to experience life through at this time. You are not already that sign. You are learning to be it.

There is an old saying, *Your problems would not cause me any difficulty at all, but my problems in turn would be easy for you to overcome as well.*

Each one of us chooses a life pattern that presents challenge to us. This challenge is most evident in the Sun Sign that we are born into. By looking first at a person's Sun position, by sign and house, we can get an inkling of what that soul has come into life to learn. Then, by looking at how the other planets in the chart behave relative to the Sun, we can determine fairly easily how that individual will approach meeting and dealing with his challenges.

This is why the solar chart you learned to construct at the end of Chapter 2 is so important. Although it does not give you the actual house the Sun would be in in the natal chart, it does allow you to see how all of the other planets in the chart relate to it, by sign and house. An analysis of the solar chart can give you good insight into the character of an individual, as well as what crises he is likely to encounter in his life.

The Sun in the chart represents the ego or sense of self. It is the lens through which the Higher Self focuses its energy. In Vedic Astrology it is seen as the Atmah or soul of the person incarnate. It is as if the higher self is saying, "I think I will incarnate as a Gemini in this life and learn about communication," or, "This problem with material values I have been working on through the last several incarnations needs the perspective of Taurus. I think I'll try Taurus this time around."

The Sun is always generative. In fact, it rules only one sign— Leo, which has a masculine polarity. Since it is so generative, we often associate it with creativity, with spontaneity, and with the clarity and honesty of the child within us.

Interestingly, the Sun also tells us something about your father. Usually, the sign and/or house that the Sun is in shows the way you saw your father when you were a young child. Perhaps this says, in a subtle way, that we all attempt to pattern ourselves upon our perspective of Dad.

The Sun light-ups the sign and house it falls into in the actual natal chart (a chart constructed for the day, place, and time of birth). It shows, by its sign and house placement, what the primary areas of life are that the individual will be focusing on.

Associate the following concepts with the Sun:

- Vitality—Image you have of your father
- Ego (sense of self)—Point the higher self acts through
- Creativity—"Lights up" its sign and house
- It's where your interpretation should start!

The Fifth House

The 5th House in the astrology wheel derives its meanings from the qualities of the Sun. It is an energetic, vital house that shows the areas in life wherein you will be the most creative, spontaneous, and childlike. As a matter of fact, the 5th house tells the astrologer how you related to your own childhood.

With Aries on the 5th, you were aggressive, the leader of your group of friends, and found sports competition to be important. With Taurus there, you may have felt that everyone wanted you only for your things that you could share with them. With Gemini, your childhood situation and friends shifted like quicksilver. With Cancer, you were just plain insecure throughout your childhood, but you were intensely creative. With Leo, you were honest, idealistic, over-emotional, and often hurt by the expectations you had of others that they failed to meet. With Virgo, you chose your friends and companions very carefully, yet you always felt critical eyes upon you. With Libra, you buried yourself in your friends and peer group and saw yourself through their eyes. With Scorpio, you felt pushed out and unwanted throughout much of your childhood, and you were very secretive. With Sagittarius, you were always on the go and carried a positive attitude throughout childhood. With Capricorn, you never had a childhood—perhaps you were required to look after everyone else. With Aquarius, you felt like you didn't fit in, you felt separate and apart, even though you may have had a host of friends. And finally, with Pisces on the 5th house cusp, your childhood was a time of dreams and illusion and intense emotionalism.

Since the 5th house tells something about your own childhood, it quite naturally tells us quite a bit about the children you will have. By the sign on the cusp of the 5th house, the astrologer can get a clue as to your attitude toward having and raising children, and any planets in the 5th house will give further insight as to the manner in which you will nurture your children. This is especially true of the oldest child, since that is the one you are likely to strive the hardest with and the one upon which siblings will have the least effect.

Again, with Aries on the 5th, you will expect your child to be the best. With Taurus there, you will give your child everything you felt you lacked. With Gemini, you will expect your child to be bright and a good communicator. With Cancer, you'll expect them to be sensitive and emotional, and you may fear that your own parenting abilities are not good enough. With Leo, you expect your child to live up to the expectations you have of them. With Virgo, you may be over critical of them. With

Libra, you make no decision concerning your child without consulting your mate. With Scorpio, you have an intense emotional bond with your child, but you may be mutually manipulative. With Sagittarius, you have a happy-go-lucky attitude toward your offspring but secretly want them to be like you. With Capricorn, you expect them to be responsible, but seen and not heard. With Aquarius, you encourage them to be different. And with Pisces, you feel the guilt of obligation and your child may feel the same toward you.

Since the 5th house rules the child within us, it also rules what we do to have fun. Recreation, gambling, speculation, and romance are all 5th house affairs.

Since the 5th house is a fire house in the natural zodiac, any of the fire signs (Aries, Leo, and Sagittarius) do particularly well here, helping to make a person lucky. The air signs are not bad to have here either, since they work well with fire; but the earth and water signs, when they appear either on the 5th house cusp, or even in the 5th house, give clear warning to stay away from gambling and speculation.

The 5th house is a succedent house (2nd house in the quadrant) and as such, demonstrates fixed and often internally directed qualities. In the area of romance this is particularly true, since our attitude toward dating is largely formed by our upbringing. Do not confuse the 5th house with attitudes toward sex; the 5th house is romance, not sex.

When one of the fire signs (Aries, Leo, Sagittarius) appears on or in the 5th house, you can expect attitudes toward romance to be traditional. In other words, the prince on his white charger is coming to save the princess in her lily-white tower. If you are a man, you are the prince. If you are a woman, you're the princess.

It is the fire signs that are in love with love. Unfortunately, these people are often playing out roles, not seeing one another as they truly are, and so often they either are hurt themselves in the dating game or cause hurt to others.

The earth signs (Taurus, Virgo, Capricorn) want stability and predictability in their romantic relationships. They want to do things like working on the car together.

The air signs (Gemini, Libra, Aquarius) relate to romance in a more social, intellectual way. They want to be friends, to share experiences and socialize with their respective romantic partners.

The water signs (Cancer, Scorpio, Pisces) want intense emotional involvements.

Interestingly, we often see water sign 5th house people romantically involved with fire sign 5th house people because the water person sees the fire person's prince or princess charming role as the emotional relationship they're seeking. This lasts only long enough for the fire person to get a jolt of reality and the water person to get hurt.

Associate the following concepts with the 5th house:

- Your childhood
- Your creativity
- Your attitude toward raising children
- Your oldest child
- Fun and recreation
- Romance
- Gambling and Speculation

Leo

Polarity

Leo is a positive sign which means that it, like Aries and Gemini, is essentially generative, and that the most important role model in Leo's early development was the father or some other dominant male figure.

What is of particular interest is that the Sun, ruler of Leo, rules only one sign. It does not rule a negative or feminine sign at all. Since the Sun itself is generative, and the sign Leo is as well, that means that Leo is the most generative, masculine-oriented sign in the zodiac!

Leo men certainly have no problem with this orientation, being quite comfortable with their masculine view of things and often become body builders and whatever else stimulates their masculine ego.

But the Leo woman has a very difficult time. She is a female in what is essentially the most masculine-oriented sign in the zodiac.

Until the Leo woman accepts fully the generative, male side of her character and integrates it with the feminine side, she will remain unbalanced. In the Leo woman, this unbalanced sexuality either produces a very masculine tomboy type, or its opposite—the ultra-feminine, super-soft female. Either extreme represents an imbalance in the Leo woman's persona.

When the polarity is finally balanced, it produces a female who is both male and female in equal parts, who will be comfortable in both male and female roles.

I have known many Leo women who have achieved such a degree of wholeness and completeness within themselves that they are content to live their lives as single people. Of course, there are many more whole Leo women who are married with families.

Quadruplicity

Leo is the second of the fixed signs, the first having been Aries.

Like Taurus, Leos' fixity will cause Leos to stick with whatever they start out to do. They are not good self-starters, needing someone else (ideally a cardinal sign person) to get them going. But once they are motivated, they are dedicated for life. And since Leo is a fire sign, that dedication can be total. Often Leos' beliefs in something or someone causes them to go down with the ship, so to speak. This is when they need someone with a mutable nature to let them know it is time to move on.

Triplicity

Leo is the second fire sign as well, the first having been Aries.

Like Aries, Leos' fire quality causes Leos to be physical, idealistic, achievement-oriented, and often obtuse concerning the needs and wants of others.

But in Leos' case, it is the idealistic side of the character that is dominant. Because of this, Leos might inadvertently hurt your feelings, but when you let them know it, they will do all they can to make it up to you.

Leos live up to a traditional set of ideals usually passed onto them by their fathers, or a father figure. So, their need to achieve is usually not as obvious as Aries. Instead of directing their achievement urges toward an outer goal, they are directed toward the attainment of the perfected ideal.

One of their lessons is to make the ideal they reach toward their own, not the one with which they have been brainwashed.

The Sign Leo

Leos are usually born into a traditionally oriented family where the father plays the dominant role. Often the mother plays a very minor part in a Leo's early life, taking care of all of the child's needs in the expected manner, but taking such a back seat to Dad's rulership of the roost that Leo focuses on Dad to the exclusion of her.

Leos are very physical children, often one of the hardest children to keep up with. Leos are climbers and they are curious. They are creative in the many ways they can get into trouble.

But this period in Leos' lives usually ends fairly quickly, since it is attention they want, and they quickly find that the way to get it is to please Mom or Dad.

It is Dad that Leos look to for their love. And they learn early on that love equates with approval. So, Leos strive for Dad's approval, and often for Mom's, too, since they are often one and the same thing.

In Leos' efforts to earn parental approval, they automatically assimilate those things that appear important to Mom and Dad, and attempt to achieve them themselves. If money and status were the focal point of Leos' parents' lives, Leos will seek money and status for themselves. If family ties and activities were the focal point of Leos' early lives, Leos will focus their attention on the creation of their own involved family life, and they will want to include their parents in it. If Leos' parents upheld a good education, Leos will get one.

Often, Leos are so intent on seeking parental approval by achieving the goals they think will earn them Mom and Dad's love, that they neglect their own basic needs. Some Leos never have taken the time to evaluate what their own goals for themselves would be; if only they weren't so busy living up to everyone else's.

When Leos fear that they are unable to live up to the expectations of those they love, or when the approval they seek is withheld in spite of their attainment, Leos develop an ego problem. They may appear egotistical, self-centered, overbearing, and seek center-stage status in every area of their lives. They may become physically aggressive and be constantly angry.

Most Leos transfer their tendency to seek approval from their loved ones to other important people in their lives as well—their spouse, their children, their friends, their boss, and so on.

And of course, since Leos spend a good deal of their time living up to everybody else's expectations, it's only natural that they should assume that other people should live up to theirs. This attitude has several interesting results:

To begin with, it sets the stage for Leos to beget more Leos. That's right. Leos tend to run in families. And of course, since everyone is looking for everyone else's approval and living up to all of those expectations, family traditions, attitudes, and emotional patterns tend to be passed down through Leos' families almost intact. And each succeeding generation adds a few new ones. Leos sure have a lot to live up to!

The other result is that Leo expects other people not of their family and traditions to live up to the same set of values that they do. This is called projection. And Leos are always hurt by it; they are let down, time and time again, by people that they have made incorrect assumptions about.

When Leos finally learn not to project their own values onto others, not to make assumptions, and to set aside their need for approval from others in favor of self-approval, they are well on the way to realizing themselves.

Leo is the sign that is learning self-love. It is the sign in spiritual astrology that is opening up the door to universal love. And self-love (not to be confused with selfish love) is a prerequisite to universal love!

Leos can be one of the most creative signs of the zodiac. They can be natural leaders. But they can only tap their own creativity and leadership abilities when they have learned to let go of their need for outside approval.

So many times I have seen Leos, while having the love and approval of everyone else in their lives, fixate on and strive for the approval of the one person who withholds it. For Leos, this is totally self-destructive and supplies the means by which other people can control them!

Likewise, Leos' constant drive for the perfection of the ideal within themselves, if carried to an extreme, is self-destructive. Often, if Leos also have some planets in Virgo, we see them constantly striving for both the ideal (Leo) and then seeking to criticize whatever progress toward it that they may have made (Virgo).

If Leos do not let go of the need to live up to impossible ideals and the approval of others, they become merely tools to be used by those others. As long as the dream they are attempting to manifest is someone else's and not their own, they live in a glass house—and it is only a matter of time before someone throws a stone to shatter it.

On the lighter side, there is often something cat-like about Leos—from their mane of hair, to their kitten or cat face, to their lithe and graceful movements.

The Leo Woman

The Leo woman enjoys the companionship of men and often most of her friends are male. As with other positive sign women of the zodiac, one of the ways Leo knows that she is accepting her feminine side is when she begins to have lots of female friends, too.

Like her male counterpart, she is living up to the expectations of those around her. On the job, she will be a faithful employee who does her job well. As a mother, she will be conscientious and applaud her children's successes. As a wife, she will put her husband's needs above her own and expect that he will return the favor.

But often the traditions of her upbringing have not prepared her for the realities of life. In her first romantic relationships, she expects to be saved, and she and her prince will live happily ever after. Her Prince Charming usually turns out to let her down. But, of course, she does not readily admit to that. She believes the entire world is watching her and she must make no errors. She covers her errors, pretends the world is perfect, and goes on with life. Remember, she is a fixed sign, so she can hold on and pretend that all is well—even when it is not—for a long, long, time.

On her job, she is idealistic; she works to please the boss. But when the boss passes over the praise she knows she deserves, she is devastated. When she is taken for granted again and again, she feels like a failure. And when he takes her to task in front of the other employees for a mistake she has made, she feels as if she could die. She may even remain working there—remember, she is a fixed sign—but she'll never forget, and she'll get even with him, too. Eventually, she becomes a realist about life, and this is when her real potential is ready to be developed.

She has a strongly physical nature. She often loves sports, and sometimes she even gets into bodybuilding. She likes positions that place her in the public eye—the attention of an audience can be like manna from heaven. And yet, sometimes she is shy, and she must overcome that shyness to attain her own goals and see herself as successful in her own right.

Her interests will vary broadly; you can find her in any field or circumstance that her family traditions may have prepared her for. If she has brothers, she often competes with them and may enter into a primarily male profession.

She commands respect and admiration, and so usually rises quickly in her employment to middle management level, but rarely beyond that unless she has grown beyond the need for the approval of everyone else.

Many times we see the Leo woman drawn to those who are already successful, basking in their reflected light. In these cases, Leo will grow to dislike her successful friend, who holds the position she secretly desires. This inner envy (that Leo cannot admit to because it is an imperfection) cannot be overcome until Leo has become successful in her own right, doing her own thing.

She is energetic, can be vivacious, and when she wants to, she can exude a special something that warms the heart of everyone she knows.

The Leo Man

The Leo man, like his feminine counterpart, is friendly and well liked. Like her, too, he is a very physical person who usually is involved in team sports when young. As he grows older, his love of sports generally continues, but sometimes he changes from participant to observer. Some Leo men refuse to play unless they can win. It is also of note that the way to get the best out of your Leo man is to praise him.

Leos are all concerned with their physical appearance. In the Leo man, this often shows up as his interest in bodybuilding, in wearing the latest male fashion clothing, and in his attention to the details of his appearance.

He also comes from a traditional sort of background and will usually be quite traditional in his approach to the various aspects of his life. This means that he wants to marry and raise a family because that is the way you do things.

Leo men seem to fall into two categories concerning the way they choose their life-mate:

The first type of Leo is Prince Charming to the Damsel in Distress. After he saves her, she is supposed to be forever beholden to and in love with him. There is usually something boyish and sweet about this type of Leo, who is so obviously in love with love. Sometimes he even finds his Damsel. More often, though, he ends up getting hurt. Women have a habit of using this Leo as a salve to tend their own wounds before they move on.

The second type of Leo is much more world wise and sees marriage not as an end in itself (as so many Leos of both sexes do), but merely the means to an end he has in mind. This Leo will choose his mate carefully, according to pre-specified criteria: Is she wealthy? Can she further my career? Is she the type of girl my family will accept?

In a sense, both types have the same failing. They are expecting their life mate to fill a specific role. That expectation results in many Leos marrying other Leos. It also results in many Leos getting hurt as they gradually realize that their life mate has expectations of her own that do not necessarily mirror theirs.

Since Leo usually has traditional values, his ability to achieve a respectable position in his career is just as important to him as having a happy and stable family and home life.

Some Leos will have their own business, but most work for business concerns where they can be assured of recognition and respectability. They like to work for someone whom they can look to for approval, yet they need a business or department small enough in which they can shine. The Leo man loves to shine; he loves to be the center of attention, and he often has cultivated a most charming way of dealing with people. He seems to be able to command women's attention by appealing to their romantic or motherly natures, and to men's attention by appealing to the common ground of their manliness.

He makes a good politician, performer, actor, salesman, and manager.

Since his values are usually traditional, whether he is loyal in his marriage generally depends on the familial and cultural background he comes from. But one thing is certain: If he does cheat on his wife, the woman he chooses will either live in another town, city, or state and she will be so far removed from his family that the affair does not affect his family life at all. For him, what other people think is terribly important, and he will not expose himself or his family to the ravages of rumor and gossip.

He will be proud of his children and will like to romp with them when young and share his interests with them as they get older. But he is not much of a nurturer. Often until the little ones are able to walk or talk he barely notices them, unless it's to exclaim over something like how strong that baby's grip is! Sometimes a Leo man will use his children as a magnet to gain attention for himself.

Occasionally, we see a Leo man who is the rebel. He has evaluated the family expectations and supposedly thrown them away, deliberately doing everything that he knows will make their traditional hair stand on end. Do not make the mistake of thinking that this Leo has grown beyond that need for approval. Buried deep down within each of his individualistic actions is the same need for approval, in spite of what he has done, that all Leos share. He, too, is looking for love. In his case, it was easier to get the love and attention he required by acting opposite to the parental expectations. Usually, when his individualized actions receive approval from some quarter, he reverts back to the more traditional role because inside, he is a traditionalist.

Associate the following concepts with Leo:

- Proud
- Traditional
- Idealistic
- Devoted
- Learning Leadership
- Romantic
- Seeking love and approval
- Creative
- Expects others to act according to his or her values

Virgo — Service with Discrimination

Virgo is the 6th sign of the zodiac

Glyph or Symbol — ♍ — The Virgin

Mode — Mutable

Ruling Planet — ☿ — Mercury

Element — Earth

Corresponding House — 6th

Orientation — Feminine

Corresponding Body Parts — The Excretory System

Mercury

We already discussed Virgo's ruling planet, Mercury, at length when we discussed the other sign it rules, Gemini.

To refresh your mind, please refer back to that discussion before you proceed.

In its rulership of Virgo, the receptive side of Mercury is dominant. Virgos have minds equally as active as Geminis, but usually the mental activity is turned inward in Virgo, as opposed to the outer-directed mentality of Gemini. This is because Virgo is a negative sign, whereas Gemini is positive.

In Virgo, Mercury's action is logical, practical (remember, Virgo is an earth sign), and discriminating.

Since Gemini and Virgo are mutable signs, they both tend to use Mercury's mental nature and communication urge to stir up a change of some sort, in their environment, their family, their work situation, or in themselves.

Therefore, in the sign Virgo, Mercury often takes on a critical edge—critical of both the self and the environment. Virgos, too, are learning a Mercury lesson, but theirs has more to do with thought itself, as opposed to Gemini's lesson in communication.

Here's a review of concepts to associate with Mercury:

- All forms of communication including how you communicate
- How you think
- Telepathy and psychic skills
- Foundation education
- Communication services; Communication equipment
- Flexibility
- Short distance travel
- Siblings, especially the oldest

The Sixth House

The 6th House, like the 3rd, derives its meanings from the planet Mercury. But since Mercury is acting through the element of earth in this house, its effect on the 6th is quite different than its effect on the 3rd.

As you already know, all of the earth houses deal with practical, materially oriented areas of life.

All of the earth houses (2nd, 6th, and 10th) are receptive or negative in polarity, which means that these houses are where the results of your efforts ultimately materialize. The 6th house is where your thoughts (Mercury) materialize.

I realize that this covers a rather broad range of areas, but you might sum it up by saying that the 6th house reflects your daily life. It truly is the House of Manifestation.

For school-age children, day-to-day life generally concerns what's going on in school—how they get along socially, as well as how they relate to the daily activities they experience in school. Remember, the other Mercury-ruled house, the 3rd, shows how you learn. The 6th house is not concerned with learning; it's concerned with doing, with the activities with which you fill your life. I have found, in practice, that when you really want to see how a youngster is going to do in school, you have to consider both of these houses.

For the working person, the daily life aspect of the 6th house describes the work he does and the type of employment he would do best. Mind you, this does not describe his title or profession, but what he actually does.

For example, people with the cardinal signs of Aries, Cancer, Libra, or Capricorn on or in the 6th house need to be in work situations that allow them to pioneer or lead. People with the mutable signs of Gemini, Virgo, Sagittarius, or Pisces on or in the 6th house need work that is constantly stimulating their interests by changing the environment or the people they come in contact with. When the fixed signs of Taurus, Leo, Scorpio, or Aquarius appear on or in the 6th house, the individual will be capable of long hours of work that require sustained attention.

You can also look at the individual's work needs from the point of view of element. The fire sign people (Aries, Leo, Sagittarius) do best at employment that is physical and contains an element of excitement, perhaps something that stimulates their idealistic nature. The earth sign people (Taurus, Virgo, Capricorn) are best suited to tasks that require good, solid judgment and perhaps physical skills. The air sign people (Gemini, Libra, Aquarius) do well in employment that requires people skills and mental creativity. Finally, the water people (Cancer, Scorpio, Pisces) excel at work where they feel they are wanted and needed, as well as where their strong intuitive and creative abilities will shine.

For the stay-at-home-mom or—wife, or the retired individual, the 6th house still shows daily life activity. Again, the sign that occurs on the 6th house cusp, as well as any other signs and/or planets that are in the house, describe the manner in which they will pursue their day-to-day life activities.

Since the 6th house is where your thoughts tend to manifest, it quite naturally follows that it is also the house of health. Even the scientific community has grudgingly come to agree that attitude affects both your likelihood of contracting an illness, as well as your ability to overcome it.

Once again, the sign(s) that are on and/or in the 6th house, and any planets that might fall in it, create whatever natural predisposition you may have toward certain illnesses and the body parts that might be the most readily affected (Note at the beginning of each sign that we cover, the body part it rules is noted).

The study of medical astrology is a complete field unto itself, and it would be an error to mislead you into thinking that this information alone will tell you every illness a person may be subject to. But for the beginning astrologer, looking at the 6th house is a good place to start.

Since the 6th house rules your health, it follows that it also rules the natural healing ability you have. I believe that everyone has some form of healing ability, even if it is only good for self-healing. Again, the signs that appear on and/or in the 6th house, and any planets that are in the house, describe that ability.

For example, earth sign 6th house people will have a grounding and calming effect on others and would make good caretakers of the sick. Fire sign 6th house people are good at handling emergency situations and often make dynamic psychic healers, using a laying on of hands. Air sign 6th house people are wonderful at counseling and talking people through their problems. Water sign 6th house people are often psychic healers without even knowing it, empathically answering the needs of the ill people around them.

The 6th house is also the house we associate with service. What greater service could we do for others than to aid them in their healing? And yet this house rules all types of service, from healing to working in a service field to the simple, everyday services we perform for those we love. Again, the sign on the 6th tells your attitude toward service, as well as your willingness (or lack of willingness) to perform it.

Probably one of the greatest pure services we perform is in caring for the animals of the earth. The sign on the 6th house tells us the pros and cons of your nature concerning ecology, both of the land and its animal life. It tells us if you like pets, and if so, what kind you're most likely to have. Needless to say, the 6th house also rules veterinary medicine.

Also, if in your imagination you turn the natural astrology wheel so that the 4th house (house of the mother) is on the ascendant, you will see that her third house is now what used to be the 6th. The 6th house is the third one from the 4th. This means that your mother's sisters and brothers, your aunts and uncles on her side of the family, show up in this house, too. Remember the concept of spinning the wheel—it will help you tremendously in your actual reading of the chart as you gain experience.

Associate the following concepts with the 6th house:

- Daily life activities
- Health
- Work
- Manifestation
- Healing ability
- Service
- Ecology
- Pets
- Mother's siblings

Virgo

Polarity

Virgo, like Taurus and Cancer, is a feminine or negative sign. That means that in childhood the dominant parental figure was either the mother or some other powerful female. It is from her that Virgos get their most prominent personality traits. It is she that had the greatest impact on Virgos' early development.

Quadruplicity

Virgo is the second of the mutable signs, the first being Gemini.

Virgos' mutability makes them motivators of change. Virgos have an insatiable urge to expose anything that is wrong, worn, broken, corrupt, or just plain not working any more. Once the problem has been exposed and the need for change identified, Virgos either happily move on to their next target or offer their services to assist the change.

This quality does not endear Virgos to most of their colleagues, but it does make them invaluable assets to any person that is seeking self-improvement or any situation that needs renovation.

Needless to say, Virgos excel at all kinds of work that allows full use of their mutability—psychiatry, surgery, critic, proof-reader, dentistry, demolition work, and so on. We also find them all throughout the construction and art fields because once they are done ripping apart the existing foundation, they are more than happy to help rebuild the new one

Triplicity

Virgo belongs to the earth triplicity. The first sign of the earth triplicity was Taurus. Like Taurus, we find Virgos involved in finance, and with physical and material issues as well.

But while Taurus is fixed, Virgo is mutable, so the way in which Virgos utilize their earth quality is quite different.

In Taurus we saw a strong urge to accumulate. Virgos certainly like material things, but they are more likely to see themselves as the caretakers of them than the accumulators of them.

However, they are perfectionists and what they do accumulate needs to be the best. It is not unusual to see Virgos thoroughly investigate a purchase before they make it and then get more mileage out of what they bought than the manufacturer ever believed possible.

What in Taurus is acquisition, in Virgo becomes service. Virgo is the nurse who is there to take care of your physical needs when you are infirm. She is the best of housekeepers and the most detail minded of your clerical staff.

Virgos organize. They are the behind the scenes set-up men that no business or political or performing group could be without.

When Virgos do accumulate stuff, it is always for a reason— not because it is pretty. Virgos like things to have uses. They are likely to have their basements, garages, and storerooms cluttered with interesting stuff they are saving because they might need it one day. And they can spout off a potential use for each object they have saved.

Virgos are difficult but interesting people to live with. They are generally both extremely neat and extremely messy. These extremes could follow one another as Virgos swing back and forth at different times in their lives, and sometimes can co-exist at the same time with Virgos keeping their whole house spotless while maintaining a messy back room. Some Virgos just get stuck in the slob mode for life, while others turn into such neat-freaks that Felix from *The Odd Couple* would envy them!

Virgos need to learn that nothing on this physical plane of existence is ever truly perfect. Every Virgo is, at heart, a perfectionist and constantly tries to make what she sees around her in the physical look like the image of perfection she holds in her mind.

There are two clichés that come to mind that both fit Virgo, and that Virgos should contemplate: the first is, *If it's not broken, don't fix it.* The second is, *Beauty is in the eye of the beholder.*

The Sign Virgo

As mentioned above, Virgos are born into a family situation where, at the time of their birth, the mother or some other strong female is the dominant figure.

Virgo's mother is a sharp woman, both mentally and verbally. She is a perfectionist who sees the world around her, including her husband and children, in need of constant criticism and direction. Often she is an unhappy woman around the time Virgo is born. Being unhappy with herself, she seeks to make those around her correct in themselves those deficiencies she sees in herself.

As seen from Virgo's perspective, Mom is a goddess. She is both benevolent and wrathful at the same time. She is strong and powerful and can ferret out the major fault in anyone and anything.

It is from her that Virgos learn the work ethic, the ability to serve others, the desire to fix whatever they find wrong around them, socially, ethically, materially, and morally.

From Mom, Virgos learn their extremist behavior. For Virgos, life is all or nothing.

Mom is not afraid of work, and since she is a perfectionist, she does everything perfectly. She expects the same perfectionism in her husband and children and rarely is rewarded with it. They rarely know what, exactly, is in her mind until after they have already done whatever she wanted incorrectly.

Usually in Virgo's early childhood, Dad has experienced some sort of disappointment that leaves him feeling undermined. Perhaps he has lost his job or failed to get a promotion or has in some other way been left to feel let down.

Mom's reaction to this is to criticize Dad for his failure. She feels let down because of his inability to achieve her idea of perfection. And, as a result, she criticizes and undermines him throughout Virgo's childhood. In essence, Virgo's Dad is a henpecked husband.

And Virgo gets the clear message—women are strong, men are weak. But Virgo's Mom does not end her critique with her husband. Indeed, she has just started. Everyone in her life is subject to her evaluation, her Virgo child included. So, Virgo grows up with constant criticism and evaluation.

Occasionally, Dad even criticizes Virgo. After all, water runs downhill and it is only fair to pass the buck by criticizing the next guy in line.

The result of all this criticism is that Virgo develops a highly critical and discriminating nature. Virgos never take anything at face value. They have to dig and scratch at it until they know all of its weak points before they can allow themselves to live with it.

Virgos may be critical of those outside themselves, but they are most highly critical of themselves. Mom has taught them that until the outer package clearly expresses the inner ideal, it is simply not perfect. Many Virgos, as a result of having very poor self images, can be even more undermining to themselves than they can to others.

Sometimes their discriminating nature works against them, and they become frozen by the myriad details of the job facing them, or so absorbed into one of those details that they forget the big picture.

But when Virgos finally come to terms with their own nature, they are tireless workers, not afraid to get their hands dirty, and no job is too large or too small to daunt them. Their attention to detail and their organizational ability make them a boon in any work situation.

They make wonderful teachers, since their ability to give concrete form to ideas allows them to present difficult concepts in simple terms, and their eye for detail and dedication to service makes them well aware of how each of their students is fairing. They shine in any service-oriented job.

Virgos have surely been known to be in business for themselves, and when they are, their fine minds, well attuned to financial matters, make them quite successful. But it is more usual to see Virgo working for someone else, where he or she can have the fulfillment they find in serving and the satisfaction they can only get from re-organizing and fixing all of the problems they find (complaining all the while, of course).

Virgos are quite capable of managing people, too, yet most Virgos who opt out of management do not like to be held responsible for other people's shortcomings. As a matter of fact, I have often seen Virgo managers doing the job themselves while the employees stand around and watch because the managers could not trust the employees to do it correctly.

Virgo men and Virgo women react very differently to their early family experiences. Let's see how.

The Virgo Woman

The Virgo woman bases her personality upon the strong role model her mother provided. She may or may not like her mother. Remember, she grew up with lots of criticism, and she, like her male counterpart, is an extremist. If she liked Mom and sided with her, she is probably still very close to Mom, even in adulthood. But if she did not like Mom, she probably has broken most ties to her by adulthood. Either way, her strong personality is based upon Mom's role in her early childhood.

Like Mom, she feels that if it is going to be done right, she has to do it. She is a hard worker who sometimes needs to be reminded to leave herself some playtime. She drives both herself and those close to her to exhaustion, always reaching for perfection and being unhappy with anything that falls short of it.

She knows that women are the stronger sex. Indeed, she may have loved her father, and she probably loves her husband and children, too, but inside she believes that they can only be successful through her intervention and urging.

To this end, she criticizes, guides, cajoles, and manipulates the men in her life toward the success she knows they are capable of, if she can just drag it out of them.

She can be very undermining to the men closest to her. In the extreme, she can, in effect, castrate the men she loves most, undermining their masculinity by constantly pointing out their weakness.

Sometimes she proves this weakness by seeking out and marrying a man who truly needs her dominance. But other times she marries a strong man and systematically undermines him, without ever realizing she is doing so.

Her intentions are good; she never sets out to undermine those she loves. In fact, it is her very desire to improve upon what they have to offer, which ends up re-creating the marital situation she observed between her parents.

It is her lesson to learn the wisdom of not offering criticism until she can offer it constructively, be encouraging, and not discouraging.

Sometimes she marries someone like her mother, who can be highly critical of her. This happens because to feel that you love her, she needs your occasional criticism. You see, she has learned that when someone loves you, they criticize you. It is a challenge to keep that criticism positive, not negative, so that she can feel your concern, but not that you are diminishing or undermining her. This is particularly important if, like some Virgo women, her self-concept is not good. You can help her to develop a strong and healthy self-concept through encouragement and constructive criticism Likewise, accept her criticism in the spirit of love. If she did not care, she wouldn't bother.

Because she is an extremist, the home she keeps may be very neat or incredibly messy; there is no in-between. She will always be on time or will always be late. She will pay attention to details or ignore them totally. She will be concerned with proper health habits, like eating properly and getting enough sleep, or she will throw health concerns to the wind and be a junk food junkie.

She has a wicked sense of humor, and has lots of friends. And when her friends need her, she is always there. She loves to party and she loves those club functions, although she tends to get involved in gossip, constantly, wherever she goes.

She is the female in the zodiac most likely to decide to have a child out of wedlock and bring it up on her own. She is also the female in the zodiac who most readily prostitutes herself for a living—seeing men as the weaker sex, this is not demoralizing for her.

She makes a wonderful mother, looking after her children's every need, both physical and emotional, provided she can keep her critical urge under control.

The Virgo Man

The Virgo man is quite different than the other negative-signed men in the zodiac in that he seeks out and generally enjoys the company of other men. In fact, since he has a healthy suspicion of most women, he feels much more comfortable among men than women. Although, like other negative-signed men, he often finds himself in circumstances where he is literally surrounded by women.

In him, we find that the Virgoan traits take a different form than they do with the Virgo woman because the childhood experience common to all Virgos affects him quite differently.

You see, his natural role model is his father. And in his case, he sees that role model, at best, as a henpecked martyr and, at worst, as a weak and incapable do-nothing.

The Virgo male is all male. He does identify with his father in his maleness, but he sees the strength of character his mother exhibits and copies it. On some deep inner psychological level he takes a vow to be so strong that no one can do to him what he sees his father going through. So, he copies all of Mom's most powerful traits, since she is the power parent. And all the while he views her as the enemy, even if it is on some deeply buried subconscious level.

The Virgo man is in a love-hate relationship with his mother. He respects her, admires her, and copies her. He may be her friend. Yet he fears her because she both has what he needs, so he has to keep coming back to her, and has the power to undermine and destroy him.

As the Virgo boy grows to manhood, he develops all the sharpness and detail-oriented abilities characteristic of Virgo. But, in addition, he develops a nature that is highly suspicious of all of the women around him. Are they all seeking to undermine or control him?

His fine mind plays chess with all of them. He stays one step ahead of all real or imagined ploys to snare him. Often he marries late in life, successfully avoiding deep emotional entanglements until he can hand pick the perfect mate that he can control. Sometimes he seeks a mate who is a good deal younger than him—he mistakenly thinks that her youth and inexperience makes her safe. Of course, she grows up, and that is his mistake. He still has to deal with a woman after all.

Virgo needs to be needed, too. And so often we find him wooing a woman he secretly feels is far beneath him or in trouble, believing that since she needs him and is dependent upon him that he will maintain the upper hand. Guess again, Virgo.

The Virgo man's biggest accomplishment in life is to outgrow his fear of his mother and to stop projecting her characteristics upon every woman he meets. For as long as he believes all women to be like his mother, he will attract highly critical and undermining women just like her. He can only escape this vicious cycle by understanding Mom, by recognizing that it is from her that he got the majority of his most powerful personality traits, and by growing beyond the need to fear her. At that point, the Virgo man can finally enter into and enjoy wholesome relationships with females whom he respects, rather than fears.

The Virgo man, like his female counterpart, tends to be a workaholic. For him, work can be almost a religion. He often feels guilty if he's just sitting and relaxing. He feels the need to be constantly busy, constantly productive.

He loves to work with his hands. For Virgo, hard outdoor manual labor is almost a therapeutic experience. Even Virgo men who work indoors at desk jobs need to set aside outdoor time to ground and center themselves. Virgo's spirit seems to settle down and find a home in the natural environment of the out of doors, be it in the woods, on the water, or just in the back yard.

If you are married to a Virgo, expect him to have his moments of total unreachability. He needs a lot of alone time and can just disappear for hours at a time.

All Virgo men are moody. And when Virgo is in one of his deep, dark moods, the worst thing you can do is dote on him and try to bring him out of it. At these times he needs to be left alone. By withdrawing your attention and your energy from his mood, you help him to break it. All by himself he will work it through and be back to his normal self in no time at all. But if you feed the mood by doting on it, you will perpetuate a cycle of recurring moods that neither one of you will care much for.

His weird health habits may also drive you crazy. He may be a vegetarian, or he may be on a strict diet all week but eat nothing but ice cream on the weekends. And he probably will expect you to join him in his health and dietary experiments. His all or nothing extremist character tends to make him a binger.

Interestingly, since Virgo opposes Pisces, the sign of addictions on the astrological wheel, sometimes Virgos can be the alcoholic or addict in the age-old co-dependent/enabler pattern. Other times they may be the enablers. This applies to both Virgo women and Virgo men. When Virgo is the addict, it is usually a controlled addiction (for example, the weekend binger). Usually when Virgos come to terms with themselves and let go of their fears of Mom and their own self-criticism, they can finally accept their feminine side and let go of their addictive patterns. (Addictions foster escapism or self-punishment.) I believe that one reason people are born into the sign Virgo is to learn to deal with addictive patterns.

The Virgo man can be quite eloquent when he wants to be, yet once you get to know him, he tends to be quiet and is often a better listener than talker. He can find a home in almost any field, yet like his female counterpart, he is best suited to the service-oriented or helping or teaching fields. He is only happy in his work when he feels that he is accomplishing something or fulfilling some purpose.

As a father, the Virgo man is indifferent. He usually does not want children, although he may have a natural ability to handle them. If he does have children, he will be wonderful at attending to their needs if asked; but if left to his own devices, he won't want to be bothered with them until they are old enough to follow along behind him.

Associate the following characteristics with Virgo:

- Critical nature
- Extremism
- Mental
- Service oriented
- Concerned with health issues
- Ultra sloppy or neat

End of Chapter Exercise

1. Be familiar with the Sun sign qualities of Leo and Virgo.

2. Know what the Sun, Mercury, and the 5th and 6th houses represent.

3. Referring back to the chapter as necessary, continue your analysis of the chart we are working on by adding in the new signs and houses you have learned. Answering the following questions will help to guide you through your analysis:

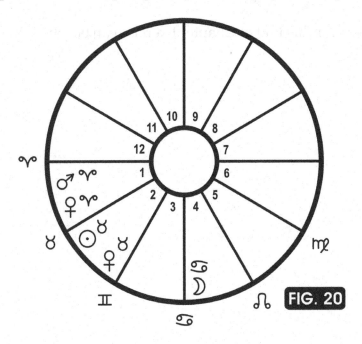

a) What does Leo on the 5th house cusp tell you about how this person will deal with the issues of the 5th house?

b) Since the Sun rules Leo but is in the 2nd house in this chart, the 2nd house will be tied to the 5th. How do you think this bridge will affect the affairs of both the 2nd house and the 5th house? What affect do you think it will have on the Sun sign qualities this person exhibits?

c) What does the sign Virgo on the 6th house tell you about how this person will deal with 6th house matters?

d) Since Mercury rules Virgo but is in the 2nd house in this chart, another bridge is created between the 2nd and the 6th houses. How do you think this might affect the affairs of each house and cause them to work together?

e) Mercury, being so close to the Sun, is bound to have some effect on the Sun sign qualities. What do you think this effect might be?

The key for this End of Chapter Exercise can be found on page 313.

Chapter 6

Introducing Libra and Scorpio

Introducing Libra and Scorpio

Libra is the 7th sign of the zodiac.

The Libra-Aries axis and the 7th house-1st house axis together represent the relationship axis in the astrological wheel.

Glyph or Symbol—♎—The Scales

Mode—Cardinal

Ruling planet—♀—Venus

Element—Air

Corresponding House—7th

Orientation—Masculine

Corresponding Body Part—The Kidneys and Renal System

Venus

The various meanings of the planet Venus have been covered in detail in Chapter 3 when we discussed Taurus, the other sign that Venus rules. Please refresh your memory by reviewing that before continuing further.

The concepts we associate with Venus are:

- Possessive love
- Desire for acquisition
- Receptivity
- Decision-making

- Self-concept
- What we want
- Mom's "role"
- Attitude toward material things
- The perfect woman

As with all of the original planets, Venus rules two signs: one negative and one positive. In Taurus, Venus energy works in a receptive, negative way, while in Libra, her energy works in a generative, positive way, even though Venus, as an innately feminine planet, is naturally receptive.

Librans are constantly looking outside of themselves and toward others to define themselves by comparison. Therefore, Librans' self-concept results from how other people react to and relate to them.

Libra is the sign of opposites. Librans must belong to the group and set that group apart from the outer world by defining its limits. An us-against-the-world attitude results, which enables Librans to define their place in it.

In this way, Venus uses generative force to create opposing poles. Her natural receptivity and reactive nature cause Librans to react to the opposition and thereby define themselves, while encouraging them to merge into the group mind.

It is almost as if Venus causes Librans to set up oppositions to create resistance. The very resistance Librans feel causes them to reach out, to merge with the focus of their resistance.

In Libra, the urge for acquisition that we associate with Venus changes form. Since Libra is an air sign, it is transformed into a desire to belong, an urge to merge. In belonging to a family

159

or a group, Librans both continue to define their self-concept and, at the same time, acquire or merge with the people within the group.

Their possessive love can sometimes make them a one-friend-at-a-time person. The receptive action of Venus causes them to desire to merge so closely with the object of their love, that they may lose all identity outside of the relationship.

Carried to the extreme, this urge to merge can be extremely self-destructive, leading to codependency and placing enormous stress on the relationship partner.

Librans need people. Yet Venus continuously sets up opposing forces in Librans' lives so that each time they acquire one set of friends they must polarize themselves to another set. They are continually forced to take sides, to make choices.

Libra is the sign most often associated with indecision. You can easily see the action of Venus here again, causing Librans confusion when they are suspended between the very opposites they have created and are forced to make a decision.

Librans are faced with dilemmas: If I go to the movies with Sally, Jennifer will be mad because I'll miss her party, or I would like to buy the red shirt, but my boyfriend likes the green one.

For Librans, every decision is monumental because they realize that, ultimately, each decision further polarizes and redefines who they are.

So, Venus causes every Libra to be constantly looking outside of themselves, toward other people. How they love, how they feel about themselves, what they think is worth acquiring, what they think the "perfect woman" would be, and even their values concerning money and things are based on their interaction with others.

Add the following concepts to your understanding of Venus:

- The urge to merge
- Codependency
- The principle of attraction through polar opposites

The Seventh House

The 7th house in the astrology wheel derives its meanings from the planet Venus, just as the 2nd house does.

In the 7th house, Venus is concerned with one-on-one relationships of all kinds. This house defines all partnerships, the relationship you have with your mother, father, sister, brother, best friend, boss, co-worker, spouse and child, as long as only the two of you are involved. The 7th house even defines the relationship between you and those who may be your open enemies. And of course, any written or verbal agreements or contracts you may have with another person are 7th house matters as well.

The sign that appears on the 7th house cusp tells the astrologer both how you are most likely to act in a relationship, as well as the type of partner you will attract.

For example, if you have Aries on the 7th house cusp, you will tend to be outspoken and aggressive, even competitive in your relationships. And you will attract someone who also is a competitive and individualistic person. You may not see yourself as competitive and wonder how you attracted that mate who is. But remember, they could not compete if there was not someone there willing to compete with them.

It is interesting to note that often someone who has Taurus on the 7th house cusp, will complain that their mate or partner is stubborn, fixed, and perhaps even a couch potato, never realizing that the mate is acting out his (or her) own pattern of relating or its opposite. Perhaps that person sees the mate as materialistic and overly concerned with money, but what he needs to see is that the person he has attracted is merely a reflection of himself, being either the same as him or exactly his opposite.

Remember, the 7th house is where, through your relationships, you are forced to come face to face with yourself.

So, the sign on the 7th house describes the type of person you are likely to be involved with in partnerships, whether that partnership is business, friendship, or marriage. Any planets in the 7th house further define the personality of that individual. And both the sign on the house cusp and any planets in the house describe how you will relate in turn.

The 7th house describes the process of relationship. By paying close attention to this house, you can pinpoint the major relating problems that a person will have. For example, with Aries on the cusp, the major problem with the mate will be competition, until the native recognizes his own competitive nature. With Taurus on the cusp, the major problems will involve money and things until the native recognizes his own attachment to them.

With Gemini on the 7th, you will attract a mate who is either a strong or weak communicator, and major relationship problems will focus on communication. With Cancer there, you will attract a mate who needs nurturance but has difficulty giving it until you freely give of yourself and make your own needs known in return. With Leo on the 7th, you will attract a mate who is very concerned with appearance and tradition—and your major problem will be getting both of you to admit there might be one. Virgo on the 7th attracts a mate who is critical and the problem will be to avoid being mutually undermining. Libra on the 7th is a yes man (or woman) who gives all of his power over to the mate and then gets mad when the mate does not do the same in return. Scorpio on the 7th attracts a secretive mate, and their major problems will arise out of mutual suspicion. Sagittarius on the 7th attracts a gregarious and social mate with major philosophical differences, out of which most of their problems will arise. Capricorn on the 7th attracts a mate who is a workaholic and opportunist, or is one himself. The solution here is to be workaholics together. Aquarius on the 7th attracts a mate who is unique and offbeat, a reflection of himself. The challenge here is to move to the same rhythm while you each dance to your own drummer. Pisces on the 7th attracts a martyr, and is one as well. The major problem here involves guilt and blame, and is resolved when the mutual martyrdom is ended.

Associate the following concepts with the 7th house:

- One-on-one relationships
- Marriage
- Contracts between partners
- Open enemies
- The way you relate
- The partner you attract
- The type of problems your relationship will have

Libra

Polarity

Libra is a positive, or masculine, sign. Therefore, the dominant parent in the childhood was the father or another male figure.

Remember, though, that Libra's ruler, Venus, is an innately feminine planet.

And realize, too, that Libra's mother is also a strong figure.

The result of all of this is that although Libra is both positive and masculine, all Librans seem to carry something of the opposite sex within them.

Male Librans are usually very pretty people, often with a demeanor that some think is effeminate. Yet rarely do you find a gay Libran.

Female Librans usually have an appearance and demeanor that, although feminine, projects something masculine at the same time. They may attract lesbian interest, but rarely are they themselves lesbian.

Perhaps this tendency to project something of both sexes that all Librans have has something to do with Venus and her tendency in this sign to cause the individual to seek unity by being caught in the tension of resolving opposites.

Quadruplicity

Libra is the third of the cardinal signs. You know now that the cardinal signs are supposed to be self-starters and pioneers.

But Librans do not do their pioneering alone, and they cannot seem to get started with anything unless there is some resistance from outside of themselves, forcing their reaction and thereby getting them moving.

Libra is a re-active sign. Their cardinality is only apparent once they get moving, once they have been motivated. When working as part of a team, they are innovative and even brilliant. When faced with resistance, they find unbounded reservoirs of energy to overcome it.

If you have a Libran child and want that child to do something, all you have to do is make sure he has a support system in standing against you, and then tell him to do the exact opposite of what you want. Or tell him he cannot do what it is that you really want him to do. When given the support of a partner, and faced with adequate resistance, Librans can accomplish the impossible.

But without a partner and without resistance, Librans will take the easy way out (remember, Venus is innately lazy); they will vegetate.

Therefore, the partners Librans choose in life are of utmost importance. If those partners become the opposition themselves, Librans will, in essence, not have partners and will not move forward. But if Librans' partners work with them in facing resistance outside the relationship, Librans' cardinality begins to work, and before long they are well ahead of the pack.

Triplicity

Libra is the second air sign, Gemini being the first. As you know, the air element deals with the mental nature, thought and communication, and socialization.

In Libra, we see the air element at its most intense. Libra is the most mental sign of the zodiac. Their minds are always active, and they're constantly playing and replaying in their own minds their interactions with others.

Librans are wholly concerned with people, communication, counseling, mediating, and any other people interaction.

Librans spend time in the realm of thought, theorizing and hypothesizing, usually about human relations.

They make wonderful poets and authors, and shine in any work where delicate people management is required.

The Sign Libra—Learning to Relate

Librans, being an air sign like Gemini, are also born into home environments where there are mental and verbal battles going on. Usually the battle is between the parents, but sometimes it is a sibling and a parent, sometimes a grandparent and a parent, or it may even switch around.

But the part Librans play in these battles is quite different than Geminis', and the way the battles are conducted is different as well. Librans are the go-betweens for the two parties engaged in battle; however, Librans are permitted no active part in the battle. It is as if first parent places his missile of destruction on the Librans' shoulders, directing Librans to carry it to the other, and when the second parent receives the missile she reacts by sending one of her own, again, via the Librans.

For example, a Libra's Mom tells him, "Go tell your Dad dinner's ready." Libra trots into the other room and announces to Dad that Mom says it's time for dinner. Dad loudly replies,

"I told your Mom I didn't want to eat until after the game was finished!" He turns up the TV. Libra returns to Mom and jauntily tells her that Dad will be in when the game is over. Mom, red-cheeked and sweaty from slaving over the hot stove, gets a wicked look in her eye, puts her hands on her hips, and in her most authoritative tone of voice says, "Well, you just tell him that if he can't get his you-know-what in here right now, he'll find his dinner in the trash can!"

By now, Libra is beginning to sweat himself. Nervous and tense, fearful of Dad's reaction, he makes his way back to Dad and somehow, between football plays, manages to give Dad Mom's message, as gently as he can. Sure enough, Dad bellows in anger, "You know what your mother can do with dinner, don't you? Well, you just tell her . . ." And so the arguments go, Libra being the go-between, being forced to absorb the anger of the parents toward each other, and never given the opportunity to release it himself, always fearing that one or the other parent will finally get mad enough to leave, feeling the burden that the success or failure of the parents relationship is his responsibility.

Libra grows up with an intense anger inside, the accumulated anger of both parents toward each other that he or she was forced to absorb, the anger he feels toward his parents, who forced him to be the go-between, the anger he has built up as a result of years of fearing that one or both parents would leave.

And all of this anger he carries inside, where no one can see it. Because in his early home environment, everyone was allowed to express their emotions except him. He was taught to suppress them. And it was only one step further for Libra to disassociate from his emotions all together!

167

By the time Libra is a teenager, he no longer knows why he feels what he feels. He may be angry and act out, and not even know that he is doing it or why he is doing it.

In extreme situations some Librans born in the first 10° of the sign may have actually been physically abused, as one parent took out their anger at the other by brutalizing the child. These children can separate so far from their emotions that they need extensive therapy to recover. These Librans, trapped in their childhood pattern, may grow up to be unconscious yellers and screamers who terrify their own children, as they unconsciously repeat in their own parenting what they felt as a child.

For Librans to become emotionally healthy people again, they must first be allowed to express their anger. They should be encouraged to express anger the moment they think they feel it. This is important because, so many times, Librans disassociate from their angry reactions at the moments of occurrence only to blow up later at some totally unrelated thing.

The problem is, that when Librans disassociate from their anger, they disassociate from all of their other emotions as well. They must not only accept their anger, but also track it down, pinpoint it, and learn to express it openly as it occurs, in order to unblock all the other emotions that they have suppressed.

It often takes Librans many years to work through this dilemma. In the meantime, their early childhood training carries over into every aspect of their lives.

In the workplace, they are the mediators of every inter-employee conflict. Never showing a hint of their own emotions, they carefully guide both contending parties to an understanding of the issues. They become marriage counselors and mediators in all of the dilemmas their friends bring to them. They spend hours trying to understand the people around them, always alert to feathers that need to be soothed, hands that need to be held.

In their marital and familial relationships, they continually stir up the same war-like situations they experienced as a child, only to play the mediator once again. It is as if each time they are able to successfully mediate another argument, they are reaffirming their success—through their sacrifice, Mom and Dad will stay another day.

Librans' greatest fear is desertion. And they will continue to have that fear until at some point in their adult relationship there is a wild argument, or some other dreaded thing happens that they cannot prevent, and the mate does not leave. This experience is necessary for all Librans because it sets them free from having to be responsible for the happiness of all the other people in their environment. It also sets Librans' families free from the co-dependent situation that the attitude created.

You see, before this in their relationships they were so over-considerate of the other parties that they put all of their partner's most casual needs above their own, no matter how unimportant. They martyred themselves. They were so busy giving to their partners and being there for them that when the partners realized their inability to keep up with giving back, they gave up and began to take Librans for granted. That's when Librans got mad.

Unfortunately, most Librans wait until they feel so used and abused by the person they have created this co-dependent relationship with, that all love has died long before they allow themselves to get angry and assert themselves. Their fear of desertion prevents them from fully expressing their emotions, as long as they still care. It is not unusual to see Librans drop the wad of everything that has bothered them for the last ten years in their mates' laps all at once, and then walk out the door. By then it is too late to save the relationship, even though the partner is willing now to do their share—Librans no longer care.

It may take Librans a lifetime or two to work through this pattern, but when they finally do, they are masters of relating, who thoroughly understand human nature and the whole process of relating. They are in touch with their emotions again, and understand others' as well. In fact, they are no longer afraid of those emotions or their open expression. They have learned to balance the need for give and take in a relationship and have no fear of speaking up to demand their fair share. They won't fight others' battles for them.

The Libra Woman

In the sign Libra, we see very little difference between the experience of the female as opposed to the male. Both have essentially the same experience described above. But perhaps the social aspects are a little more important for the Libran woman than the Libran man.

As the Libran woman is growing up, it is very important to her to belong to the elite group. She must not just belong, she must be in the inner circle. It is important to her to fit in: to have the same clothing and hair style as the other girls. If it is a fad and everyone has it or is doing it, she experiences deep feelings of deprivation if she cannot do it, too.

Dating is incredibly important to the Libran girl. Both having a date and having the *right* date are of utmost importance. Often her social life is of far greater importance to her than her work or her schoolwork. She is very concerned with status.

As she grows older, this gives her a keeping up with the Jones appearance. She attracts people who compete with her and who think she competing with them. This sets in motion the us-against-them syndrome that was discussed earlier.

She likes to socialize, and so her home is often a place of meetings, parties, and other odd gatherings. And, of course, since she is so status conscious, she is certain to have the latest music, color-coordinated plates and napkins, and the finest table settings the event will allow.

Her eye for balance and appreciation of color make her a fine decorator, and she will love art, whether in the guise of an artist or as an art appreciator.

If she has children, she will make a better friend than mother, since to an air sign, nurturance does not come readily, whereas communication and social interaction are quite natural. She will be an active parent, being class mother, confidante to her children's friends, and involved in all of their physical and emotional crises. Her family will be very important to her, and she will strive continually to maintain a harmonious atmosphere in her family life.

As a matter of fact, she hates anything that produces anger, disharmony, and imbalance in her home situation, and yet, more often than not, introduces these things herself, only to be forced to play mediator once again.

If she works, she is wonderful in the literary field, as well as in any work that works with or for organizations. She is a wonderful mediator, personnel manager, union representative, or artist.

The Libra Man

The Libran man's experience is similar to the Libran woman's.

As a child, he usually has a sense of initially belonging and then being cast out. The result is that as he is growing up it is very important to belong. Depending on his character, we may find him leading the student government or out smoking behind the storeroom with the other guys who are cutting class.

He is just as status-conscious as the Libran woman, but his idea of status and belonging may be somewhat different than hers. We find a considerable number of Librans in motorcycle gangs!

Dating is important to him, too, but he is self-conscious in the extreme and is therefore often overly shy in his pursuit of women. He seems to make friends with them easily enough but has a lot of trouble turning the friendship into a romantic relationship. In his desire to please and keep his romantic partner, he often gets used and hurt.

It is common for Librans of both sexes to become involved in the proverbial love triangle. But it is the Libran man who tends to be most often used as the shoulder to cry on while the object of his adoration pours out her heart to him all about her other lover.

He is very impressionable, even more so than the Libran woman, and will adopt the values of the group he has determined to belong to. If you are the parent of a Libran child, please be aware of this: The friends he has are likely to have a greater affect on his value system than you are.

He, like his female counterpart, is looking for acceptance, for a feeling of belonging. And he is looking for himself.

He can merge into the group so strongly that his own needs are submerged within the group needs. He may feel that when his own personality is totally submerged, he has found himself, but what has actually happened is that he succeeded in running away from himself.

He is much more mental than the Libran woman, and as a result, it is even harder for him to work through the problem of disassociation of emotions than it is for her. In his case, his disassociation is sometimes so complete that he actually projects his emotions onto others, never recognizing them as his own.

One of his most important lessons is to learn that those traits he dislikes most in other people are probably the very ones that he does not like in himself and is denying.

The Libran man is a gentle person who seeks peace and balance in his environment. For this reason, it is a shock to see his anger, which can storm up for no apparent reason and often takes physical form. I know parents of several Libran children, as well as Libran adults, who have wisely invested in punching bags for these moments.

Often the Libran man fears having children because he does not want to repeat his own childhood experience. If he does have children, he makes a good father, supplying authority and gentleness in equal balance. However, you will find him impatient with children, especially the young ones who upset his sense of harmony. If you are married to a Libra, expect him to share in all of the work involving the kids when you ask his help, but don't expect him to like it.

The Libran man does well in many different types of work. His mental nature and thoughtful mind make him a good teacher, writer, and researcher. His mediation abilities make him a good politician, arbiter, counselor, or coach. Add to that his people skills and you find him particularly good at those middle management jobs that the rest of the world hates. He is a good salesman, too. And I have even known Librans who have run very successful companies of their own.

Associate the following characteristics with Libra:

- Mediation
- Resistance
- Learning to relate
- Resolving opposites
- Disassociation of emotion
- Balance
- Love of harmony and art
- Co-dependency
- Mental
- Need to belong

Scorpio — Born to Transform

Scorpio is the 8th sign of the zodiac.

The Scorpio-Taurus axis and the 8th house-1st house axis together represent the power axis in the astrological wheel.

Glyph or Symbol — ♏ — The Scorpio, Phoenix, Eagle

Mode — Fixed

Ruling planet — ♂ — Mars

Co-ruler — ♇ — Pluto

Element — Water

Corresponding House — 8th

Orientation — Feminine

Corresponding Body Part — The Reproductive Organs

Mars

We have already discussed the action of Mars astrologically when we covered the sign Aries in Chapter 3. Please refer back to that to be sure you understand Mars in its rulership of Aries before continuing.

Here is a review of the associations we make with Mars:

- Energy
- The way you act
- Anger

- The way your father acted
- Aggression
- Sex
- Competition
- Impatience

Scorpio is a negative, receptive sign. In Scorpio, the action of Mars is turned inward, as opposed to the outward-directed action of Mars in positive Aries, the other sign that it rules.

When Mars energy is turned inward, it creates the sometimes brooding yet magnetic personality we associate with Scorpio. It is as if Mars creates a pressure vessel out of Scorpio. All of that energy focusing inward results in Scorpios being secretive, behind-the-scenes people. They may appear calm on the surface, but underneath, Scorpios are seething with emotion, with ideas, with pent up energy seeking release. It is that inward focus of energy that causes Scorpios to be such magnetic, often sensual, people.

That sensuality, combined with the obvious sexuality of Mars, causes Scorpios to be pre-occupied with sex. It is as if in the sex act, Scorpios sense life energy itself. Perhaps they feel that at the moment of orgasm they are on the brink of true self-discovery, true union with the higher self. Scorpios are getting to know the sexual side of Mars, and in so doing, they often end up dealing with both their own and others' sexual problems.

Because the focus of Mars' energy is inward, when Scorpios are angry, the anger is harbored and nurtured as a grudge that may take years to be released. Indeed, the lower evolved Scorpio might take years to arrange, orchestrate, and fulfill their proper revenge.

Like Aries, Scorpios compete, since they are Mars-ruled. But Scorpios' competition is subtle, and is more in evidence as games involving power and control rather than direct competition. When your competitor is a Scorpio, expect massive strokes of genius that appear out of nowhere and leave you defenseless. Scorpios will not let their actions become seen until the last moment. Remember, in Scorpio, Mars energy is inner directed.

Mars is naturally generative, masculine. It seeks outward expression. So, all of Scorpios' internally directed energy ultimately seeks to act upon the world around them.

This is why, for Scorpios, the sudden stirring to action that has been brewing for years can seem like an explosion. That explosive quality of Mars in Scorpio is responsible for the power of transformation that all Scorpios possess. Through it, they transform themselves, and in transforming themselves they transform the world around them!

Add the following concepts to your understanding of Mars:

- Explosive
- Transforming

Pluto

Pluto is the outermost body in our solar system, taking 235 years to go around the Sun once. It was discovered in 1930.

Although in 2006 Pluto lost its planetary status among astronomers, astrologers still use it in as a planet in astrological analyses.

Shortly after Pluto was discovered, World War II was fought, the atomic bomb was developed and used, and nuclear energy use evolved, all of which substantially changed our world.

In the astrological community, these events were seen to give insight as to how Pluto would function. Since the sign that most clearly related to all of these things was Scorpio, astrologers generally agreed to assign Pluto as a co-ruler of Scorpio and the 8th house, adding it to the traditional rulership by Mars.

However, there is still not total agreement upon that assignment, though it is the one used by most astrologers today. Spiritual astrologers generally only use the original traditional rulerships, not specifically assigning the three outer planets (including Pluto, Neptune, and Uranus) to any one sign.

Still other astrologers focus on Pluto's relationship to the masses, and in particular the unconscious of the masses—the group mind. These astrologers prefer to see Pluto as a co-ruler of Pisces and the 12th house, which rules the unconscious. Some astrologers even associate Pluto with Aries, assuming that Pluto's co-rulership with Mars in Scorpio should apply to Aries, too. But no matter where you choose to apply it, Pluto's characteristics are clearly defined.

Pluto is primarily a planet of transformation. After all, what is nuclear fission if not the transformation of matter into energy?

Wherever Pluto falls in your chart, by sign and house, is where you will transform yourself in this lifetime. That sounds rather profound and spiritual, doesn't it?

But the process Pluto uses, in its effort to transform you, is far from spiritual, and certainly not easy. Pluto leads you systematically into the deepest, darkest parts of yourself, those you have buried the deepest, and then forces you to recognize and eliminate them.

On its lowest level of expression, Pluto is obsession. It shows by its location in your chart where you are most likely to become obsessive. By obsessive I mean being so single-mindedly absorbed by a person or issue that you cease to be able to think about anything else. It is as if you've become addicted to whatever the object of your obsession is.

As Pluto hooks you, you become progressively more obsessed, until you find yourself needing to control the object of your obsession due to your over concern and insecurity with it. In fact, the more obsessed you become, the more out of control you feel, and the more you feel the need to control the situation.

And so you begin to manipulate it. Pluto, by its sign and house, shows you where you are most likely to be manipulated (through your obsession) and do your own manipulating (to regain control over the object of your obsession).

This power struggle involving manipulation and control can go on for a long time. But eventually, Pluto shows you that the very thing that you are trying to control is actually in control of you. By the time you realize this, you have usually made a fool of yourself and sacrificed everything else that was important to you, through your neglect, during your obsession.

The only good thing to come out of this is that by the time Pluto is done with you, your obsession is gone. It is like you were an addict who could no longer stand the sight or smell of the drug. And when you are no longer an addict in that area of your life described by Pluto, you can finally draw on the higher side of Pluto and use its magnetism, intensity, power, and transformative ability to change your own life and help to uplift the people around you.

Let me show you a common example:

Suppose you are a man who obsesses over whatever woman you are involved with (I'll bet you even know a few people like this).

Your obsessive kind of love makes you think of her constantly. And because all you can think about is her, you find yourself calling her constantly, finding excuses to drop by her house or work, and so on. And of course, a good deal of the time you call or drop by, she is not there!

This stirs up the insecurity you feel because of your obsession with her. So, you begin to manipulate and control her by telling her when you are going to call late each night to make sure she is home.

You make dates with her on all of her days off so that she does not have the time to be with anyone else. Whenever she goes out, you insist she call you when she gets back so you know she is home safely.

You may create emotional crises with her in order to draw her into your obsession. If she gets drawn in, the two of you might continue this game of obsessive-manipulation for a long time.

But one day, you realize that you do not go out with your friends anymore because you never have any time; your free time is all spent following her around. You realize that you are waiting for her to call and report in, when you could be out having a good time yourself. You realize, in effect, that you have no life of your own anymore, outside of the manipulation game that you are playing with her. That which you had sought to own now owns you! You have let everything else in your life slide and the quality of the relationship you have developed with her, based on no firmer ground than an obsessive need to control, is just not worth the sacrifice you have made.

Once reality hits, you face your own obsessiveness and let it go. And all of the emotional energy that you had tied up in it is freed up for you to use constructively in other areas of your life.

As a welcome fringe benefit, your future relationships will also be happier and healthier.

Additionally, Pluto is said to rule death, and, indeed, it does. But as you have seen, Pluto kills off what is no longer needed and leaves vast stores of energy behind. So, Pluto is really a good guy after all!

And remember, too, that Pluto rules the unconscious habit patterns of an entire generation of people. After all, it stays in a sign from anywhere between 11 years (Scorpio, the short end of its orbit) and about 35 years (Taurus, the long end of its elliptical orbit).

Its house placement in your chart will show you where you are working out the deeper psychological problems of your entire generation. The sign it is in shows what those problems will be.

Some astrologers also consider Pluto to be the dark mother, where you fear to be engulfed and overwhelmed by the female side of your own nature, as depicted by the devouring mother in mythology.

Associate the following concepts with Pluto:

- Transformation
- Regeneration
- Death
- The "Devouring Mother"
- Obsession
- Manipulation
- The collective unconscious

The Eighth House

The 8th house, like the 1st, derives its meanings from the planet Mars, but in the 8th, Mars is acting through the element of water, with a fixed or succedent mode, as well as a negative polarity. This makes its effect on the 8th house quite different than the 1st. The 8th house is also co-ruled by Pluto, which further accentuates the differences between the two houses.

The 8th house rules death and regeneration through its association with Pluto. All kinds of deaths occur here, from the little deaths that occur all throughout our lives whenever it is time to end something in our lives, to the major, physical deaths of people who are important to us.

The sign on the 8th house cusp indicates how you deal with death and all kinds of losses.

With a fire sign here you might be a daredevil, defying death when you get the chance. An earth sign here will be very matter of fact about death-related issues. An air sign might be very intellectual about it, but might not be able to actually deal with the physical fact. A water sign on the 8th will be highly emotional about anything concerning death, but will also have an intuitive understanding of it.

Since the 8th house deals with death and dying, it stands to reason that it also rules wills and all of the circumstances, both legal and medical, that might surround a death.

Both Pluto and Mars contribute to this house being one of the *power houses* of the astrological wheel. In fact, the 2nd-8th house axis is considered the *power axis* in astrology. The sign on the cusp, as well as any planets in the house, reveal how you are likely to approach power, both your own and that of others. Do you deal with it directly, or are you just attracted to it like a moth flitting around a flame? Do you avoid power and powerful people? Do you see yourself as the power person in your life? Do you find yourself continually engaged in head-on conflicts and confrontations with either people you see as power figures, or with the establishment in the form of big business and government agencies?

The 8th house deals with power and control in all of its forms, from big business to government to labor unions to the banking system, and even to the Mafia. It concerns itself with all legal issues between more than two parties, and rules the actual practice of law.

Often people with heavy 8th houses (by heavy, I mean having a lot of planets in the 8th house) work for these large institutions, where they are constantly working with and managing other people's money and developing other people's abilities.

I have often noted that when a woman has a lot of planets in her 8th house, she usually ends up being the support system for someone else, either emotionally or financially, even though her innermost desire is to be taken care of herself. It is like she is being required to help others to develop their own abilities in whatever way she can, and in so doing transforms her own tendencies away from dependency.

When a man has a lot of planets here, the result is quite different. These gentlemen usually seem to end up in a situation, whether by accident or design, where they are dependent upon someone else. In this case, it is their dependency that is forcing the development of new abilities in the person they are depending on.

Because of the Mars/Pluto influence here, there is also a very strong secretive aspect to the 8th house that places secret fraternities of all kinds in this house. So, societies like the Rosicrucians, the Masons, and the Ninja belong to this house, along with all magical fraternities.

The 8th house, therefore, is the house of the occult, since occult means hidden. This is the house that we associate with all types of magic, the practice of astrology (not the science itself, but the *practice* of it), séances, and the practice of all kinds of psychic work where the non-physical world is being tapped in some way. This house is especially strong in people who are psychic mediums.

Lastly, the 8th house rules your second child, should you have one. The pattern here is that the children appear around the chart in the fixed or succedent houses in their order of birth. In this case, the sign on the 8th house cusp and any planets in the 8th house will determine your relationship with the child and how you will see the child.

Associate the following concepts with the 8th house:

- Death
- Regeneration
- Big business
- Government and Law
- Banks
- Other people's money
- Other people's abilities
- Power
- Secrecy
- Secret organizations
- The occult
- The second child

Scorpio

Polarity

Scorpio is a negative or receptive sign. Like the other negative signs we have covered—Taurus, Cancer, and Virgo—Scorpio is female-dominated in childhood, and receptive and reactive in nature.

Because Scorpio is Mars/Pluto ruled and is a water sign, the negative polarity causes Scorpios to direct their extreme emotionalism inward, where it may not be evident to others, yet where it exerts a constant pressure on Scorpios to react intensely and emotionally to all of the circumstances of their lives.

Quadruplicity

Scorpio is the third of the fixed signs. In Scorpio, the strong energies of Mars/Pluto combined with the negative polarity of the sign cause an inward direction of energy that is then held onto and permitted to brew.

It is this fixed quality of Scorpio that allows them to hold onto a grudge for years and that creates the build-up of tension, which ultimately results in explosions that transform their lives.

It is also Scorpios' fixed qualities that, when combined with their extreme emotionalism, allows them to make life-long commitments to a partner, whether that partner is faithful or not.

And it is this same quality of fixed emotion that results in Scorpios' tendencies toward obsession—a tendency that ultimately gets them into trouble and causes them to transform.

Scorpio is learning about commitment, and about the danger of obsession. And yet it is through obsession that Scorpios learn how to make commitments. I believe one of the reasons that someone incarnates as a Scorpio is because, in other lives, he or she refused to be committed to anyone or anything.

Through their fixed emotion they are led into obsessive behavior. That behavior teaches them about the value of commitment. Once that new value is learned, their obsession reaches explosive proportions and they must let go of the object of obsession to regain freedom for themselves.

In the process, they learn to make and keep commitments, and to follow through on what they promise.

Triplicity

Scorpio is the second of the water signs, the first having been Cancer. In Cancer, the water element was cardinal. This causes Cancers to wear their emotions on their faces, and their emotional responses are quick, spontaneous, and easily forgotten.

But in Scorpio we see an entirely different kind of water. Scorpios' fixed qualities slow down their emotional responses. Scorpios save up those trading stamps—the things that bother them, merely, get filed away for future reference. They are never forgotten, but just stored away until the proper moment comes to resurrect them.

Scorpios are famous for their poker faces. They will never let you know if you have scored. They conceal their emotions, both positive and negative. It is hard to ever really know exactly how Scorpios feel about something because they are so busy hiding their emotions from you (along with everything else, too).

They love secrecy. They keep so many secrets from so many people that it is hard to keep them straight. And just because Scorpios keep something a secret does not make it important. Even small, negligible things can make a good secret, if there is someone out there who wants to know it. Remember, too, that Scorpios easily fall for their own games. If you want to get their interest, just let them know you're keeping a secret from them.

However, on the more serious side, many Scorpios do have deep, dark secrets to hide, and they know the art of burying something so deep that they have almost forgotten it themselves. And they will keep your secrets for you long after you have forgotten what it was you wanted to conceal.

187

Scorpios' concealment of their emotions, their secrecy, and their tendency to think through their emotions over and over make them appear very mental. But they are not. Always remember, Scorpio is a water sign, so every decision that Scorpios make in life, no matter how well thought out and organized, no matter how firmly based in actual physical circumstance, will, ultimately, be made emotionally or intuitively.

The Sign Scorpio

In childhood, Scorpios are most strongly influenced by their mothers, copying her strengths and powerful character traits, both good and bad.

Scorpios are the unwanted children in the zodiac. I know that sounds harsh, and many of you reading this who have Scorpio children disagree because you know how much you love your child, but this is the basic fact of Scorpios' existence. Usually at the time a Scorpio is born, no matter how much the child was wanted prior to conception, something is going on in the family that makes Mom have second thoughts about this child.

Perhaps the parents had to get married because of the pregnancy. Or perhaps Dad lost his job right after Mom got pregnant. Perhaps Mom just went through a severe pre-birth depression and had doubts about her mothering ability. Or perhaps the pregnancy was not wanted.

The cause varies. But usually, even while Scorpio is still in the womb, the unborn infant is already being affected by Mom's second thoughts concerning the birth. He or she feels unwanted.

The effect of being unwanted is to make Scorpios feel guilty, because of their intrusion into the parents' lives. This is the root of the almost instinctive guilt we see in all Scorpios even in their adulthood.

Scorpios will do almost anything to prevent themselves from being in a position of obligation and guilt. Intuitively they know that the easiest way for them to be controlled is through their guilt. This is interesting because they seem to draw circumstances to themselves in which they feel guilty over and over again, until they realize that it is they, themselves, who create those circumstances. They must forgive themselves before they can forgive anyone else.

One of the methods I usually suggest to Scorpios to help them to deal with their tendency to feel guilty about everything is for them to take the time to think through the probable results of each of their actions. If they are prepared for the result that their actions create, they will either change their minds about acting or take action and resolve not to feel guilty afterward.

If you expect Scorpios to let you know they feel guilty, guess again. They are far too aware of how easy it is for you to gain control of them through their guilt. The most you will get out of them is a grudging apology and a chip-on-the-shoulder attitude.

But the scenario of Scorpios' early life continues. Shortly after a Scorpio is born, Mom's attitude completely reverses itself. As a matter of fact, when she realizes how she has hurt this poor Scorpio infant she often feels guilty and tries to make it up to the child. She may then lavish love and attention on the child or try to bribe them into an acceptance of her love; in essence she is asking the child's forgiveness.

Scorpio's response to this is interesting. The Scorpio child, being no fool, looks at this change in attitude and reacts to it in a highly suspicious manner. It is as if the child is saying, "OK, you didn't want me to begin with, and now all of a sudden you're hanging all over me and trying to give me things. Well, let's see . . . There must be something you want from me. I think maybe I'll just sit back and wait to see how high you're willing to jump to get whatever it is you're after!"

This reaction takes place so early in Scorpio's life that many will not even remember it. But from it arises Scorpio's innate suspicion of people, his tendency to manipulate people emotionally, his concealment of his own emotions, his need to look beneath the surface of every action to determine its motive, and his suspicion of anything that is offered to him, even when it is offered with good intentions.

Scorpios are so sure, deep down inside of themselves, that they are unwanted, that they often feel the need to buy the person or people they care about, just as Mom did in the scenario above. In this way, they create dependencies of loved ones on them, thereby assuring themselves that the loved ones cannot leave. The problem here is that because Scorpios have bought them, they never can believe that the people in their lives really love them. And because of Scorpios' innate suspicion of the true motives of everyone, they never show the people they love the most how they truly feel because, they fear so deeply that their feelings are not returned.

Scorpios' suspicious nature causes them to look deeply into everyone they meet. Most Scorpios are aware of their penetrating stare, and some are hesitant to make eye contact—it scares off too many people.

As a result of their observation of everyone, they become excellent judges of character, recognizing the potential in a person almost as soon as they meet them. Unfortunately, they often then try to change the person in order to release the potential, whether the person is ready or not. Usually, their efforts to change others result in their own changing.

As Scorpios grow up they become adept at hiding their feelings behind their poker faces, and yet they seethe inside with buried intensity. They relate to everything in life emotionally and are given to brooding and mooning over every emotional slight, whether real or imagined.

Some Scorpios are so afraid of being bought that they refuse all offers of help, and are even uncomfortable receiving gifts. And yet this same Scorpio might deeply resent and secretly be jealous of the other people they see accepting the same help they were offered and did not take.

Scorpios often get into power plays with Tauruses over the issue of stuff. Taurus wants it; Scorpio withholds it. Or Taurus has it and Scorpio is jealous of it.

Scorpios are not really interested in material possessions for themselves, and yet they intuitively recognize the power potential inherent in the manipulation of money and things and are attracted to them for that reason. Scorpios are never happier than when they are wheeling and dealing, manipulating money and/or people, and finding a way around the system that they are a part of.

All Scorpios are obsessive, and no matter how you look at it, ultimately, the obsession is nothing more than a need to totally control that which they care about. It is their obsession that will ultimately lead them to letting go of their need for control and lead them back to themselves.

Scorpios are attracted to power, and so we find them in and around every powerful position to be found in our society. There have been many presidents of our country who were Scorpios, many generals, many chairmen of large corporations—the list is endless.

I personally tend to think of the Scorpio personality as being layered like an onion. There is a thick skin on the outside, which, when peeled away, reveals layer upon layer of walls that Scorpios have erected between themselves and the world as a protection. As you get to know them, the layers slowly peel away. But do not kid yourself if you are friends with or married to a Scorpio—even after all those years of peeling your way in, you are still not really inside. In the interest of their own self-preservation, Scorpios make it a point to know everything about everyone, while keeping that inner core of themselves completely secret.

The Scorpio Woman

The Scorpio woman's early development leaves her uniquely open to her own psychic sensitivity. It is perhaps for this reason that we see so many Scorpios, particularly women, in the psychic fields. And even those Scorpios who are not practicing psychics seem to have particularly well-developed intuition. Those not involved in metaphysics are often very religious people because their natural awareness is that there is more to life than the physical world we see.

Scorpios' sensitivity is probably due to two factors: First, Scorpios' suspicious nature causes them to use all of their capabilities and psychic sensitivity including hunches to find out all they can about others. Second, Scorpios' secretive nature causes them to keep most of the information they obtain, as well as how they obtained it, to themselves. This means that in early life the surrounding adult community did not have a chance to shoot down all of Scorpios' psychic experiences because the Scorpios did not tell anyone they were having them!

So, to most adult Scorpios, it is so perfectly natural to use the various psychic senses that we all possess, and they probably do not even realize, most of the time, that they are using them!

In the Scorpio woman this psychic sensitivity is directed toward whatever she is emotionally involved with at the moment, be it her children, work, lover, or husband. Often she is so emotionally involved that the Scorpio obsessiveness comes into play, and because of her need to control the object of her obsession she creates a psychic link to it or them.

It is not at all unusual for the Scorpio woman to know that her husband or lover is having an affair or that her children are breaking the rules or in trouble. Having a mother who is a Scorpio is not something I would wish on any child—and if you're dating a Scorpio, think twice about cheating on her.

Yet in spite of this well-developed sixth sense, Scorpio seems to get herself into one emotional problem after another. She seems to fall into the Scorpio pit of guilt all too often, and when she does, instead of cutting her losses and moving on, she either punishes herself or seeks out someone who will make her life miserable to even out the score (penance).

All too often we see Scorpio women involved with men who use and abuse them in one way or another, emotionally or both physically and emotionally. Scorpios born into the first decan (first 10° of the sign) are often emotionally, physically and sometimes sexually abused as children. And here, I am speaking of both males and females.

The Scorpio woman who is involved in an abusive situation will remain there until whatever guilt she carries is paid off. Unfortunately, she sometimes also gets into power struggles with the abusive party and when she does, the situation can go on indefinitely because one partner will always either be making it up or getting even, depending on who has the upper hand.

She is often involved in relationships where there are sexual problems. In fact, when a client comes to me to discuss sexual problems, I automatically look to the 8th house, the sign Scorpio, and the planets Mars and Pluto to determine their root. The important thing to remember about the sexual problems that all Scorpios, both men and women, will experience is that they will continually attract people to them who are sexually unhealthy until they recognize the problem as their own, projected onto others.

Scorpios have a tendency to confuse sex and love. Scorpio women are particularly likely to do this. They want you to love them so badly that they see the tradeoff of their bodies as the means to buy your love. Scorpio is the sign most likely to feel that they own you simply because they have had sex with you or in reverse, that you now own them. They may confuse sex with love and love with ownership. They may use sex in order to make you dependent upon them, or in reverse, they may become sexually obsessed with you.

The Scorpio woman is the one woman in the zodiac most likely to use sex in her control games. She wants you totally committed to her, but she withholds her commitment to you, needing to keep you off balance to ensure her control of the situation. And, of course, since opposites attract, she often attracts the exact opposite situation in which she herself is controlled.

Depending on how comfortable she is with herself, the Scorpio's relationship with her children will vary widely. Some Scorpio mothers are both psychically and emotionally in tune with their children, while recognizing and fulfilling their needs almost automatically and offering her love freely. But other, more insecure mothers, while taking care of their children's physical needs automatically, neglect the children's emotional needs by withholding love. And sometimes they will go as far as deliberately creating both emotional and material dependencies so that the child cannot get away.

We see Scorpio, most often, in banking or big business, in any position from which she can move up. She makes a wonderful boss or business owner, able to recognize the needs of the business easily, as well as which employees can best fulfill those needs.

She loves intrigue, so we find her involved in the behind the scenes planning, as well as the gossip, involved in every move her business makes, large or small. She shines forth in any field where her intuition, her quick and accurate assessment of people, and her instinctive use of power and the barter system can come into play.

The Scorpio Man

The Scorpio man, similar to the Scorpio woman, is more in tune with his intuitions than the average man. This quality, combined with his being a male in a female-dominated sign, sometimes makes him uncomfortable with his masculinity.

He is the male most likely to have sexual issues, but they vary widely.

He may have experienced sexual relations at a very young age. He often sees himself as having been the initiator of these activities, which may result in considerable guilt. He sometimes has a very manipulative-dependent, love-hate relationship with his mother that continues into adulthood and interferes with healthy heterosexual relationships with women his own age. Sometimes in his childhood, need for emotional fulfillment led him to prostitute his body in some way. For instance, he might have allowed himself to be sexually used by an older sibling or friend he admired. He might carry extreme guilt into adulthood as a result of such a relationship.

He might have been punished for normal sexual behavior, like masturbation, when he was a child and was made to feel that such normal behavior was dirty.

I find it interesting that when Pluto, the planet that rules the generational group mind, transited into Scorpio, AIDS was discovered. The discovery and subsequent discussion and fears concerning this disease have colored the unconscious sexual thoughts of an entire generation. As the children born between November of 1983, when Pluto first entered the sign Scorpio, and November 1995, when Pluto left Scorpio, reached adulthood, they carried with them fears concerning the sex act and their sexuality that are more profound than ever before. Since Pluto rules transformation, it is likely that this generation's obsession about sex will ultimately change the world's attitudes toward it.

As a result of the childhood experiences, whatever they were, the adult Scorpio man may adopt a macho role to cover his fear of sexual inadequacy in a normal heterosexual relationship. Or, once he recognizes it, he may use his Scorpio magnetism to attract women (or men) and keep them hanging.

Like the Scorpio woman, he obsesses about love and sex, and often confuses the two. Also, like the Scorpio woman, he becomes extremely possessive about anyone he is involved with or otherwise emotionally concerned with, though he may hide his feelings well. Since in him, the aggressive, male side of Mars is more apparent when he is emotionally upset, he may sometimes turn to violence, which can erupt suddenly and with no apparent cause.

Scorpios may be the only men in the zodiac who can fixate so strongly on the woman of their dreams (often someone who uses or hurts them) that they have literally no desire to pursue any other woman. Scorpios can go celibate for years, waiting for the woman they have obsessed over to finally notice them.

Scorpios make good fathers, but again, the point in their development that they have their children is important. The father who is still insecure and lost in obsession will be an erratic parent at best and may use the child as a tool to control the wife. But the father who has grown beyond those negative traits will be solid and loving and will give his children constant support, although he will probably always fight his desire to buy them.

He shines in the medical field, where he is assured of the recognition and love of his patients, and where his intuition and sensitivity work for him. He makes a great general, knowing the best way to use his forces. He is drawn toward intrigue, so we find him on both sides of the law, as well as in

Government, Secret Service, and ferreting his way through and around corporate structures.

Scorpio is the only sign that actually has three different symbols associated with it. The Scorpion, the insectile part of Scorpio's psyche, is the insect that will sting itself to death. This is reflective of the lowest-evolved Scorpio, who will often cause himself harm to get even. The next level of Scorpio is the Phoenix, the mythical bird who dives into the fire, is consumed, and rises from the flames renewed. Most Scorpios reading this passage have already done that once or twice in their lives, figuratively speaking. The highest evolved level of Scorpio is the Eagle—the bird that flies high above the battlefield of life, seeing all but involving in nothing, until the moment it is time to take action. Then it is swift and deadly.

Associate the following characteristics with Scorpio:

- Obsessive
- Manipulative
- Emotional
- Need to be in control
- Intuitive
- Secretive and private
- Transformative
- Sexual problems and sexuality
- Good at recognizing, utilizing and developing other people's skills

End of Chapter Exercise

1. Be familiar with the Sun sign qualities of Libra and Scorpio.

2. Review your understanding of Venus, adding what you have learned of how Venus relates to Libra.

3. Review your understanding of Mars and add the new concepts you have learned in studying Mars' rulership of Scorpio.

4. Know the meaning of Pluto.

5. Know the meanings of the 7th and 8th houses.

6. Understand the difference between the personal signs and the we or socio-intellectual signs.

7. Continue your analysis of the chart we have been working with, adding the 7th and 8th houses, the signs Libra and Scorpio, and the planet Pluto. Questions a) through g) will assist you with your interpretation.

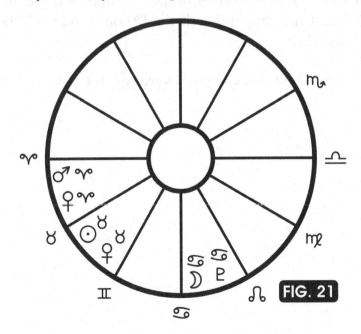

FIG. 21

a) What does Libra on the 7th house cusp tell you about the relationships that this person will have and about the type of person he or she will choose to marry?

b) Venus, ruler of Libra, is in the 1st house. This forms a relationship between the 1st and 7th houses. What effect do you think this Venus placement will have on the affairs of the 7th house?

c) What does Scorpio on the 8th house cusp signify?

d) The ruler of Scorpio, Mars, is in the 1st. This ties the 8th house to the 1st. How might they work together?

e) The co-ruler of Scorpio, Pluto, is in the 4th house, in Cancer. How do you think it will act there?

f) How do you think Pluto, being in the same sign and house as the Moon, will affect how the Moon acts?

g) Since Pluto is co-ruler of the 8th, but is in the 4th in this chart, how might that tie the 4th house and the 8th house together?

The key to this End of Chapter Exercise can be found on page 315.

Chapter 7

Introducing Sagittarius and Capricorn

Introducing Sagittarius and Capricorn

With our discussion of Sagittarius and Capricorn, we enter into the last third of the zodiac. These last four signs, including Sagittarius, Capricorn, Aquarius, and Pisces, are called the philosophical signs of the zodiac. They are, unlike the personal *me* signs or the socio-intellectual *we* signs, objective to much of the world around them. I like to think of these so-called philosophical signs of the zodiac as the *them* signs.

All of the philosophical *them* signs are characterized by a tendency to set themselves apart from the group and from whatever events and circumstances are transpiring. The connection they feel is to a far greater whole, as if they are on an outside platform from which they can view life. They look at what is happening to others with great concern, since they do see us all as children of one world. Yet with their objective approach to life, they have no need for involvement. They feel an affinity to no single group, and can be objective to circumstances affecting themselves or their own families, looking to a greater cause philosophically, behind every situation, whether negative or positive.

This philosophical approach toward life, which is typical of the *them* signs, is generally passed down through the father, whether the sign is inherently negative or positive. Therefore, it does not matter which parent had the overall greatest impact on the child. In this last group of four signs the father still impacted the child philosophically, even if it was via the mother's action.

As with the socio-intellectual we signs, the philosophical *them* signs are represented by each of the four elements—one sign to each element. Sagittarians (fire) base their ideology upon their father's persona and belief system and constantly search to expand upon it. Capricorns (earth) work toward a pinnacle of material success wherein they create a foundation and structure that can support those they see as less fortunate, Aquarians (air) objectively move from group to group, philosophy to philosophy, spreading the ideas and philosophy they absorb from one group into the next. Pisceans (water) feel an emotional urge to reach out to any unfortunate soul they come across, empathically experiencing the same hurts as the individuals they succor.

Sagittarius—"In Unending Search for Truth"

Sagittarius is the 9th sign of the zodiac.

Glyph or Symbol—♐—The Archer

Mode—Mutable

Ruling Planet—♃—Jupiter

Element—Fire

Corresponding House—9th

Orientation—Masculine

Corresponding Body Part—Hips, Thighs, and Lower Back

Jupiter

Jupiter completes its cycle around the Sun in twelve and a half years.

Like all of the original planets, it rules two signs, one negative or feminine and one positive or masculine. Pisces is the negative sign it rules and Sagittarius the positive one.

Therefore, in Sagittarius, the energy of Jupiter is expressed outwardly, in a generative manner.

Jupiter, in any sign, is primarily a planet of expansion. In fact, it is the largest planet in our solar system—probably large enough to contain all of the other planets within it and still have room for more.

Jupiter is the only planet in our solar system that actually gives off its own light. All of the other planets shine only by reflected light. Jupiter has a light all its own.

Astronomers generally believe that Jupiter was close to becoming a star, but failed. They feel that had Jupiter succeeded, our solar system would have been a binary (2-star) system and, of course, there would have been no life on Earth—we would have been burned to a crisp!

I am not alone among astrologers in believing that Jupiter did not fail, but is still on its evolutionary journey toward stardom and that eventually, if indeed it occurs, is so far into the future that mankind will probably have evolved beyond the confines of this planet by then.

Jupiter also has twelve moons, some of which are currently being explored through our space program, and Jupiter also has a series of rings surrounding it. Indeed, it does sound like it has the makings of its own solar system already.

Another interesting feature about Jupiter astronomically is its physical location. The first four planets we covered—Mercury, Venus, Earth, and Mars—lie relatively close to the Sun. Jupiter is just about as far out from Mars, furthest of these, as Mars is from the Sun. That means that there is quite a jump from the four 'inner'planets to Jupiter (Refer to Figure 5.)

Yet Jupiter cannot really be considered an outer planet either. It is not even halfway between the four inner planets and the four outer, being closer to Mars than Saturn.

So, Jupiter lies in a sort of spacial no-man's land; it cannot really be considered a personal planet, but it is surely not an outer planet either. This becomes very symbolic as we analyze Jupiter's meaning. It is as if Jupiter perceives both the larger picture and the smaller, but is not truly a part of either. In a sense, we could easily see this planet as the means by which we move from old to new, from lesser to greater, from death into life and life into death. Jupiter is the connecting tissue.

If we look at Jupiter's place in mythology, we find him listed in the Roman pantheon of gods as the ruler of the gods. He could be gentle and sensual. And although he was a god born of gods, he took many mortal women to him and gave birth to many sons and daughters who were half god and half man.

In this summation, again, you can see Jupiter's point of balance between higher and lower aspects of creation and personality. In leading us toward that which is greater than ourselves, he changes us toward our god-self.

Likewise, mythological Jupiter was the son of Saturn, who was a Titan. Saturn represented the old order in the universe, Jupiter the new. Saturn was the last of the old Gods while Jupiter was the first of the new. Again, we see planetary Jupiter's bridging and expanding effect.

The mythological Jupiter was a ruler, concerned with law and he saw his law as the ultimate spiritual authority over man and Gods alike. The planet Jupiter is concerned with Universal Law, which, on its lower end, sometimes turns into man's zest for creating, upholding and enforcing his own laws.

When mythological Jupiter's law was broken, he became a violent god, capable of throwing lightning and creating thunder. Again, on its lower level, this becomes the Jupiter's tendency toward over-reaction, over-protectiveness, and its dynamic and physical nature as well.

Mythological Jupiter considered himself not just a ruler but father of the gods; and likewise, the planet Jupiter is concerned with guiding and teaching all those it sees as its children. Mythological Jupiter was given to frolicking, over-eating, over-drinking, and excesses of all kinds, including sex. Likewise, the planet Jupiter is involved in every excess mankind thinks he has invented.

The ancient astrologers used to look upon Jupiter strictly as a benevolent force, always seeing more as better. Indeed, Jupiter is involved in luck and the expansion of your finances and material assets, but it may, just as easily, become involved in expanding the trouble that loses you those same assets.

Modern day astrologers are perhaps somewhat wiser concerning Jupiter's action. We realize that more is not always better, that moderation is often the wiser course of action. So, although Jupiter always expands anything it touches, it is not always to the benefit of the individual. It does depend upon just what is being expanded. It is a joke among astrologers that when transiting Jupiter crosses over the ascendant in your chart, you generally are prone to weight gain. Likewise, someone with Jupiter on or near the ascendant in his natal chart is likely either to be very big and tall or prone to being overweight.

Any time you reach out to expand beyond the limits of your own self in any way—be it to a person, to a philosophy, to a religion or spiritual belief, or to a system of law and order—you are seeing your Jupiter in action.

And where you reach out, to expand naturally, is shown in your chart by Jupiter's sign and house placement. Your attitude toward other races, cultures, religions, philosophies, higher education, and long distance travel, which expand these areas, also is shown in your chart by Jupiter's sign and house placement.

Associate the following concepts with Jupiter:

- Big and expanded
- Religion and spirituality
- Long distance travel
- Philosophy
- Astral traveling
- Higher Education
- Luck and money
- Teaching and guiding
- Weight gain
- Law
- Excesses of all kinds
- "Channeling"
- How other people think
- Prejudice
- Sisters and brothers-in-law (and the extended family)

The Ninth House

The 9th house, in the astrological wheel, derives its meanings from the qualities of Jupiter. Because of this, the 9th house rules all types of expansion, both personal and social.

The astrologer can tell from the sign that appears on the cusp of the 9th house whether you are religious, and if so, where those religious values came from. Likewise, the sign on the cusp of the 9th and any planets in it will describe whether you are open minded about religion, race, cultural values, legal and political issues, educational issues, and so on. It also will tell the astrologer if you like to travel and if you are likely to do any great amount in your lifetime. It tells if you would benefit from a higher education and even gives insight as to whether you will get one and, if so, what area(s) you are most likely to be interested in.

This house also rules astral traveling and channeling, due to Jupiter's rulership of travel and the expansion of higher mind. Essentially, in ruling the way other people think, Jupiter expands your consciousness through the 9th house as you encompass and explore new ways of thinking.

Unfortunately, where there is resistance to new thought and new attitudes and anything that is different, there is always prejudice. And so the 9th house also rules prejudice, as Jupiter expands the narrowness of thinking.

Also, since the 9th house is the third house from the 7th (the mate), it rules the mate's brothers and sisters, as well as your extended family.

Here's an example for you:

Suppose you had Cancer on the 9ᵗʰ house cusp. It's likely that you would be emotional about religion. Your religious values were formulated by your mother, or some other woman, and you are either very religious or very anti-religious depending upon how you reacted to her way of thinking. Since Mom and family were so important in the formulation of your ideas, you are quite traditional. You are somewhat insecure about your ability to grasp higher concepts and so you might avoid higher education. However, if you do pursue a higher education, it will probably be in a nurturing field such as nursing or teaching.

You will be very family-oriented in your philosophy of life, so whether you are open minded about other cultures or religions will depend upon the family values with which you grew up. However, you are always insecure whenever you are faced with a new idea or cultural values different than your own. You will have a very emotional relationship with brothers—and sisters-in-law and the extended family, which will be either good or bad in the extreme. Long-distance travel will probably not be your bag unless you own a house at your destination, or unless your family lives there.

A lot more can be said about this, but I think you have the idea.

Associate the following concepts with the 9ᵗʰ house:

- Higher education/teaching
- Long distance travel
- Other cultures/values
- Astral travel
- Other races/values
- Law
- Prejudice

- Religion
- Philosophy
- "Channeling"

Sagittarius

Polarity

Sagittarius, like all of the positive, generative signs before it (Aries, Gemini, Leo, and Libra), is most strongly affected in childhood by a male figure, usually the father. Since Sagittarius is Jupiter ruled, the positive polarity in this sign is especially fun to watch. Remember, Jupiter expands whatever it touches.

This combination tends to make Sagittarians naturally outgoing and social people. they are the people who just walk right over and start up a conversation with someone they do not know. And, of course, since they have the obtuseness typical of all fire signs, they may not even have noticed that the person they just initiated this conversation with was previously engaged in something important, like sewing up a wound or having a heated discussion with someone else, or, maybe, pulling out a gun and getting ready to rob a bank. Needless to say, they have a knack for getting themselves into interesting situations.

They also are the people famous among the astrological community for blurting out whatever is in their minds to whoever is listening. They are not known for keeping secrets. The cliché foot-in-mouth disease was invented to describe a Sagittarian. Indeed, it often seems that even when Sagittarians are aware they have said too much, the more they try to extricate themselves from the situation, the deeper into it they propel themselves.

Sagittarians' positive polarity makes them very physical people who may also sometimes be klutzy or, if they are big people (Jupiter sometimes makes Sagittarians over-large), they may sometimes feel like the bull in the china shop. They love activity of all kinds, as long as it is for fun. They are much too lazy (remember, Jupiter likes those creature comforts in excess) to engage in work-related physical activity, if they can possibly help it.

Sagittarians are among the people most adept at getting out of work. Their outgoing, fun loving, almost puppy dog demeanor helps them to find people to do it for them. And they are so lavish in their praise, that usually their slave is more than happy to accommodate them. Remember Tom Sawyer?

Jupiter's positive orientation in this sign makes Sagittarians naturally lucky people. I have done considerable thinking on this because not being a Sagittarian but knowing a lot of these lucky types tends to makes me think about just why they are so lucky. My conclusion is that their luck stems from their positive attitude.

Sagittarians can be so incredibly trusting that events and circumstances are all working out just right for them that they actually draw all kinds of help and support to themselves.

It is the Sagittarian who plans a picnic when it is supposed to rain, and, of course, the rain holds off until the picnic is ending. The rest of us would never have such luck. It is Sagittarians who lose home, family, security (occasionally they do have some bad stuff happen to them), and even then, they are taken in by a friend or long-lost uncle who leaves them their entire estate to make up for their losses.

It sort of makes us all wish we were born Sagittarians, doesn't it? The probable reason Sagittarians have this safety net of sorts is that in this life they are supposed to be searchers and pioneers. They need to be able to constantly move forward into new situations, exposing themselves to new people, ideas, religions, and so forth, without fear.

Quadruplicity

Sagittarius is the third of the mutable signs, following behind Gemini and Virgo.

Sagittarius' mutable quality makes it, like the other mutable signs, changeable.

In Sagittarians' case, this changeable nature is what keeps them constantly moving throughout their lives, whether physically or just mentally. And it is this constant reaching out to new experience, the constant need to change, that many of us see as Sagittarians running away from their responsibilities, that eventually gives them a wealth of experience far beyond what the average person's experience encompasses.

Triplicity

Sagittarius is the third and last of the fire signs, following Aries and Leo.

Like the other fire signs, Sagittarius is idealistic, and like them, these ideals are rooted in the philosophy and the attitudes of the father. But since Sagittarius is also a philosophical sign, the quality of idealism is even more apparent in Sagittarius than in the other two fire signs.

In the first two fire signs, the quality of idealism was in living up to an ideal projected by Dad. In Sagittarius, the ideal is Dad himself. Sagittarians, male and female alike, attempt to become whatever their perception of Dad is.

I say perception of father because since Sagittarians are a philosophical or *them* sign, it is unlikely that their perceptions of Dad are accurate—it is most often an idealized version.

And again, as with all of the fire signs, the idealism they encompass keeps them constantly looking out of themselves, either to project their ideals outward, or to compare their own to others. In sifting through these new ideals, they develop and refine their own.

The Sign Sagittarius

Sagittarians are born into families where Dad is the dominant figure. Sagittarians have warm memories of being held in Dad's strong, protective arms, and of being loved unconditionally by him.

However, there is something about Dad that makes him unapproachable to Sagittarians. Sometimes Dad is much older than the other kids' dads. Sometimes he is a businessman whose interests leave him minimal time for the child. Sometimes Sagittarians' parents separated when they were very small, and they stayed with Mom. In some occasional situations, the child did not know Dad at all, only the stories that Mom told about him. The reasons will vary, but Sagittarians develop a deep and abiding love for Dad and, at the same, don't know who Dad really is.

Many Sagittarians, at a very early age, erect a pedestal and often place Dad upon it. Sagittarians admire Dad greatly. They pattern their belief systems, values, and attitudes toward people and world events, upon their impression of Dad's values and beliefs. They see Dad as special and try to reach out to others in the same way they imagine their fathers do.

Through this action, all Sagittarians, at some time in their lives, will either directly or indirectly experience prejudice. They might either be the objects of that prejudice, or the prejudice may be their own, directed outward. This is part of the experience necessary to force them to look at other cultures, races, etc., and learn from them.

Part of the reason that Sagittarians have an idealization of Dad is that at the time Sagittarians were born, Dad was usually doing particularly well. In astrology, we know Sagittarians as the golden-spoon children, which makes them one step up from Taureans, the silver-spoon children

Sagittarians perceive Dad to be successful in every way, so that Sagittarians are able to have nice things, to go to great places, and to feel loved in that unconditional way we all wish we were loved by our parents. As a result, they develop a love of those nice things, a love of travel, and to go with these, an easy and outgoing nature. You might say that the Sagittarian childhood, barring interference from other signs and planets, is the idyllic childhood. And Sagittarians perceive that their idyllic world is made possible by Dad.

What they do not see is the years of scraping and struggling and hard work that Dad put in to reach this pinnacle of success that Sagittarius chose to be born into.

For that reason, Sagittarian men and women often expect the best things in life to be handed to them, not realizing that it was good, hard work that really created their early circumstances, and it is only through their own equally hard work that they can achieve equally affluent lives.

But hard work does not come naturally to Sagittarians. We often find Sagittarians in relationships with Tauruses because their mutual attraction to money and things draws them together. But always remember that while Taurus is emotionally attached to these things and will work for and save toward them, Sagittarius is not and does not. Sagittarians want things to come easily, they want to enjoy them, liking their creature comforts every bit as much as Taurus. But when they become bored, they will move on, looking for new toys to play with.

Life is generally good to Sagittarians, and though they may never become rich unless they learn to work, the Sagittarian who chooses to drift through life can actually get away with it. There will always be someone, or some circumstance that presents itself, to show him the way to his next meal or to share their affluence with him. This Sagittarian may be slippery, he may lie freely, he may even be prone to drug use and excesses of all sorts, including sex with anyone he can interest, even your husband or wife.

The problem is that Sagittarians really do want to be like Dad, as strong and as successful in every way. It is only when a Sagittarian develops a sense of responsibility, that is initially absent, a recognition that the good things in life must be worked for, that he can truly live up to his ideal of Dad.

Once the Sagittarian has done this, he can finally be free of the limitations his singular goal placed upon him and grow beyond even his idealized image of Dad. Not too many Sagittarians make it to this stage of development, but for those who do, anything is possible.

We see these special Sagittarians involved in all aspects of world politics, of big business, of law enforcement, and of organized religions. Now that they are not afraid of that hard work, their luck works to bring them to the pinnacle of success, while their developing values keep them constantly reaching for something just beyond the sight of their peers.

One last generality about Sagittarians: statistically, they are the longest-lived sign—that positive and easy—going attitude is probably what gives them their longevity!

The Sagittarius Woman

Like the other positive-sign women of the zodiac, the Sagittarian woman is somewhat uncomfortable with her femininity. Also like them, she enjoys being with men more than women, at least until she has learned to balance the masculine/feminine components within herself.

The Sagittarian woman is looking for Dad. She unconsciously compares every man she meets to the perfect Dad she holds in her mind. Likewise, she is constantly looking for Dad's attention—whether it is attention from her actual father, or from all of the men she meets.

Sometimes in her childhood, she competes with mother or sisters for Dad's attention. This may carry over into adult life by causing her to unconsciously place herself in competition with other women for whatever male is present.

In her efforts to attract Dad's attention, she copies Mom's feminine wiles. Unconsciously, she often adopts decidedly sensual mannerisms, which she has noted Mom used to get Dad's attention.

In adult life this often gets her into trouble, as she uses these same sensual mannerisms and covert sexual invitations to attract the attention of the men around her. It is their attention, friendship, and comradeship that she really wants. But what she often ends up with is the man who treats her as a sexual object, or men she wants to be friends with calling her a sexual tease. Once she becomes aware of the problems these unconscious action patterns cause her, making her the object of women's jealousy and men's sexual desire, she can modify them. When she does, her relationships with both men and women will improve.

Often the Sagittarian woman has a hard time making a successful marriage because of her tendency to compare her husband to her pedestal image of her father.

What she usually doesn't realize is that she has married her father. What I mean is that while Sagittarius carried in her mind a storybook father image that she was seeking to manifest in the man she married, her unconscious mind was busily drawing the real thing to her. So, Sagittarius finally gets to know, understand, and work through her problems with Dad, by recognizing them in the man she has married.

But she is an idealist, and she tries to put her man up there on the same pedestal Dad occupied for so long. Dad's is an impossible image to live up to. So, if you are thinking of marrying a Sagittarian woman, do not let her put you there.

The Sagittarian woman does make a good mate once she has worked through these Dad deal problems. She is supportive of her husband, works with him very well, and will often go out of her way to share in his dreams and goals.

217

She has an active mind and is physically active as well, so in her work she needs constantly changing circumstances to be content. And if she is not, she usually will move on without a glance back.

She is capable of doing challenging work and is a wonderful hostess or liaison person, once she gets past the idea that things are supposed to be just given to her. But even when she learns to work, the best way to motivate her is still to have a man ask her to support him in his efforts to achieve his dream.

Her man will be the center of her life, and even if she has children, she will still put him first. But do not neglect her for too long—she just might succumb to the attentions of one of those men who have been chasing her.

The Sagittarius Man

The Sagittarius man is also living up to Dad. But since he is a male, his approach is somewhat more direct.

It is not uncommon to see the Sagittarian man unconsciously reproduce all of the actual components of Dad's life in his own, though it is the idealized Dad that he is seeking to live up to.

For example, I know a Sagittarian man who was the only son of his father's third, and only lasting, marriage. As he was going through his own second divorce, he loudly announced that he knew the marriage would not last, but that he was ready for a real marriage now.

Another Sagittarian man I know had a father who lost all of his teeth due to gum disease and refused to get false teeth. When My Sagittarian acquaintance lost all of his, while still in his forties, he also refused to get false teeth.

The same Sagittarian's father also died within months of his retirement, leaving his wife with no means of support. This Sagittarian also retired without the benefit of a pension, and died within months as well.

The extent to which the Sagittarian male will copy his father is staggering, especially since it is wholly unconscious. Most Sagittarian men reading these passages will deny that they have copied their father.

But please be advised, if you are a Sagittarian man, be aware of your father's real life patterns, not the ones you have idealized, so that you can choose whether you want to bring them into your own life. If you remain unconscious of them, they will surely become yours.

The Sagittarian man usually does not truly come into his own until after he has lived up to at least a part of the real Daddy-pattern in his unconscious and has become aware of it. Once he has this awareness, he can begin to make his own life, encouraged by the early values instilled in him to constantly reach out and grow beyond the confines of his own limiting worldview.

He is a physical man and is often big because of his Jupiter rulership. He is usually outgoing, with lots of friends. He also is known as the Don Juan of the zodiac, chasing and usually getting as many women as he cares to. Women are attracted to his he-man quality, coupled with his puppy-dog sweetness and apparent guilelessness.

If he marries too early in life, his marriage will not survive because he takes longer to grow up than the other signs do. It is important that the Sagittarian man gets his playing and experimenting done before marriage.

He often has a problem with responsibility, especially if he tries to step into a responsible situation too early in life. If his responsibilities begin to drag him down, he will betray your trust by running away. But if he explores fully his character and capabilities while he is young and waits until he is ready for the responsibilities of life, he will be more likely to be successful.

He wants a home and family, although he may rarely be there. He loves his children, but believes them to be the wife's responsibility. So, if you are married to him and want his help, you had better tell him what you want.

He is physical and continues to like sports of some kind for most of his life. And he loves to play at everything, keeping that childish quality of his, no matter how old he gets.

Associate the following concepts with Sagittarius:

- Gregarious
- Big or lanky
- Lazy
- Idealistic
- Fun-loving
- Don Juan or Femme Fatale
- "Daddy" problems
- Philosophical
- Questing
- Prejudice

Capricorn — Born to Learn the Correct Use of Power; Born to Build

Capricorn is the 10th sign of the zodiac.

The Capricorn-Cancer axis and the 10th house-4th house axis together represent the Mommy-Daddy axis of the astrological wheel. This axis deals with family patterns that may have originated in childhood, or even have been passed down through the family for generations. It represents the struggle between our identification with the nucleus family in which we grew up (Cancer) and the greater world family we develop later in life (Capricorn). This axis represents the unconscious struggle between Mom and Dad. On a deeper level, it is the battle of the sexes; and on a deeper level still, it is the struggle to balance the masculine-feminine portions of our own being.

Glyph or Symbol—♑—The Mountain Goat

Mode—Cardinal

Ruling Planet—♄—Saturn

Element—Earth

Corresponding House—10th

Orientation—Feminine

Corresponding Body Parts—Back, Bones, Teeth, and Skin

Saturn

Saturn completes its journey around the sun (and therefore the astrological wheel) in about twenty-nine years, returning back to its natal position in your chart when you are somewhere around 29 years old. It is because of Saturn's return to its natal position that so many people go through major life changes when they are somewhere between 28 and 30 years old.

These changes may be wholly internal, or they may be internal changes that result from external events. It is not unusual at all to see individuals get married, get divorced, have a child, change a career, go back to school, make a major move, or even lose a loved one during their Saturn return.

It seems that at or around age 29, Saturn brings into your life whatever is necessary to refocus your attention on why you are here. If you have strayed from your chosen life path during the previous twenty-nine years, Saturn straightens you out with a big club. If you have remained pretty well on target, Saturn just adds a little responsibility to your load but otherwise leaves you alone. Either way, according to astrologers, you are not truly an adult until after you have had your first Saturn return.

Saturn, as a planetary energy, deals with responsibility, authority, work, career, structure, and teaching, experiencing life lessons and with the principle of karma—that is, the principle that says whatever you have started, in this or other lives, you must continue until it is completed.

In your natal chart, by its sign and house, Saturn tells you what your biggest struggles in early life will be and what you are bound to have the biggest problems dealing with.

Saturn in Aries is forced to be independent and are terribly afraid of their own shortcomings. Saturn in Taurus want money and things but cannot have them unless they earn it all themselves. Saturn in Gemini has severe problems with communication that must be overcome in order to achieve their goals. Saturn in Cancer are desperate for nurturance, but are forced to give it rather than get it. Saturn in Leo sacrifices all for respect and love, only to learn that if they have no self-love, whatever they receive is empty. Saturn in Virgo picks at everything around them until they learn the surrounding world is only a reflection of themselves. Saturn in Libra has major problems with relationships of all kinds—they cannot be independent until they learn to relate. Saturn in Scorpio has problems with control issues and with sex—they will learn that the only way to gain control is to let it go.

Saturn in Sagittarius has trouble with values and searches until they find those that work for them. Saturn in Capricorn wants to be top dog but must learn patience and diligence to get there. Saturn in Aquarius cannot fit in anywhere but wishes they could—they are learning the value of objectivity. And Saturn in Pisces is constantly supporting someone else or being supported by them until they learn discrimination.

Saturn in your chart, is the primary life lesson you have come in to life to learn. And Saturn's lessons are a life-long affair.

Approximately every seven years, you have Saturn squaring or opposing its natal position. (Look at the math: 29 divided by 4 = 7 and change.) That means that every seven years, your natal Saturn is activated and you experience a minor Saturn correction of your life direction. The first of these occurs around 7 years old, the next at age 14, then age 21. Then, of course, around age 28-29, comes the Saturn return itself. But Saturn's journey and its lessons for you do not stop there

At age 35, you have your next Saturn square, at age 42 you have a Saturn opposition, at age 49 you have another square to Saturn, and at age 56 (approximately), Saturn returns back to its natal position again for a second Saturn return. And then the cycle begins again. Your Saturn lessons never end. They become more refined, subtler, but you will continue to have them until the day you die.

Of course, that does not mean you are a slow learner. Indeed, once the early lessons are learned, you become so good at them that you begin to teach them to others, though you might not be aware of it. They, then, become your very strongest points. And then you go on to learn Saturn's more subtle lessons.

Since Saturn in your chart represents authority, it also often refers to that parent in your early childhood that you saw as the authority. The relationship to authority in your childhood set the stage for how you will deal with all authority figures throughout life. If Dad, for example, was your early authority figure and he had trouble dealing with authority, so will you.

Saturn also has a lot to do with age and longevity. Remember, in mythology, Saturn (the Greeks called him Cronos) was one of the Titans; he was the father of the lesser Gods. It is also noteworthy that he ate all of his children until his wife finally got wise and hid one from him—that was Jupiter (Zeus, as the Greeks called him) who became the king of the gods.

Because of Saturn's connection to age, it sometimes reveals the relationship that you had in early childhood with an important older person—perhaps a grandparent.

Its relationship to time caused the ancient astrologers to relate it to the life cycle, and even to the end of life. Modern day astrologers relate Saturn to your perception of time itself, as well as to how you will end or finish up karmic issues in your life.

Associate the following qualities with Saturn:

- Structure
- Your major "life lesson"
- Foundation
- Karmic Patterns in your life
- Age and Longevity
- Authority parent (usually Dad)
- Work and Career
- How you deal with authority
- Building
- Your sense of timing
- Teaching
- Grandparents and old people
- Restriction
- How you end things

The Midheaven

The Midheaven or MC (Latin for Median Coeli) is actually the cusp or line that shoots up through the top of the chart at the start of the 10th house.

You already learned in Chapter 2 that the Midheaven-Nadir axis shows the action of spirit entering life at the Nadir, crossing the material plane (the Ascendant-Descendant axis) where it gives birth to the spark of life that is you, and continuing on its developmental journey out through the top of the chart at the MC (See Chapter 2, Figure 4.).

It logically follows, that the Midheaven represents something toward which the spirit within you aspires to and reaches. I like to think that it is the very best and highest qualities of the sign that appears on the Midheaven that you aspire to develop, deep down within yourself. It is as if this is the type of person, hypothetically speaking, that you would most like to become.

For example, Aries on the Midheaven aspires to independence of thought and action. Taurus there aspires to stability, imperturbability, and material success. Gemini there aspires to seeing and understanding both sides of every issue. Cancer aspires to be nurturing and creative. Leo aspires to be recognized and loved for who he is. Virgo aspires to be analytical, objective, and relied upon by others. Libra aspires to be the artistic mediator. Scorpio aspires to transform himself and others through example. Sagittarius aspires to the truth. Capricorn aspires to succeed in building something of value. Aquarius aspires to be or become part of a humanitarian project or effort. Pisces aspires to receptivity, sensitivity, and being of help to others.

Associate the following concept with the Midheaven:

- Your highest aspirations

The Tenth House

The 10th house is an angular house, so it is a very active house. It also is an earth house, so you know that this house and any planets in it will deal with material issues and concerns. The 10th house is ruled by Saturn, so the qualities of Saturn color and give form to the meanings we associate with it.

Firstly, the 10th house in traditional astrology represents your father, just as the 4th house represents your mother. This is because, traditionally, the nurturing parent is seen as the mother (4th house), while the authority and support parent is seen as the father (10th house). In actual practice, this sometimes reverses because for some people in today's society the parental roles have shifted.

We also often see the husband in a woman's chart as her 10th house and her 7th (traditionally the house of the mate) because some women relate to their husband as an authority or father figure. And since the 10th house is the fourth house from the 7th, the 10th house becomes your mother-in-law, while the opposing 4th house, being tenth from the 7th, becomes your father-in—law."

This technique of locating various people in your astrology chart is called spinning the wheel. To do it, all you do is use whatever house involves the primary person you're looking at as the 1st house, and then count forward from there to whatever house normally shows the relationship in question.

In the above example, the 7th house is the house of the mate. So, if we use the 7th house as the first and start counting from there, the 4th house is the mother (in this case, the mate's mother and your mother-in-law) and the 10th house is the father (in this case, the mate's father and your father-in-law).

Spinning the wheel is a somewhat advanced astrological concept; if you had difficulty following this discussion, just set it aside for now. For those of you reading this who are more advanced, this tool will help you define who people are more readily when reading a chart.

Probably the most important thing to associate with the 10th house, though, is the idea of career. Needless to say, our idea of career is largely influenced by the parent we viewed as the support parent, but as we move through life, it is an idea that grows and develops.

The sign on the 10th house and any planets and perhaps other signs that influence the 10th, all tell the astrologer something about your career aspirations. They talk about the type of career that you will most aspire to, as well as the way in which you will probably conduct yourself in your career. They give insight as to just how important career issues will be to you.

And of course, the sign on the 10th house cusp tells the astrologer the way you want to be seen by the world around you. You will pursue that image until, eventually, the world sees you less like the Ascendant of your chart and more like the Midheaven, or 10th house cusp.

Associate the following concepts with the 10th house:

- Career
- Authority/Support parent (Dad)
- Mother-in-law
- The way you want to be seen
- Husband as authority figure (for women)

Capricorn

Polarity

Capricorn is a negative, receptive sign. Like the other negative signs, Capricorn is female dominated in early life, and, therefore, becomes receptive and reactive in nature.

The rulership by Saturn combined with this negative polarity, often causes Capricorns to be retiring and somewhat non-communicative, a quality that many people interpret as being secretive. This combination also makes them planners and builders who work toward a position of authority.

The receptive-earth quality of Capricorn causes people of this sign to be involved in material issues. They are concerned with acquisition and with a consolidation of power. Capricorn is the third and last of the power signs of the zodiac.

Quadruplicity

Capricorn also is the fourth and last of the cardinal signs. Since Capricorn is cardinal, we tend to think of Capricorns as being self-starters. But if you take a moment to remember that Capricorn is Saturn ruled and is a negative sign, you will realize that Capricorn is more reactive that active. It is cardinal in that once it gets moving, it takes the lead and pioneers new ground; but Capricorn is not self-starting. Actually, Capricorns' cardinal mode shows up more in their opportunism—that is, their ability to recognize and hitch a ride on the right vehicle to success—than it does in any ability they might have on their own to get things rolling.

Over the years, I have had many Capricorns and Capricorn types get angry when I pointed out their opportunistic nature, since automatically there is a tendency to associate the quality of opportunism with being a bad person. Do not make this error. Capricorns' ability to recognize promising opportunities and act on them, almost intuitively, is an extremely important and positive quality. Without it, there would be no true entrepreneurs and many people, who have innately good ideas, would never get the necessary support to make them work.

Capricorn's opportunistic nature is only considered bad when it leads Capricorn to take advantage of an opportunity and give nothing back in return. These Capricorns are generally seen by the rest of the world as users. But for the most part, Capricorns, more than adequately, pay for any advantage they may be given by their hard work once they are on board.

Their cardinality does often present them with problems, though, once they have come on board of a project, business, etc. Their reactive nature makes them appear like an easy-going follower to their employer, but very quickly, the employer notes Capricorns' cardinal nature, which surges to the fore now that they've gotten moving. Capricorns become the dynamic employees who the boss cannot do without, but who also may pose a threat to the boss if the boss has any feelings of inadequacy concerning his own ability.

Triplicity

Capricorn is the last of the earth signs, following behind Taurus and Virgo.

In Capricorn, the earth element is cardinal, which explains something of why Capricorns are always engaged in building or creating a business, a financial empire, or something else of a material nature. Capricorns' cardinal nature causes them to be as achievement oriented as Aries, but for them, the pinnacle of success is measured by what they have built—be it a house, a business, a corporate structure, a financial empire, and so on—because of their earth-sign orientation. And like Aries, it is not unusual for Capricorns to set their sights on a new project the instant the current one is done, or to suffer the same fear of success that some Aries do, destroying whatever it is they have built just before it is completed.

Capricorns' earth orientation coupled with their Saturn rulership causes them to seek respect and admiration for what they have built or are in the process of building. They like to be relied upon and see the structures they have created, whatever they may be, as both supporting and developing the people around them who they want to look up to them.

It is Capricorns' cardinal-earth orientation that makes them the sign of the builder. And in our world, all structures, whether political, such as a federal or state government, or a religion's hierarchy of officials, or countries and nations themselves, carry a Capricornian connotation.

Capricorn is the sign of structure on the physical plane—structure physical, like a building, or philosophical, like the structure of a corporation or government. This is perhaps what makes Capricorn both the most material of signs, and yet the most spiritual as well.

The Sign Capricorn

Capricorns, like the other negative signs of the zodiac, are most influenced by their mothers during the formative first three years of life.

However, unlike the other negative signs, Capricorn also has a strong father whom he admires and respects, although his effect upon Capricorn's childhood development is more philosophical than actual.

Typically, Capricorns are born into traditional family environments in which Mom plays the dominant role in rearing the children and running the household, while Dad is expected to direct his attention to work and the outside world—receiving the proper respect from children and wife for his worldly accomplishments but otherwise taking no active role at all in home life.

Capricorns admire and copy Mom's strength of character, her practical nature, her serious approach toward life, her tendency to look at any new crisis in life as merely one more obstacle to be overcome, and her healthy work ethic. They see her as the strength and glue that holds the family together. They see her as the nucleus energy that enables everyone in the family to achieve their various successes. They also see her as knowing and carefully manipulating the minutest details of the lives of all of those she loves and cares for, so that they can become happy and successful.

Whether Capricorns' Mom works or not, she runs her household with an iron hand. Her children have manners. They may fight among one another, but certainly not when Mom is around. They are expected to stand up for one another—after all, they're family. And of course, the oldest are always supposed to look out for the younger ones.

Capricorns respect their father, not because they know him or understand what he does or even because he deserves it, but because Mom's traditional ethics say that Dad is to be honored and respected. So, when Dad returns home, regardless of whether he spent the day at the office or playing, the children line up at the door to greet him, dressed cleanly and neatly, and make sure that he is comfortable in his favorite easy chair. At dinner, Dad gets served first, and, of course, he gets the largest portions. After all, he is the breadwinner in the family (whether he really is or not is relatively unimportant). If the kids are too rowdy or noisy, one look from Dad will silence them because they know what Mom will do if Dad gets angry. After dinner, the well-behaved children file by to say goodnight because Dad has earned his peace and quiet.

So, Capricorns develop a healthy respect for Dad, and indeed see him as an authority figure not to be contended with. But underlying Dad's authority, they recognize Mom's power and control, even though she defers to Dad. It's her traits they copy.

From this early family experience, Capricorns develop very traditional attitudes toward home and family and a strong sense of responsibility toward the family. Grandparents may well play an important role in Capricorns' early lives as well, since the family experience is so traditional. Lineage is important, and patterns of behavior are seen to be passed down intact for generations.

Also, from this early upbringing, Capricorns are imprinted with an understanding of authority—both how to accept it and how to manage it. Just as Mom defers to Dad, Dad defers to his father, and so on. There is an instinctive understanding of the chain of command, as well as an intuition for who the power person in any situation really is.

In some rare cases, the Capricorns will be unable to accept authority from anyone else, automatically setting themselves up in a position antagonistic to any authority in their lives. This Capricorn is the rebel.

It is not unusual for Capricorns to experience periods of financial deprivation in early life, regardless of Mom's good financial head and willingness to work hard. Capricorns almost have to have this experience in order to force them later in life to focus their attention on the material concerns of developing and building a career.

So, in later life, as they build their career, they are concerned with material security, for themselves and their family, as well as gaining respect and recognition, and a position of authority.

It is very common for Capricorns to go to work at a young age. Most will see whatever money they can bring in from their youthful career as being an aid to the family's financial circumstances.

The recognition and acceptance helping the family brings them stimulates Capricorns to greater and greater efforts. In fact, it is not usually until Capricorns are past middle age that they finally feel successful enough to let go of the need to build, and build, and build.

And finally, having lived their lives backward, the adult Capricorn begins to find some time to be a child, to have some fun, to lighten up. It is as if Capricorn, born old, learns the lightness of youth only with age.

Capricorns, like Tauruses and Scorpios, are attracted to power. In Capricorns' case, there is an almost intuitive or instinctual recognition of where the power is in any situation. Their opportunistic nature combined with their intuition manages to place them in positions where they will have a stab at the power position themselves, if they are very tenacious and very patient. They enjoy control and are most comfortable when wielding it themselves, since they find it difficult, if not impossible, to trust other people, unless those others have gone through the necessary years of trial to prove themselves reliable as family members.

For Capricorns, impatience is the greatest threat to their accomplishment. I know of countless Capricorns who have come within arm's reach of their goal, after years of careful and patient planning, only to throw it all away in one moment of brashness and impatience.

We find Capricorns in all types of job and career situations, but rarely do we find them in entry-level positions, since their eye for opportunity coupled with their diligence moves them up through the ranks quickly.

Capricorns do well owning their own businesses, working for large businesses, corporations, or government, or even working in religious organizations. They often work for small businesses as well, but will not fare as well here since their innate business sense and ambition often creates envy and jealousy in fellow employees, and threatens those in positions immediately above them.

The Capricorn Woman

The Capricorn woman is one of the strongest females in the zodiac. Having copied her powerful personality traits from a strong and inspiring mother, she will have all of the business acumen, practicality, manipulative ability, long-distance planning ability, reliability, and resourcefulness of her mother.

She sees the female of her species as the foundation, the earth mother, the point of stability her world revolves around. As far as she is concerned, the female is the dominant member of the species.

However, she, unlike many of the other negative-signed women of the zodiac, likes and respects men, and enjoys their company enormously, as well as their attentions. She sees no reason why she can't do the same jobs as them, perhaps, even better than they can.

And like Arian women, she enjoys working with men, perhaps because they generally take their jobs just as seriously as she takes hers. Unlike Aries, she does not compete with men; rather, she sees herself as their equal or better already, and merely enjoys their companionship and comradeship.

She will never see any man to be as big a threat to her position as she might see an equally capable woman. This is probably because she instinctively sees the woman as having the killer instinct that the man lacks. She also quite artfully depends upon his tendency to see her as just a woman in order to wrap him right around her finger.

I often think that the Capricorn woman would fit nicely into a pride of lions. Fiercely protective of her young (which could encompass anything she has built or created, including her actual children) and her territory, she is the patient and deadly huntress—who yet defers to her mate after she has brought his meal back to him.

Being a traditional sort of person, the Capricorn woman usually marries and raises a family. However, if she is smart, she will continue her career after her children are born.

The Capricorn woman who decides to stay home and raise the kids the old fashioned way usually tends to keep a strong and controlling hand on kids and husband alike. She may either alienate them from her or possibly deprive them of their ability to think and act for themselves, which causes them all to be totally dependent upon her. The ancient matriarch who lives on in old world novels is undoubtedly a Capricorn of this type.

All Capricorns feel the need to manipulate and control something. When the thing they are controlling is their family (usually it is the female who is guilty of this one), you can expect both material and emotional manipulation.

Capricorn fully understands the principle of divide and conquer, so a tiny act like giving one child something that another dearly wants manages to neatly entrap both of them. Capricorn is full of little ideas like this one.

Capricorn is a master tactician, who understands the importance of never telling her corporals what the real game plan is. After all, if they knew, they might want to push her out and take the spoils for themselves.

All of these traits make mincemeat out of family relationships, but are worthy skills in the game of corporate politics, which is where the Capricorn woman belongs.

In business she shines and can reach any position. And although she is not always well liked, she is always highly respected.

When she vents her need for tactical expression in the business world, she is able to go home to husband and family and makes a warm and loving mother who is able to stand by her family in a supportive, not controlling, way.

The Capricorn Man

The Capricorn man also learns his strength of character, his drive for success, and his tactical abilities from his mother. But he also learns from his father, even if the lessons are sometimes indirect.

He learns that a man is the lord and master within his family, but that he is required to play no active role in the family at all, other than being the breadwinner. He expects his word to be law and that his family will automatically follow his directions, without his intervention.

He learns that a man commands the respect and admiration of his family by sitting at its head and by earning a revered position in his work outside the home.

He expects his wife to be as powerful and capable as his mother was and to run his home as smoothly as she did. From his perspective, everything at home is supposed to be taken care of so completely that his involvement, as authority or in any other guise, is totally unnecessary.

He is, like his female counterpart, a traditionalist. And so, like her, he will probably have children. And yet, unlike her, he does not feel the necessity for children to complete his life. He is more likely to be peripherally aware of them in the proud sense of the king surveying those who will carry on his line.

The Capricorn man's primary focus in life is his career—his work and life outside the home. And he expects that everyone in the family will automatically understand this and be totally supportive. As long as he is responsible to them, they are supportive of him.

Within home and family, the Capricorn man is gentle and quiet; his home is his safe retreat from the dynamic world outside. He is even sometimes non-communicative, telling wife and family only the essentials of what they need to know about his life outside the home.

Some Capricorn men pull from the sign Cancer, which is the opposite sign on the astrological wheel. These Capricorns are more emotional and need the support of wife and family even more. They may be unnaturally close to mother as well, and may even follow the Cancerian trait of acting badly to get their wife's emotional attention.

But no matter which Capricorn you are looking at, out in the working world he is a dynamo. He is responsible, capable, and ambitious. His tactical ability comes into play on the job, where he jockeys and manipulates for the power position again and again, until finally he achieves it.

The aspect of impatience is even more of a threat to his accomplishment than it is to the Capricorn woman. He can become so consumed by career plans that he attempts short cuts to the position to which he aspires. His short cuts are always met with failure. Capricorn succeeds only through the virtues of hard work, merit, and patience.

Like his female counterpart, he finally learns to enjoy life and take it less seriously as he ages, and after he has been able to achieve some degree of success. And also like her, he is, at sometime in his life, given a degree of power over other people—for how else is he to learn the Capricorn lesson of the correct use of power?

His lesson is not just in the acquisition of power, but in its proper use. When he gains authority and control over another being, will he revel in what he can make them do? How he can make them jump? How the exercise of power sends excitement through every nerve in his body? Or, will he truly become the all-father image he has worked to become, never forgetting the responsibility he now has toward those he holds power over?

Remember the old adage, *Power corrupts, and ultimate power corrupts ultimately*? Well, this is Capricorn's real challenge—to maintain perspective while exercising the correct use of power.

Associate the following qualities with Capricorn:

- Responsible and serious
- Family oriented
- Career oriented
- Seeks power and position
- Needs respect
- Lives life "backwards"
- "Earth Mother" or "King"
- Materialistic

End of Chapter Exercise

1. Be familiar with the Sun sign qualities of Sagittarius and Capricorn.

2. Know the meanings of Jupiter and Saturn.

3. Know the meanings of the 9th and 10th houses, and the Midheaven.

4. Understand what the theoretical signs are.

5. Continue your analysis of the chart we have been working with, adding the 9th and 10th houses, the signs Sagittarius and Capricorn, and the planets Jupiter and Saturn. Questions a) through f) will assist you with your interpretation.

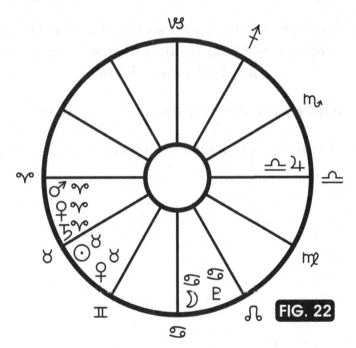

FIG. 22

a) What does Sagittarius on the 9th cusp say about the type of religious and philosophical views this person will have?

b) Jupiter, ruler of the 9th house and Sagittarius, is in the 7th house in Libra. How will this affect the type of mate this person will attract, and the relationships that will form?

c) Jupiter naturally rules the 9th house, which has Sagittarius on the cusp in this chart. How will this join or bridge the affairs of the 7th house and the 9th house?

d) Capricorn is on the Midheaven (MC). What does this tell you about this person's greatest aspirations? What does Capricorn in the 10th house, as well as on the MC mean?

e) In this chart Saturn, who is ruler of the 10th house and Capricorn is found in the 1st house. How does this combine the affairs of the two houses?

f) What effect will Saturn have on the 1st house?

The key to this End of Chapter Exercise can be found on page 317.

Chapter 8

Introducing Aquarius and Pisces

Introducing Aquarius and Pisces

Aquarius is the 11th sign of the zodiac.

The Aquarius-Leo axis and the 11th house-5th house axis together express how love is given (Aquarius) and received (Leo). It is through Aquarius that mankind is learning the objectivity and humanitarianism that is a pre-requisite to the development of the ability to love unconditionally.

Glyph or Symbol—♒—The Water Bearer

Mode—Fixed

Ruling Planet—♄—Saturn

Co-ruler—♅—Uranus

Element—Air

Corresponding House—11th

Orientation—Masculine

Corresponding Body Part—The Ankles

Saturn

The various meanings of the planet Saturn have been covered in detail in Chapter 7 when we discussed Capricorn, the other sign that Saturn rules. Please refresh your memory by reviewing that before continuing further.

The concepts we associate with Saturn are as follows:

- Structure—Major life lesson
- Age and Longevity
- Building—Karmic Patterns
- Authority figures
- Teaching—Grandparents—Dad/authority parent
- Career—Sense of timing—Endings
- Restriction—Dealing with authority

In Aquarius, which is a positive air sign, Saturn behaves somewhat differently than it does in Capricorn, a negative earth sign, even though its meanings remain essentially the same.

The foundation and structure that Capricorns build is a physical one because of their earth element and their innately receptive nature. But the structures that Aquarians build are of the mind. Their positive nature makes them constantly reach out, and their air element directs them toward new ideas, new concepts, and new methods of social expression. It is as if Aquarius builds the mental constructs that Capricorn gives form to on the physical plane.

Both Aquarius and Capricorn are traditional. But in Capricorn, the traditions are easy to see—they are physical, like the family unit itself. However, in Aquarius, the traditions, the patterns, are less discernible because they are patterns of thought and ideas.

Many people make the mistake of thinking that because Aquarians are innovative thinkers that they are open minded in their thinking. These two qualities are not the same at all.

It is Aquarius' positive air orientation that gives this sign their innovative thinking ability, while Saturn itself gives pattern and structure to those thoughts, making Aquarians very traditional indeed.

Aquarians will only be as open minded as the ideas and values learned in their early lives allows them to be. Saturn gives Aquarius the same traditionalism and structure it does Capricorn, but in Aquarius, the result is mental, which results in Aquarians being extremely dogmatic concerning whatever their values and ideas are. This quality is further enhanced by the fixed mode of the sign.

If you hold the image of all of Saturn's qualities in your mind, and then imagine these qualities to represent the mental make-up of a person, including how they reach out to and inter-react with other people, you will have a good understanding of Saturn in its rulership of Aquarius.

Uranus

Uranus was discovered in 1781, around the same time as both the American and French Revolutions, and at the beginning of what we now refer to as the Industrial Revolution.

For this reason, astrologers attribute the process of change or revolution and all forms of technology to Uranus, including everything from electricity (discovered, again, around the same time as Uranus) to mechanical equipment, engines, aircraft, and computers.

Astrologers assigned Uranus to be a co-ruler of Aquarius because so many of the world events surrounding the time of its discovery were Aquarian in nature. Everything relative to

Uranus is different, both unexpected and out-of-step with the rest of the world—or even a step ahead.

The planet itself justifies this interpretation of its being different, for Uranus is the only planet in our solar system that actually spins sideways on its own axis. That is, it revolves at right angles to all of the other planets. No wonder it represents all of those things in our lives that separate us from the norm, that bring out our individuality and uniqueness.

Uranus takes approximately eighty-four years to complete one revolution around the sun, so it spends approximately seven years in each sign. This means that Uranus, like Pluto, is what we call a generational planet. That is, the sign it is in affects a whole group of people.

In essence, then, the sign in which Uranus is located in your own chart represents where your entire generation will be unique and individualistic in its thinking. Its house placement in combination with its sign is where you will be most unique. It is also where your greatest opportunities will be presented, and where you will undergo the greatest personal change.

Interestingly, Uranus, like Saturn, is often associated with time, age, and longevity in a chart. This is probably partly due to its eighty-four-year cycle, which today is very close to the average human life span. But when we associate Uranus with time, there is an inherent understanding that there will be something different about time relative to Uranus, as opposed to time relative to Saturn. It is as if Uranus represents the idea" of time, while Saturn represents its actual flow.

When Uranus is seen to represent a grandparent or older person through its association with age and longevity, there is an automatic inference of either very great age or something equally unique about them that sets this particular older person apart from others.

In mythology, Uranus was the father of Saturn; this places Uranus in the position of the great-grandparent. Also according to mythology, Uranus was the husband of Gaia (Earth) who gave birth to the Titans. One of these, Saturn, overthrew him.

A very subtle relationship between Earth, Saturn, and Uranus is revealed here. Many astrologers relate Uranus to the higher mind. I would like to suggest that it is the bridge formed between Earth and Uranus—that is, the arena of physical life and higher mind—by the planet Saturn that allows use of higher mind or higher intuition in everyday life.

For those individuals in whom Saturn still holds supremacy, higher intuition will be blocked. For those individuals in whom Uranus dominates, higher intuition will function in an out-of-control way, allowing no possibility for application. It is only when a balance is formed between Saturn and Uranus that the higher mind will function freely in the individual.

It is interesting that in the sign Aquarius we see examples of both types of personalities. The dogmatic, Saturnian Aquarian permits no intuition or leaps of logic to interfere with his linear logic. But the free-minded Uranian Aquarian goes off on flights of absent-minded fancy without hope or even intent of applying his ideas.

It is only when these two planets are merged in the Aquarius type that we see true higher intuition or higher mind functioning. Where Uranus is able to supply the leap of logic necessary for true discovery and creativity, Saturn is able to supply the structure and organization of thinking necessary to make the idea practical.

Uranus is often thought of as being a higher octave to Mercury, since it obviously also has a great deal to do with our mental faculties. It is also considered the ruler or father of modern astrology.

Associate the following concepts with Uranus:

- Revolution and change
- Uniqueness
- Higher mind/intuition
- Technology
- Great-grandparent/old age
- Speeding or slowing time
- The ruler of Astrology
- The unexpected

The Eleventh House

The 11ᵗʰ house, like the 10ᵗʰ, derives its meanings firstly from the planet Saturn, since Saturn is its primary ruler, and secondly from the planet Uranus, its co-ruler.

As mentioned earlier, Saturn's action in the 11ᵗʰ house and the sign Aquarius is positive or generative. And since this is an air house, in the 11ᵗʰ house, Saturn generates ideas and socialization.

The 11ᵗʰ house deals with friends and with groups and organizations, and even more importantly, with the ideals, ideas, values, and aspirations we learn from our interaction with them. Every group is formed of like-minded individuals, and Saturn's influence in the 11th house is to bind groups of individuals together to become a mobile force in society.

Yet, Uranus also has influence in this house. Uranus brings about the dissension and the insertion of new ideas that prevent groups from stagnation. Indeed, it is Uranus' influence that causes various groups or organizations to merge and share ideas and influence before separating and taking on whatever they have learned with them.

Saturn's influence makes us want to form deep and lasting friendships. Yet, Uranus' influence makes us want to constantly move on, make new friends, and add new insights to our interaction with others.

The combined action of these two planets makes the 11th house a very active house socially. We all are constantly reaching out to others in new and innovative ways, while attempting to hold on to and nurture old and valued friendships.

The combination of Saturn and Uranus rulership also makes this the house associated with universal law—kind of a scientific approach to deity. As second house from the 10th (by spinning the wheel), the 11th house also rules our self-concept relative to our profession, as well as the abilities we have that we can apply to our profession and the wages we may earn directly from it. As the third fixed or succedent house, the 11th house also describes both who our third child will be (if we have one) and what our relationship with him or her will be.

Since the 11th house is opposite the 5th on the axis of giving and receiving love, it shows our ability to love and the ways in which we actually do give love (as opposed to the 5th house, our ability to receive love).

This 5th house-11th house expression of giving and receiving love is very important, especially when you are looking at two people in a relationship. For example, someone with an air sign on the 11th house cusp tends to give his love by listening to his loved one and sharing his or her thoughts and ideas. Social interaction, like going to parties or sharing group activities, with the loved one is very important and is a direct means for him to express love. When giving a gift, he might spend more time picking out the card than the gift or he might write his own card.

Now, imagine that you are this air sign 11th-house person married to a person with a water sign on his 5th house of love received.

The water sign on the 5th-house spouse wants to have an intense emotional interaction with you. He wants to fight, cry, hug, and laugh together. He does not care what you say—he just wants you to do it emotionally, to let him know you love him. He does not want to share you with a group of friends. He wants a relationship that is mutually nurturing and close. The gift he would prefer from you is to have you to himself for a night, to eat the candle-lighted meal you prepared, and then cuddle together in front of the fireplace. He will love your card because you wrote it, but do not expect him to read it.

If two people, compatible in every other way, do not have compatible 5th to 11th houses, they will not be able to understand how their partner needs to be loved.

If your 5th house is fire, you will find that people with either a fire sign or an air sign on the 11th house will satisfy your need for love most easily. If your 5th house is earth, look for someone with earth or water on the 11th. If your 5th house is air, look for someone with air or fire on the 11th. If your 5th house is water, look for someone with water or earth on the 11th.

And if you're already with someone whose 11th house is not compatible with your 5th, then you both will have to study astrology so that you can be more understanding of one another's needs.

Associate the following concepts with the 11th house:

- How you give love
- Friends
- Groups and organizations
- Aspirations, ideas, values
- Professional wages
- Professional self-concept
- Professional ability
- Third child
- Universal law

Aquarius

Polarity

Aquarius is a positive, generative sign. Like the other positive signs we have covered, it is male dominated in early childhood and is outer directed.

The combination of positive polarity and Saturn/Uranus rulership tends to make Aquarians the scientists of the zodiac, always directing their mental attention outward to understand their world and constantly seeking to interact with and change it.

Quadruplicity

Aquarius is the fourth and last of the fixed signs. Since Aquarius is also an air sign, the fixed nature is on the mental level.

This mental fixity gives Aquarians the ability to fixate on ideas, to work with them for years, sometimes, until they thoroughly understand them. This is another reason why we so often find Aquarians engaged in research activities and in scientific fields. I remember my Aquarian grandmother going into the hospital for surgery and being more interested in how all of the equipment worked than in what they were going to do to her.

Of course, since their positive orientation also makes them outer directed, Aquarians often direct their research-oriented mind toward people and social situations. They love to study people.

And in their social interactions, Aquarians' mental fixity can cause them to immerse themselves so deeply in the need to understand a person or a situation that the result is very similar to the obsession associated with Scorpio through its rulers, Mars and Pluto.

The chief difference is that Aquarians' obsession is mental, whereas Scorpio's is emotional. Scorpios cannot let go, but must work through the emotions until they are forced to push the object of obsession away. Aquarians can let go at any time, if their intellectual curiosity is satisfied. Often, this sudden cessation of interest on the part of Aquarians is confusing to others. But once you understand that it was never really an emotional obsession you were seeing, but rather, an intellectual fixation, this phenomenon is much easier to understand.

Unfortunately, this tendency to fixate on ideas gives a superficial similarity to Scorpio. Hence, we find many Scorpios involved with Aquarians. I say unfortunately because Scorpios can go on being obsessed long after Aquarians' curiosities have been stilled and their interest ended.

This intellectual fixity created by the positive polarity of Aquarius also gets many people in trouble with Aquarians. You see, Aquarians are mental and outer directed, so all too often they are so busy trying to understand your ideology and values that you make the mistake of assuming that not only are your ideas similar, but also that they can accept everything there is to know about you.

This is not so. In seeking to understand you, Aquarians adopt the objectivity of the scientist. However, they are not truly objective, since their fixed nature prohibits this. And after they have finished their research, they will drop back into their own fixed values. This is when you find out that they are holding against you something you may have confided or done in good faith, while counting on what you misinterpreted as their open mindedness and similarity to you.

In their fixity and sometimes rigid-mindedness, Aquarians can sometimes be judge, jury, and even executioner, objectively serving sentence on all comers—even themselves.

In addition, Aquarius is the only sign of the zodiac that actually keeps a list of non-existent people. People whom they may have been close to at one time but have in some way stepped out of the Aquarian's acceptable limits of tolerance are assigned to this list. In an Aquarian's mind, they simply no longer exist.

If you have Aquarian friends, their fixity forces them to be your friend forever, even though you may not have seen them in twenty years. That is why your Aquarian friends tend to pop up every so often, picking up the friendship exactly where it left off, as if nothing had changed—because, for them, it has not. So, in your Aquarian friends' minds, the only way they can stop being friends with you is for you to stop existing.

Triplicity

Aquarius is the third and last of the air signs, following behind Gemini and Libra. The air element is mature in Aquarians, which effectively means that, for most Aquarians, the world exists more truly in their minds than in the physical reality around us.

Aquarius' fixed nature gives their thoughts the quality of strong focus and concentration, unlike the other air signs. Often, because of this, Aquarians appear intense and magnetic, and in many ways mysterious.

What is interesting is that since Aquarians are so thoughtful and because of their Saturn rulership, they often do not express their thoughts. Again, this gives them a certain mystique.

The reason Aquarians do not express their thoughts is often because they have made an assumption that you already know what it is they would have communicated. Again, this causes Aquarians difficulty. Eventually, it becomes obvious that their assumption was incorrect. Rather than accepting this, their fixed nature makes them angry with you for not acting as expected. Be careful—this could get you added to their list of non-existent people.

One of their primary lessons is to make their expectations known to others. They need to learn to share and communicate their inner world.

Because Aquarians are so very air oriented, intellectual curiosity often replaces honest social interaction. Oftentimes, they lock away their emotions in a place so deep they almost forget they have any. Many Aquarians, especially Aquarian men, who are not as naturally connected to emotion as women, actually run from the expression of emotion.

People often mistake the strong-willed mental focus Aquarians direct at them as obsessive love or possessiveness. But it is important to remember that this has no emotional base; rather it is based on the quality of air operating through a fixed sign. All of Aquarians' decisions and actions throughout life are the product of mental analysis, which they may or may not share with you.

As a philosophical sign, Aquarians also have an inherently objective worldview. Their air element combines with this to make them automatically place themselves outside of any situation so they may better evaluate it.

Aquarians' greatest challenge is to rise above their judgmental nature, to use their objectivity not to set themselves up as unbiased judge, but rather to use it to generate unconditional acceptance.

The Sign Aquarius — Born to Learn Objectivity

As noted above, Aquarians are influenced most strongly during their formative first three years by their father or some other strong male around them. Usually, their mother is not a strong figure at all; although if the Moon is in a negative sign, she may also have been quite important.

Aquarians' early environment is marked by the fact that there is something different about their father, something that sets him apart from the community in which they live. Perhaps he speaks a foreign language. Perhaps he is a different nationality than the surrounding neighbors, or perhaps his values merely differ. Perhaps he is very well educated when the surrounding family and neighbors are not.

For whatever reason, he is seen by Aquarians as different. To Aquarians, it is Dad's differences that are his strengths. His differences are what set him apart and make him special.

Since Aquarians, like all positive-sign children, base their personality development upon Dad, they too seek to be different. By the time Aquarians are ready to start school, they have already stepped far out of pace with the other children their age. They may pick up learning more quickly or more slowly, but they will not ever be average.

There is also something unique about the way in which Aquarians' minds work, and very often this difference causes them problems in their early education—problems which tend to set them apart from the other children even further. Their clothing will either reflect last year's fad or be one or two years ahead of what everyone else is wearing now. You will always recognize the Aquarian child in the room because he or she will be the one who forgot socks or has one red shoe or is wearing the thick black glasses no one else would be caught dead in.

But the need for Aquarius to be different includes more than just their physical appearance and superficial behavior patterns. It includes their values as well.

In striving to copy Dad's different quality, Aquarians also copy a host of other qualities from him. Their Dad was stubborn and usually very traditional in his own way. It is likely that those traditions were different from the society in which Aquarians are being raised. Aquarians copy their Dads' traditional nature, his stubbornness, and his values.

Dad is usually thoughtful, a man with strong beliefs and ideas, whether or not he is well educated. Aquarians admire this and from it develop their own strongly mental nature.

Aquarians' Dad is a social animal, if not by direct involvement, then by his political or philosophical view. Again, Aquarians copy from Dad both his social activity (or lack of it) and his tendency to set himself apart from the group.

Many times, the things that make the Aquarians' Dad unique are positive; perhaps he is a famous author or movie star, or any man who has had the courage to break away and follow his own convictions. He passes on to Aquarius the legacy of his pride in accomplishment and his ability to stand apart and do things his own way.

But other times, the things that make Aquarian's Dad unique are not good. He may be a criminal behind bars throughout much of an Aquarian's life; he may be an alcoholic, or a mental patient, or an invalid.

Many times, an Aquarian's Dad is a man incapable of communication. His strong expectations of Aquarius are delivered silently through a system of reward and punishment. Occasionally, especially if the child is born in the first 10° of Aquarius, there is even physical abuse visited by the father upon Aquarius or another family member. Even where there is no abuse, Dad is usually a strict disciplinarian whose old school ethics often present Aquarius with an entirely different behavioral code than his friends have.

Often Aquarians grow up in an emotionally cold environment in which they are expected to act like adults far before they are truly ready. In early childhood, they may experience extreme pain and the loss of something or someone they love, which they are not permitted to mourn. Some Aquarians develop their humanitarian nature early on by taking care of a sick or indisposed family member. They learn to create emotional distance between themselves and others to prevent being hurt.

By the time Aquarians reach middle school, the mold is already cast, and no matter how hard they try to fit in with the other children, they cannot. Usually, they do try. By now, their need to copy Dad is superseded by a desire to copy and be like their peers.

Although they are often looked up to and admired, although they may lead the group or hang around on the fringes of it, they are never able to simply become a part of it.

Aquarians become social butterflies. They have many friends, but it is hard to know whom they are really close to. They drift from friend to friend, from group to group, being a part of every social situation available to them, yet truly belonging to none. They develop the objectivity discussed earlier that further sets them apart.

They sometimes get so involved in looking at the big picture in their objective, scientific way that they forget the small one that is of immediate importance.

Aquarians make good scientists and researchers, where their strong focus, creativity, and tenacity is a plus. They make excellent social directors and sales people, where the ability to know a lot about everyone while remaining objective is a plus. Their Uranian intuition makes them good entrepreneurs. They make good attorneys, politicians, and statesmen, where their tendency to look at the overview or big picture in a humanitarian fashion is a plus.

It is the Age of Aquarius that we are moving into now. As we do so, many of the facets of Aquarians' upbringing and general character are becoming a generalized part of our own society, both good and bad.

As we move into our own future world, technology will continue to increase, as Uranus creates quantum leaps in intuition that Saturn turns into new age technology.

Politically and economically our world will continue to look more and more at the big picture, providing things like health care and food for everyone, yet somehow forgetting the small picture that asks if this is what they really need.

The Aquarian age will take us far from the maudlin emotionalism of the Piscean age we are leaving. But it is important that we remember the Pisces lessons, so that we do not succumb to the emotionlessness exhibited by some Aquarians.

As we move forward into this new age, there is a real danger that in our effort to become more humanitarian, we will in reality become less human.

The Aquarian Woman

As with most women born into a positive sign, the Aquarian woman usually is not comfortable with her femininity until later in life.

Aquarius is one of the signs that often appears to be more like the sign that opposes it (Leo) than itself. When the Aquarian woman is drawing on the Leo end of this axis, she sometimes behaves in an overly feminine manner or may adopt a tomboy demeanor, just as many Leo women do, as a means of covering her discomfort with the female form.

However, when the Aquarian woman is behaving in a true Aquarian manner, her discomfort with her sexuality shows up in her tendency to think of herself as a walking mind. In her mentalism, she may be nearly sexless and often offers herself to the opposite sex, whom she is certainly attracted to and enamored of, as a friend.

As a matter of fact, to the typical Aquarian woman, friendship is far more important than sex and certainly must precede any real romantic relationship. Remembering that Aquarius is both Uranus and Saturn ruled, and that, in the typical Aquarian, these two planets' energies are not yet unified, the Aquarian usually leans more toward an expression of one or the other.

The Aquarian woman who leans toward the Saturn influence tends to take life very seriously; her career will be very important to her, and she will probably gravitate toward a career that requires a responsible nature.

This Aquarian will be traditional in her approach toward life; she will probably marry a man much like Dad and will surely tend to put him on a pedestal.

Her expectations of both her husband and her children will be extreme. She tends to live her life according to her own very strict code of which she expects everyone else to know and also be living up to.

This Saturnian Aquarian is materialistic. She wants a great deal in terms of material security and is very conscious of social station. She often has a keep up with the Jones urge.

But when the Aquarian woman is influenced most strongly by the action of Uranus, the picture is quite different. This second type of Aquarian woman may appear downright flaky to the rest of the world. She has to do everything her own way and in her own time. She is something of an anarchist

She is reliable, yet you may not want to rely upon her because her idea of what is needed might be quite different than yours, even after you think you have gotten your idea across with perfect clarity.

She is much more mental than her Saturnian sister, and as a result, tends to forget material things like paying the bills, cleaning the house, or feeding the family.

She is a wonderful dreamer, and she is intensely creative. She makes a good artist, but she is just as likely to exercise her creativity in the chemistry lab.

This Aquarian also puts friendship before sex, but her curious and experimental nature definitely makes itself known in the bedroom. She will try just about anything once.

Neither Aquarian type is an outstanding mother. Unfortunately, children benefit more from motherly nurturance early in life than motherly friendship. But as her children grow older, they will find that whereas they may not have been able to rely on her mothering ability, her friendship is firm and her objectivity to their issues makes her advice invaluable.

The Aquarian Man

Like the Aquarian woman, the Aquarian man often tends to draw from the sign of his opposite polarity, Leo.

When he does, he will be the romantic, physically active and aggressive. He will often find himself in the knight in shining armor role—saving some poor woman in distress. But when he acts like the Aquarian that he is, an entirely different picture emerges. Whether he is the Uranian or the Saturnian Aquarian, he is a mental chess player.

He is a born tactician, much like Capricorn, but his game board is the mind, not the material world. He can spend hours planning and analyzing anything from his stock portfolio to how a can opener works.

The Saturnian type of Aquarian tends to behave almost like a Capricorn. More materialistic than his Uranian brother, he makes a chess game of corporate politics and of finance. He gravitates toward law, politics, and administrative positions. He sees himself, like his father, as the authority figure and enjoys being in a position where he can exercise humanitarian concern for his employees and people.

In some cases, his materialistic nature and concern for social status will motivate him to focus on simply making money, and when Aquarius focuses his considerable mental energy on a single goal, he is most often successful.

We often find this Aquarian in sales, and when it comes to knowing his market, manipulating it, and developing contacts, there is no sign that can surpass him.

If he has one major failing, it is usually a tendency to closed mindedness and dogmatism.

As a father, he will be a firm authority figure who will generate admiration and respect in his children and will be a good provider.

His Uranian counterpart is usually the Aquarian who becomes involved in developmental technology, who becomes the scientist and researcher. Or, he might become an artist or writer. Perhaps he might even be a musician or composer, giving life to that music only he can hear.

The Uranian Aquarian man is the absent-minded professor. He is the brilliant scientist who works on the NASA space shuttle but cannot remember remember to tie his shoes or eat lunch. He is the inventor whose mind creates a new technological process but who doesn't fix his own doorknob.

His tactical mind is tuned solely toward pursuing whatever he seeks to understand. He, too, is a flake. Often, without someone to look after him, we wonder how this Aquarian survives because there is not a practical or materialistic bone in him.

If you are married to this one, you had better be the one to handle the checking account and all of life's practical needs. He might make good money, but he will be so involved in his latest project that he will not even remember, or care, if he has been paid. He'll gladly offer to help watch the kids, but when you come home a few hours later, he is surprised that they are not there, still watching him take apart the T.V. that suddenly caught his attention.

There is an ingenuous boyishness about this Aquarian that is most attractive—but remember, when you marry him, he just may be your first child.

Associate the following concepts with Aquarius:

- Different and unique
- Fixed and stubborn
- Scientific
- Intellectually creative
- Mental
- Judgmental
- Out of pace
- Curious minded
- Humanitarian minded
- Unemotional

Pisces—The Spiritual Martyr

Pisces is the 12th and last sign of the zodiac.

The Pisces-Virgo axis and the 12th house-6th house axis together represent the balance of inner and outer directed consciousness. In a spiritual sense, the 12th house is the House of Initiation. The 12th-6th house axis is the health axis in the zodiac; it is the axis that deals with addiction, co-dependency, service, and discrimination.

Glyph or Symbol—♓—The Fish

Mode—Mutable

Ruling Planet—♃—Jupiter

Co-ruler—♆—Neptune

Element—Water

Corresponding House—12th

Orientation—Feminine

Corresponding Body Part—The Feet

Jupiter

We have already discussed the action of Jupiter astrologically when we covered the sign Sagittarius, which it also rules, in Chapter 7. Please refer back to that to be sure you understand Jupiter so far.

Here is a review of the associations we make with Jupiter:

- Big, expanded
- Long distance travel
- Astral travel
- Philosophy
- Religion, spirituality
- Luck, money
- Weight gain
- Higher education
- Law
- Excesses
- Other people's thinking
- In-laws
- Prejudice
- Teaching, guiding
- Channeling

Remembering that, in Sagittarius, Jupiter is in a positive fire sign, while Pisces, the sign we are covering now, is a negative water sign. You can expect there to be some alteration in Jupiter's character when it is acting through Pisces.

First of all, the negative-receptive quality of Pisces causes the Jupiter energy in this sign to act inwardly, as opposed to its outer-directed action in Sagittarius. Jupiter's negative quality in Pisces causes Pisces to be more often overweight than most of the other signs.

The negative mode affects long-distance travel by either making Pisces people the victim of it or causing them to do their distance traveling by reading or through televised travel-logs.

Pisceans do not just astral travel; they often spend more time fantasizing and daydreaming in their inner world than they do taking any form of action in the outer world. The effect is to make them extremely gifted and creative people.

In Pisces, Jupiter's religious zeal turns into an inner spirituality. Many Pisces are very religious, yet they do not need the outer forms, trappings, and religious ritual that only reflect a true inner belief system. Pisces are rarely militant about their beliefs, being inherently private people, and rarely are they attracted to the study of belief systems other than their own. However, their water quality often makes them fearful of what they don't understand. Sometimes that fear results in prejudice. In fact, things like magic or psychic phenomenon often frighten them, although they have an inherent understanding of them.

Often Pisceans are raised in a religion that encourages deep-seated guilt, which results in their developing a powerful sense of conscience. As adults, these Pisces most often are forced deeper and deeper into themselves to fully understand and develop their own very individualistic beliefs.

Likewise, Pisces seem to be born with a deep-seated philosophy of life already present. They have only to look inward to discover that philosophy, unlike the constantly searching Sagittarian.

Since Jupiter's energy acts inwardly in this sign, Pisces are not known to be particularly lucky, nor are they particularly good at attracting money. However, when they learn to listen to Jupiter's voice within them, the resulting intuitive ability they can tap is a fair substitute. Their strongly developed intuition can lead them into positive situations and protect them from negative ones once they learn to listen to it.

If Pisceans can get past the inborn fear of the psychic realms, their intuitive ability combined with their wonderful imaginations and innate understanding of otherworldly things make them superior psychics.

On a more negative note, with regard to excesses, Pisces often have a real problem. This is the sign we most often find associated with substance abuse, both because Jupiter's inner-directed energy tends to promote excesses directed at the self, and also because that same inner-directed energy often makes Pisces run away into themselves from whatever they don't like—into daydreams, or books, or a complete fantasy world, as well as into drugs or alcohol.

Pisces, being a negative water sign and Jupiter ruled, is also the most receptive sign in the zodiac. This receptivity makes Pisces so sensitive to the needs and hurts of others that often it is the very emotional need they feel coming from others that makes them run away. And when they do not run, they often go so overboard trying to help others that their excesses lead to other problems, like dependency.

Pisceans' Jupiter rulership also can make them draw on the resources of the people close to them indiscriminately, to help others they see in need. Because of this, we often find Pisceans' families and friends suffering and struggling to support them, while they, in their oblivious fashion, are joyfully supporting the rest of the world.

Pisceans also are natural born teachers. Many astrologers feel that all Pisces-born people are old souls. As such, what they have to teach the rest of us is not necessarily book knowledge; they are teaching about life.

Neptune

Neptune was discovered in 1846, at a time when sailing ships gave man mastery of the sea, allowing free trade between nations and cultures from around the world. Nations were still empire building.

Along with the exchange of goods between nations came an exchange of ideas, philosophies, and religious and cultural beliefs. Ideas from the Eastern world began to become popular in the West. It was during the time period immediately following Neptune's discovery that Madame Blavatsky wrote her famous book, *The Secret Doctrines*, that introduced so many Eastern concepts to Western minds. The book eventually gave birth to Theosophy and a host of other metaphysically oriented organizations and fraternities.

However, what came back to the many seafaring nations, as Neptune was discovered, was much more than shipped goods and philosophical beliefs. Sailors brought exotic diseases and new drugs, like opium, back as well.

It was also during this period of our human history that entire cultures and religious belief systems were utterly wiped out. For example, the American-Indian wars were just coming into full swing as the Gold Rush of 1849 began and the U.S. began extending its territories. The Romantic and Industrial Revolutions also were getting into full stride at this time and the first labor strikes, as a result of unimaginably horrible working conditions, took place.

The steam engine on land and sea was developed and put into use around this time, too, and perhaps this machine most clearly represents Neptune—water, super heated to create steam, results in an explosive release of energy that has the capability to create physical change.

Neptune is usually presented as being the planet of spirituality. Yet when you look at the history of the time period surrounding its discovery, you know that Neptune means a great deal more than spirituality and that, in many ways, it is not the most pleasant planet to deal with.

Neptune takes 165 years to complete one revolution around the sun. Next to Pluto, it is our outermost planet. As a matter of fact, its orbit crosses Pluto's. From the years 1978 to 1999, Neptune was temporarily the outermost planet. It is so far from the sun that it has no atmosphere, being a completely frozen world.

In mythology, Neptune (Poseidon) was god of the sea, the mysterious lord of the deep, who was stepbrother to Jupiter (Zeus), King of the Gods, Saturn having fathered both. Perhaps this is one of the reasons Neptune was given co-rulership of Pisces, along with Jupiter.

In the various myths, Neptune is most often depicted as a mysterious and violent god, uninterested in any aspect of life that does not touch upon his deep waters. But wherever the ocean is involved, we find Neptune—protective of his kingdom, intense, humorless, all-knowing and all-seeing, cold and emotionless, yet always fair in his judgment.

It is obvious from this that Neptune is a planet that deals primarily with the waters of the unconscious mind. Indeed, it is a spiritual planet, for like all three of the outermost planets

(Uranus, Neptune, and Pluto), it is always much more positive when used spiritually than materially. But also like them, one must first work through the material aspects of Neptune before one arrives at the spiritual truths it teaches.

Neptune's material aspect is not very pleasant. On its lower level, Neptune rules drugs and narcotics, escapism, illusion, disillusionment, and lies. It toys with our perceptions, causes us to see what is not present while we misunderstand what we do see. Wherever Neptune is in your chart, by its sign and house, is where you are most likely to have unrealistic perceptions about life and where you are likely to be the most challenged to alter those perceptions.

Neptune is a killer. It gives you what you think you want but do not see clearly, and then makes you live through the resulting agony of learning step by step exactly what your misconceptions were. By the time Neptune is done with you, you no longer have those misconceptions, and you probably no longer have the slightest desire for whatever it was you used to think you wanted. Neptune has killed your desire for it.

I have noted that whereas Pluto, the planet usually associated with death and transformation, never just destroys without leaving something better behind, Neptune eliminates what is no longer needed, but gives you no replacement. It assumes you no longer need the crutch of your erroneous belief. When it is done, in one stroke Neptune has taught you to let go of a part of yourself you no longer need and has made you a master of that part as well.

On a more positive note, Neptune's escapist qualities lend themselves very nicely to the various arts. Neptune enhances imagination and gives appreciation for the arts and artistic and musical ability. Neptune is often very active in the charts of creative writers and is especially strong in the chart of anyone in the field of drama and acting, whether they are behind the scenes or in front. Neptune, in fact, rules photography, television, movies, and stage acting.

It is interesting how many actors have said that they only came into contact with certain hidden aspects of themselves after they had played a part that characterized that aspect. This is another one of Neptune's functions. Through our assumption of roles, we learn and develop aspects of ourselves we did not know we possessed. Neptune loves to lead us into those murky waters of the unconscious mind, so you will also see it very active in the charts of psychics, hypnotherapists, and psychologists.

Neptune does not just rule your daydreams; it has a lot to do with your nighttime dreaming as well. Neptune is associated with the process of initiation in which the veil to your unconscious mind becomes transparent, revealing to you all of the treasures of your innermost self.

The spiritual side of Neptune gives us an intuitive insight into a power higher than ourselves that we realize we can reach, not by looking outward but by exploring inward. It gives us an urge for union with the divine. For some, this urge is directed outward and they search eternally for their soul mate to supply that sense of completion that their intuition tells them is their destiny. But Neptune's true goal for you is never outer-directed. It seeks to lead you to yourself.

Needless to say, Neptune is also prominent in the charts of most spiritual leaders. It is wonderful for meditation, yoga, and any other form of spiritual development.

Neptune is said to be a higher octave planet to Venus, and is always active in the search for universal love.

Associate the following concepts with Neptune:

- Illusion
- Disillusionment
- Confusion
- Lying
- Concealment
- Drugs
- Escapism/fantasy
- Spiritual Development
- Addiction
- Soul mates
- Inner directed thought
- Drama/Arts
- Dreams
- Mastery of the self
- Meditation

The Twelfth House

The 12th house, like the 9th, derives its meanings primarily from the planet Jupiter, but also from Neptune.

The 12th house is a water house and is negative. It is also a cadent, or mutable house. So, Jupiter's effect here is quite different than in the 9th.

The 12ᵗʰ house has long been one of the most misunderstood houses in astrology, depicted by ancient astrologers as the house of your own undoing or prisons and institutions or secret enemies. If you, like me, have any planets in the 12ᵗʰ house that sounds pretty depressing.

However, modern astrologers are coming to better understand the 12ᵗʰ house, probably because of the acceptance of the study and practice of psychology during the last century. Up until the twentieth century, mankind was almost totally outer-directed. No wonder no one could understand the inner-directed 12ᵗʰ house.

Both Jupiter and Neptune direct their energies inwardly in this house. Because of that, the 12ᵗʰ house deals with your unconscious self. It is very active in the charts of psychics, psychologists, and anyone studying themselves, seeking to understand and develop themselves.

Since it is the house that rules the unconscious mind, it contains all the information and knowledge, the abilities and talents that you have acquired, both earlier in this current lifetime and in all of your previous lifetimes, if you only have the courage to tap it. Much of your psychic ability also is available only through this house, since it is your unconscious mind's link to your consciousness.

Some astrologers believe that the sign that appears on the 12ᵗʰ house cusp is actually the sign that you were in your last life. I prefer to look at this as being the sign that best displays the qualities you exhibited in your last life.

Since the 12ᵗʰ house deals with the unconscious mind, it, of course, also holds all of your most deeply buried fears and phobias. Herein lies the root of the negative associations with this house.

If you do not face and admit your fears to yourself, then you must live them. The 12th house-6th house axis is the axis of the unconscious-conscious mind. So, in essence, whatever you try to repress and not face in the 12th house is only forced out through the opposite pole of the 6th house for you to see it and work through it. This is why the ancients called this the house of your own undoing.

I believe that it is always important to remember that every time any emotion is buried (remember, this is a water house), its equal but opposite emotion is also buried. So, if you bury, for example, the extreme anger you feel toward someone who has hurt you, you also bury the opposing ability to love intensely. Looking into your 12th house is always a little frightening because of all of the negative emotion you have buried there. But it is always worthwhile, with rich rewards, as the positive opposing emotion you have forgotten how to express becomes yours once again

It is usually easier for someone with an inner planet (Sun through Mars) to tap the elements of this house than someone with only outer planets (Saturn, Uranus, Pluto) or no planets here. People with Jupiter or Neptune, rulers of the house here, are probably most comfortable with their unconscious selves, enjoying time alone and naturally searching within for answers to their outer dilemmas.

People with any planets in the 12th will always be forced by their life circumstances to take the time to delve into their own unconscious motivations and actions, whether or not they find it comfortable to do so.

Associate the following concepts with the 12th house:

- Your unconscious mind
- Your buried fears
- Unconscious abilities/talents
- Past life therapy/recall
- Psychology
- Psychic prediction
- Dreams and dream therapy
- Unconscious motivation

Pisces

Polarity

Pisces is a negative, receptive sign. Like all of the negative signs, Pisces is female dominated in childhood and is receptive and reactive in nature. This, the last of all of the signs, is also the most receptive of all of them.

Quadruplicity

Pisces is the fourth and last of the mutable signs. The mutable quality of this sign combines with the negative polarity to make Pisces the most receptive sign of the zodiac. That is, Pisces tend to absorb the environment they are in and the people they are around, almost like a sponge absorbs water. This quality does not always endear them to others because when Pisces are in their absorbing mode, they can have a very draining effect on those around them.

On the other hand, it makes Pisces naturally the most intuitive and psychic sign of the zodiac; Pisceans know what you are feeling and what you are up to because they actually became you for a few moments! This tendency to absorb people and environments is frightening to many Pisces, who cannot control the phenomenon and, therefore, feel like they are on a continual roller coaster ride of feeling and sensation. These Pisces often run away from the world, viewing it with fear and suspicion. They would benefit greatly from lessons in psychic development that include means of self-defense.

Triplicity

Pisces is the third and last of the water signs, following behind Cancer and Scorpio.

In Pisces, the water element is fully developed, making Pisces the most intuitive of all of the signs, as well as the sign in which the unconscious mind is closest to the surface.

Pisces are intensely creative. Their abilities may be in drawing, painting, music, or any other art form.

Although Pisces may have good minds, their tendency is to learn through feeling. Whereas most other signs learn by some form of logic, Pisces do not use logic at all. They combine their negative, mutable, water characteristics to absorb what they are learning and then simply do it.

It is always fun to teach astrology to Pisceans. The other signs read, memorize, and apply their knowledge to learn. Pisces get inside the planet, sign, or house they are learning about and feel it. Once they have absorbed knowledge of it, they simply bring it on to the next bit of information they absorb. They make surprisingly good astrologers—just don't ever ask them to explain where they get their information from.

Their water quality also combines with the negative-mutable character to make them the zodiac's only true empath—that is, they absorb other people's emotional states so completely that they actually experience them in the same way the person does. When Pisces say, I know what you are feeling, they really mean it!

This tendency makes Pisces so acutely aware of other people's hurts that they feel the need to fix them . . . all of them. It is for this reason that we so often find Pisceans in the medical, psychiatric, or even legal fields. Yet, if Pisces do not learn to keep their empathy on a tight leash, it can get them into major trouble. Many Pisces experience continual ungovernable mood swings as a result of their empathy. These make better patients than doctors. Many Pisces become so overwhelmed by the need to help so many people that they totally withdraw into themselves, driven by guilt and fear.

The Sign Pisces

Pisceans, like all of the negative signs, are born into families where the mother or some other strong female has the principle impact on their early development. Unless the Pisces children have positive Moon signs or ascendants, Dad usually has a very limited impact upon them.

Like Scorpios, Pisces are often unwanted children; or sometimes, even if they are wanted, they are made to feel that they are a terrible burden upon their mother. Either way, Pisces develop the same deep-seated guilt that you first saw demonstrated in Scorpios, a deep-seated guilt rooted in the feeling that in some way they have caused harm to the parent by being born.

Perhaps this is why so many Pisces actually have trouble being born. It is not uncommon for long labors or other delivery-related problems to accompany Pisces' births. It is as if Pisces stand with a foot in both worlds, looking forward to their life here on earth and having second thoughts about it.

When we reviewed the sign Scorpio, we saw a second stage of development wherein the parents recognized their impact on the children and attempted to correct it, resulting in the children feeling that there was an attempt being made to buy them. That second stage let Scorpios off the guilt hook and it enabled them to develop defensive feelings.

But Pisceans never get the second stage. If they were unwanted before birth, Mom made no bones about it. She freely admitted it to the youngster and felt perfectly justified. If Mom is struggling financially and this extra mouth to feed is a burden, she makes sure her Pisces child knows about the situation, and how hard she has to work to take care of him. Pisces is painfully aware of all of his shortcomings and inadequacies.

Pisces' Mom is a strong woman and so Pisceans copy her. Mom is often a martyr, lending her considerable strength to those she sees as taking advantage of her. Pisces copies this, too.

Sometimes Pisces' Mom uses her own illness or weakness to control and manipulate those around her. Pisceans may be victimized by this control ploy but learn to use it themselves as well. They learn that sometimes the greatest strength is in weakness.

Pisceans commonly have very painful childhoods, filled with feelings of inadequacy, fear, and loneliness. Unlike most other signs, Pisces usually have excellent recall of even very early childhood memories, unless those memories were deliberately blocked due to some trauma. Somehow, Pisceans feel guilty about being born, guilty about being a burden on Mom and the family, guilty about everything.

Pisces find themselves constantly watching the other people in their environment to make sure everything is going smoothly for them. As soon as something does go wrong, they are sure it is their fault. Pisces are almost ready to take the blame for things that have not even gone wrong yet. But even negative things always have their positive side; all of this watching and observing helps Pisces to develop that empathy I discussed earlier.

These constant feelings of obligation and guilt also make Pisces live in fear of being blamed. For some Pisces, it is terribly important to have a scapegoat lined up, just in case.

Pisceans are so busy trying to make up for everything (both imagined and real) that they usually take on heavy responsibilities at an early age and often go to work early as well. It is not unusual to see a young Pisces taking care of a Mother or Grandmother who is an invalid or a brood of sisters and brothers.

Since Pisces is the last sign of the zodiac, Pisces seem to have characteristics that comprise all of the other signs of the zodiac. And depending on the individual, any one could predominate. So, some Pisces are intellectual, some emotional, some idealistic, and some materialistic. But there is one quality they all have in common: They all need to be needed.

Pisceans seem to be drawn to needy individuals like flies are to honey. Unfortunately, they are not often discriminating about whom they choose to help. This sign, more than any other, becomes involved in all kinds of abusive situations in which they are used, until they learn to discriminate. And unfortunately, as long as they are unconsciously motivated by their own guilt, they cannot be discriminating.

I often see Pisces involved in relationships with Virgoan type individuals who force them to put the brakes on and give with discrimination. But when Pisces do not have Virgo-types around them to put those brakes on, their lesson is very hard, long and painful.

In fact, often it is obvious that Pisces place themselves in those abusive situations in order to work through those guilt feelings, to pay off some imagined debt. For the Pisces at this stage in their development, the world is indeed a fearful place. Pisces is the most fearful sign in the zodiac.

However they go about it, they cannot demonstrate the more evolved Piscean type until they have risen above their tendency toward guilt and obligation and begin to reach out to others without fear and with discrimination.

The Pisces Woman

The Pisces woman is all female. She is soft, sensuous, feminine, and very comfortable with her femininity.

She sees everything in life from an emotional viewpoint and bases all of her major life decisions upon her emotional and intuitive feelings. She has the same tendency as Scorpio to obsess about feelings and emotions. She is a strong woman, but as a Pisces, she has the strength of the willow—the ability to bend and twist and be so flexible that you don't realize the strength is there.

Sometimes she is manipulative. When Pisces chooses to manipulate, it is usually through her dependency on you. Somehow, you will feel obligated to take care of her and to fulfill her needs.

Born guilty herself, she is a master at developing those same feelings in others. It is not uncommon to see Pisces lingering in a marriage where all feelings have ended years ago because both partners feel obligated to take care of the other one.

Because of her combination of Jupiter-Neptune rulership and her mutability, she can be almost any woman required in any situation. This is probably one of the reasons people of both sexes find her so attractive.

Her extreme flexibility makes her a boon in any job situation. The Pisces woman can do well in almost all jobs, but she will derive the greatest satisfaction from a service-oriented job where she is able to help people, yet is able to maintain enough professional distance that she does not become involved in their problems.

I am always happier to see the Pisces woman fulfilling her need to be needed by getting paid for it, rather than by letting her family and friends use or abuse her. When the Pisces woman is in an abusive family situation, she can become an extreme drain on all of her friends and other relatives. Her guilt will keep her in the situation while she continues to draw on the strength of everyone else to deal with it. The Pisces woman, in this situation, needs long-term psychiatric counseling to help her.

Pisceans usually have children, and when they do, the bond between mother and child, especially the first, is usually very strong. Pisces needs to be careful that this bond does not become an unhealthy one because it is so easy for her to emotionally pass on those feelings of guilt, obligation, martyrdom, and mutual need to the child.

However, she does make a very good mother, being almost psychically in tune with her children. She is always there for them when they need her.

The Pisces Man

Being a man in a negative, mutable, water sign is not an easy task. Like most men in a negative sign, the Pisces man is somewhat uncomfortable with his masculinity.

There is a soft and gentle, very intuitive, and creative side to the Pisces man that is wonderful to see, yet many Pisces men never allow this side of themselves to be seen by others.

Remembering that Pisces was a boy raised by a strong woman who used her weakness to manipulate and create guilt, you can see both where he gets his gentle strength and why he is loathe to let anyone in to see his sensitivity.

The Pisces man loves to be around women but is terribly afraid that they will control him, as his mother did. So, he develops a hard shell around that softness. He seeks out women who need him and are dependent upon him. This gives him the upper hand; he has the control and they cannot leave him.

Often the Pisces man distances himself from his mother because he fears her control over him. If he is married, he sometimes places his wife between himself and his mother, using her as a sort of protective shield.

He often creates distance between himself and his wife, too, fearful that the emotional ties between them will undermine him. He can be a very lonely man. Too often the Piscesman fears real intimacy. He often is a very sexual person, yet here he is sometimes using his desire for physical intimacy to compensate for the emotional closeness he both fears and desires.

Pisces is the sign most often involved in addictions, and the Piscean man is more commonly the addict than the Piscean woman (who is more often the enabler). But these roles reverse as well. Pisces can be addicted to anything—sex, cigarettes, nail biting, alcohol, drugs, work, and so on. The list is endless.

As with his female counterpart, he must work through his patterns of guilt to be free emotionally. In his case, since his role model was either weak or non-existent, he might also have to overcome some fairly major inferiority complexes, too. Like her, until he overcomes these patterns, he will continually place himself in untenable situations wherein he gets used. Also like her, he might use illness, both real and imagined, to gain control and attention. Sometimes you have to think twice before asking a Piscean how they feel.

However, when he finally does overcome these patterns, he emerges a very solid, stable, loving, and gentle individual who knows his own limitations and is comfortable with them.

He does well in any career, but we see him perhaps most often in medicine or dentistry. He loves to work with his hands, too, so he is often found in construction or in the arts.

He is often afraid of parenting, but if he does have children he will be a good father, taking his parenting role very seriously. His idea of Dad's role is somewhat traditional and his emotional ties to his children will be very strong indeed.

Associate the following qualities with Pisces:

- Emotional
- Guilty
- Fearful
- Empathic
- Artistic
- Intuitive
- Flexible
- Martyrdom
- Spiritual

End of Chapter Exercise

1. Be familiar with the Sun sign qualities of Aquarius and Pisces.

2. Review the qualities to associate with Jupiter.

3. Know the general qualities to associate with Uranus and Neptune.

4. Know the meanings of the 11th house and the 12th house.

5. Referring back to the chapter as much as you need to, continue your analysis of the chart we are working on by adding in the new signs, planets, and houses you have learned about in this chapter. Answering the following questions will help guide you through your analysis:

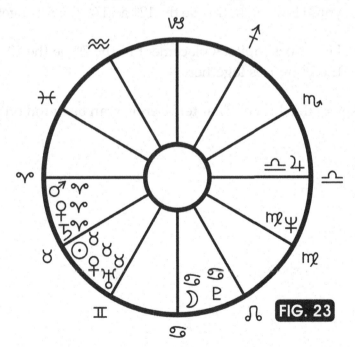

a) What does Aquarius on the 11th house cusp mean? How will this person relate to friends? What kind of hopes and dreams might he have? How will he get help from others? How will he give love to others?

b) What does Pisces on the 12th house mean? Will this person have many past life or unconscious fears or problems to deal with? What can you say about his intuitive ability and creativity?

c) Uranus, ruler of the 11th house and Aquarius, is in the 2nd house in Taurus. What does this placement signify to you? How might this tie the 11th house and the 2nd house together?

d) Neptune, ruler of the 12th house and Pisces, is in the 6th house in Virgo. What does this placement signify to you? How might this tie the 12th and 6th houses together?

e) How does Jupiter's placement in the 7th tie the 12th and the 7th houses together?

The key to this End of Chapter Exercise can be found on page 319.

Conclusion

You have just spent an extensive amount of time and energy learning the language of astrology. As with any language, initially it feels alien and somewhat difficult to grasp. But as you develop the tools, recognize the symbols, and begin to understand the concepts, the elements of the language fall into place.

For me, astrology is the primary language I use in my understanding of people. Anyone who has spent much time around me has gradually learned the language by osmosis. I think in terms of the language of astrology, and I communicate through that language, though I translate it into ordinary American English for the layperson.

Understanding astrology and thinking in astrological terms has helped me throughout my life to better understand people, to better counsel them, and to always see the big picture instead of the little, personal, selfish one that normal language causes us to focus on. Astrology is a Universal Language. And you now have the skill to communicate in that language.

So, where do you go from here? Well, some of you will continue to study the material in this book for some time. You will apply it to your understanding of friends and family members and of your relationships with them, and to how all of those factors affect all of your lives. If your study of astrology only takes you that far, that is still a wonderful use of my book, and I applaud you.

Some of you who are more technically minded are already geared up to learn about how to manually cast a natal astrology chart and how to locate and understand the various planetary aspects in it. You are ready to jump into a deeper evaluation of the chart and are already jumping ahead looking for the tools to do so. I also applaud all of you, because this is where your lifelong study of astrology really begins. You have been bitten by the astrology bug, just as I was.

To those of you who want to move forward with your studies, I recommend my *Intermediate Astrology* book to you. A warning—it is technical. You will need to be able to add and subtract to cast a natal astrology chart. But if you are willing to apply the effort, those efforts will be richly rewarded. Even in today's world where most astrologers (me included) use computers to cast their charts, it is a good idea to at least understand the process when it is done manually because casting a chart or two really gets you in touch with just what an astrology chart is, and ultimately will give more depth to your readings. Also, in that book you will learn how to find and read planetary aspects and other important points, and how to divide a chart and weigh all of the data to get a real feel for the person you are reading so you can take your reading to the next level of expertise. Presently, *Intermediate Astrology* is available through www.theastrologicalinstitute.com in its original spiral bound version.

Those of you who want to continue your study of astrology with my work should also check out *Astrology for Yourself Levels 1 and 2* currently available on my website, www.sandyanastasi. com, in MP3 and on CD. These two audio courses give you an amazing method of working with astrology straight from the ephemeris, with no charts at all involved (Honestly, not even a solar chart!). *Astrology for Yourself Level 1* will show you how to quickly find and interpret the aspects on a person's birthday, so that you can have deep insight into their personality and their relationships to their family members and friends, as well as how they will perform at work, what kind of career would be best for them, and more.

Astrology for Yourself Level 2 shows you how to identify and interpret transiting aspects so that you will be able to tell the person what is coming up in their life next, and will even give them some positive hints as to how to best deal with those events. Many of my students over the years, including the well-known John Edward who has so graciously written the forward to this current volume, have developed an excellent working knowledge of astrology just from working with the material in those two courses.

And, of course, for those of you who enjoy constant mental stimulation (like me), I have more than fifteen other astrology courses and lectures available on MP3 and CD on my website and the Astrological Institute website. Make yourself happy. Keep studying!

I am including a list of recommended reading for you. These few books are my absolute favorites for folks at your level of expertise.

One thing you will definitely need at this point is what I call a cookbook. That is an astrology book that lists the basic meanings of each planet in each house and each sign. There are many available by many different authors, so you can choose one that suits you. I have listed several in my recommended reading list. When I was first learning astrology, I spent hours working with cookbooks, comparing what they said, writing down all of the information on my own chart and charts for my friends and family. I learn and remember best by writing. If you learn that way, too, I suggest writing out your chart interpretations using a cookbook as a guide.

One of my favorite things to do is to visit new age bookstores or new age sections in main-line bookstores when I travel. I love to browse the astrology books. I often pull one off the shelf and open it to any page and start reading. If that book is for me, the passage my eye falls on will talk to me in that moment. I have an extensive astrological library and that is the way I have been led to most of my books.

There are literally thousands of astrology books in print. I once helped my good friend Mary Alice Warren, former owner of Planet Earth Book Center in Florida (and a wonderful Tarot reader and astrologer in her own right), to run a book fair for an astrological conference hosted by the (National Council of Geocosmic Research (NCGR) chapter of Orlando, Florida. She covered more than twenty conference-sized tables with astrology books. That was when I began to become aware of just how big the field of astrology is, and how widely studied.

You will note that above I mentioned the NCGR. In the United States the NCGR has chapters in just about every state, and there may be one near you. The NCGR and the American Federation of Astrologers (AFA) are wonderful membership supported organizations that periodically host some wonderful speakers and sometimes coordinate and/or host full multi-day conferences.

I attended several conferences hosted by the AFA and have loved every one of them. Expect hundreds of people at these events. It is not unusual for the AFA to host a conference that lasts for a week and on the weekend has fourteen lectures by world-renowned astrologers going on at the same time—with four or five sessions for each conference room planned per day.

I hope you are beginning to see the scope of just how big astrology is! Welcome to a bright new field with unlimited potential for personal growth, and the tools to reach out and help others!

Suggested Reading

Now that you have the basics, you'll want to build on what you know. What's your next step? Practice, of course! Do as many solar charts for as many people as you can. You don't have to be an expert yet—that will come with practice.

Apply what you know now. Read everything in the field of astrology that attracts you. Continue to study and expand your knowledge and continue to apply what you learn. You will find that you learn astrology best by doing it.

Here are some of my favorite books suitable for beginners, as well as being just plain good reading for anyone:

- *Astrology, Psychology and the Four Elements* by Stephan Arroyo
- *The Astrologers Handbook* by Sakoian and Acker
- *The Planets Through the Houses* by Robert Hand
- *Complete Astrology* by Alan Oken
- *Soul-Centered Astrology* by Alan Oken
- *The 12th House* by Karen Hammacher-Zondag
- *Saturn, a New Look at an Old Devil* by Liz Greene and Robert Hand
- *Pluto* by Jeff Green
- *New A-Z Horoscope Maker and Delineator* by Llewellyn George
- *Exploring Jupiter* by Stephan Arroyo
- *Linda Goodman's Sun Signs* by Linda Goodman
- *Astrology of Fate* by Liz Greene

- *Astrology Bible* by Judy Hall

- *Rulership Book* by Rex Bills

- *Karma and Your Sun Sign* by Joan Kilgen and Laura Glasberg

If you do not already have one, you will want to purchase an ephemeris. An ephemeris is a book that lists the sign and degree that each planet was at for each day of a year, a decade, or even a century, depending on what ephemeris you look at. There are many different ephemerides on the market, so deciding what to buy can be difficult.

I really do not have any favorite author, but I do suggest that you get one for the entire twentieth and twenty-first centuries, since many of the people whose birthdays you will want to look up were born in the 1920's, 30's, 40's and so on up to the present. Also, I recommend that you get an ephemeris calculated for midnight, because if you decide to use my *Intermediate Astrology* book, to learn natal chart construction that book uses a midnight ephemeris.

Becoming an Astrologer

Most states in the U.S. do not require licensing of astrologers, but you should check with your local government to be sure, if you plan on becoming a professional astrologer.

There are no particular requirements, at present, regulating the practice of astrology in the United States, but there are several nation wide organizations that give the field unity. Most well known among these are the AFA and the NCGR. The AFA offers their own certification classes and examination. I also created an entire series of recorded classes that constitute a complete program in astrology, currently available through www.astrologicalinstitute.com or on my own website, www.sandyanastasi.com.

Glossary Terms

Air—Signs that are intellectual and deep thinking in nature.

Angular—Refers to the first, fourth, seventh, and tenth houses. These houses are the most action-oriented houses. They correspond to the cardinal signs of the zodiac.

Aquarius—Third of the air signs. Fixed in nature. Symbol is the Water Bearer.

Aries—First of the fire signs. Cardinal in nature. Symbol is the Ram.

Ascendant—The sign on the horizon at dawn on the day you are born. An actual chart for day, month, and year must be constructed to find your Ascendant. Also known as the Rising Sign.

Ascendant-descendant line—This is the horizontal line across the birth/natal chart starting on the left side of the chart at the cusp of the first house/Ascendant and going straight across to the seventh house/Descendant. Spiritual Astrologers think of this as the line of the physical plane the soul crosses on its way into matter.

Aspect(s)—The relationship or geometric angle between each planet in your chart to the others. These explain how the planets will act in your chart relative to one another.

Astrology—The science of reading the planets and stars to understand human psychology and predict life events.

Birth Chart—See Natal Chart.

Cadent—Refers to the 3rd, 6th, 9th, and 12th houses. These houses are involved in change and transition. They correspond to the Mutable Signs of the zodiac.

Campanus System—A mathematically derived system of dividing the heavens into houses using the ecliptic.

Cancer—First of the water signs. Cardinal in nature. Symbol is the Crab.

Capricorn—Third of the earth signs. Cardinal in nature. Symbol is the Mountain Goat.

Cardinal—Signs that are self-starters.

Chinese Zodiac—A form of astrology that is based on the 13-month cycles of the Moon.

Cusp—The dividing line between houses where one house ends and the next begins. The cusp belongs to the new house.

Earth—Signs that are practical and good with the things of the material world.

Earth-plane—The material plane that we are all living on. Symbolized in the birth chart by the horizontal line between the Ascendant and the Descendant.

Eighth House—My Partner's Resources; key word: *theirs.*

Elective Astrology—A form of astrology employed to select the best date to do something.

Elements—Earth, Air, Fire, Water.

Eleventh House—Key word: *My Friends*

Ephemeris—A book that shows the location of the Sun, Moon, and planets for each day. Most encompass 100-year periods.

Equal House System—A system of dividing the Heavens into twelve equal segments of thirty degrees each. Usually, the calculated Ascendant or the degree and sign of the Sun, as in this book, are placed on the Ascendant.

Esoteric Astrology—A form of Spiritual astrology.

Fifth House—Key word: *My Creations*

Fire—Signs that are physically active and idealistic.

First House—Key word: *I AM*

Fixed—Signs that are rigid, determined, and unchanging.

Fourth House—Key Word: *My Home*

Gemini—First of the air signs. Mutable in nature. Symbol is the Twins.

Generative—All of the masculine or positive-polarity signs are considered generative or projective signs. These are Aries, Gemini, Leo, Libra, Sagittarius, and Aquarius.

Geocentric Astrology—Puts the Earth at the center. It is used for natal charts and predicting events for people here on Earth.

Hindu Astrology—A system of astrology widely used in India that is highly predictive and uses a different zodiac than we use in the West.

Horary Astrology—A form of astrology used to find things or answer specific questions.

House(s)—The astrology chart is divided into twelve pie-shaped pieces called Houses. Each House represents a different area of life. Houses are mathematically derived and man-made.

IC—Inum Coeli. See Nadir.

Impersonal or *WE* Signs—The second four signs of the zodiac: Leo, Virgo, Libra, and Scorpio. They see life from the point of view of the group to which they see themselves a part of.

Intellectual or Mental Quadrant—The third quadrant contains the 7th, 8th, and 9th houses. It is a highly social and mentally interactive quadrant.

Koch System—A mathematically derived system of dividing the heavens into houses similar to the Placidus system. Uses the surface of the Earth in its equations.

Leo—Second of the fire signs. Fixed in nature. Symbol is the Lion.

Libra—Second of the air signs. Cardinal in nature. Symbol is the Scales.

Line of the Midheaven-Nadir—This is the vertical line beginning at the IC/Nadir/4th house cusp and travelling straight up the middle of the natal chart to the Midheaven/MC/10th house cusp. Spiritual Astrologers see this as the path your soul is on as it enters life, crosses the Ascendant-Descendant line of matter, and evolves toward the tenth house/Midheaven.

MC—Medium Coeli. See Midheaven.

Midheaven—The cusp of the 10th house is otherwise known as the MC.

Modes—Cardinal, Fixed, Mutable.

Mutable—Signs that are constantly changing themselves and the things around them.

Nadir—The cusp of the fourth house sometimes known as the IC or Nadir.

Natal chart—A pie-shaped chart created for the exact time, date, and place of birth.

Natural Zodiac—The Natural Zodiac places zero degrees of Aries on the ascendant, and each sign follows in succession around the chart. So, Taurus is 30 degrees, Gemini is 60 degrees, Cancer is 90 degrees, Leo is 120 degrees, Virgo 150 degrees, Libra 180 degrees, Scorpio 210 degrees, Sagittarius 240 degrees, Capricorn 270 degrees, Aquarius 300 degrees, and Pisces 330 degrees. Of course, in actual use, it is usual to just put 0 degrees of each sign on its cusp and it is understood that it is the corresponding degree in the natural zodiac.

Ninth House—Key Words: Other People's Thoughts and Other People's Communication

Nodes or Nodes of the Moon—There are two Nodes of the Moon. Only the North Node is listed in the Ephemeris; the South Node is placed in the chart directly opposite it by sign and house. The North Node is said to be where you are growing and evolving and the South Node is where you have come from in past lives.

Personal or *ME* Signs—The first four signs of the zodiac, Aries, Taurus, Gemini, and Cancer. They see life from their own personal point of view.

303

Personal planets—These are the planets closest to the Sun. They include Mercury, Venus, Mars, Earth, Moon, and Jupiter. Jupiter is sometimes considered personal and sometimes as an outer planet.

Physical quadrant—The first quadrant contains the 1ˢᵗ, 2ⁿᵈ, and 3ʳᵈ houses and deals with the physical self and the world you create for yourself physically and materially.

Placidus System—A mathematically derived system of dividing the heavens into houses that uses the center of the Earth for its equations. This is the most common House System used in Western Astrology.

Power Signs—There are three power signs: Taurus, Scorpio, and Capricorn. All are drawn to power and often rise to positions in which they wield it.

Precession of the Equinoxes—Just as the Earth moves around the Sun, the Sun and our Solar System move around a Central Sun. One of our months would be equal to the 2,500 years it takes our Solar System to move through one of these cosmic months. The Precession of the Equinoxes (i.e., the movement of our Solar System from the Age of Pisces to the Age of Aquarius) is nothing more than our Solar System moving from one cosmic month to the next. Note that the Precession of the Equinoxes moves backward through the zodiac.

Predictive Astrology—Any form of astrology that is used to project events.

Progressions—The very slow movement of the planets in your birth chart as they evolve over the course of your life. These are used to gain insight into developing personality, growing and changing relationships, and to give more depth to predictions.

Quadrants—Each quadrant deals with a different aspect of self. One of the ancient ways of dividing the chart to be read was by quadrant.

Quadruplicity—Refers to the modes. There are four signs in each of the three different Modes of behavior. For example, there are four Cardinal Signs—Aries, Cancer, Libra, and Capricorn; four Fixed Signs—Taurus, Leo, Scorpio, and Aquarius; and four Mutable Signs—Gemini, Virgo, Sagittarius, and Pisces.

Receptive—All of the feminine or negative-polarity signs are considered receptive. These are Taurus, Cancer, Virgo, Scorpio, Capricorn, and Pisces.

Relationship Astrology—The art of comparing the charts of two or more people to explore the positive and negative issues in a relationship.

Rising Sign—See Ascendant.

Sagittarius—Third of the fire signs. Mutable in nature. Symbol is the Archer.

Scorpio—Second of the water signs. Fixed in nature. Symbol is the Scorpio.

Second House—Key Word: *Mine*

Seventh House—Key Word: *My Mate or Partner*

Sidereal Astrology—Puts the Sun at the center. It is usually used to predict cosmic events.

Sixth House—Key Words: *My Health and My Daily Life*

Solar Arc Progressions—Progressions based upon the 1-degree yearly movement of the Sun and other planets, and frequently used in predictive astrology.

Solar Chart—A chart used when the time and/or place of birth is unknown. Used throughout this book as it is a quick and easy way to cast a chart with no math necessary and the only tool needed is an Ephemeris.

Spiritual Astrology—The birth chart is looked at from the point of view of spiritual evolution.

Spiritual Quadrant—The fourth quadrant contains the 10th, 11th, and 12th houses. Planets in these houses are in search of something greater than themselves.

Star Chart—See Natal Chart.

Star Map—See Natal Chart.

Succedent—Refers to the 2nd, 5th, 8th, and 11th houses. These houses are stable and focused. They correspond to the Fixed Signs of the zodiac.

Sun signs—The sign the Sun was passing through on the day you were born is called your Sun sign.

Taurus—First of the earth signs. Fixed in nature. Symbol is the Bull.

Tenth House—Key Word: *My Career.*

Theoretical or *THEM* Signs—The last four signs of the zodiac: Sagittarius, Capricorn, Aquarius, and Pisces. They see life from an objective point of view, placing themselves outside of both their own circumstances and those of the group.

Third House—Key Words: *I Think and I Communicate*

Transits—Where the planets and stars are right now in the heavens. Often these are used for predictions.

Triplicity—Refers to the elements. For example, there are three fire signs in the Fire Triplicity, three air signs in the Air Triplicity, three earth signs in the Earth Triplicity and three water signs in the Water Triplicity.

Twelfth House—Key Word: *My Unconscious*

Virgo—Second of the earth signs. Mutable in nature. Symbol is the Virgin.

Vital quadrant—The second quadrant contains the 4th, 5th and 6th houses and is referred to as the Emotional Quadrant in this book, as so much of your vital energy comes from it.

Water—Signs that are emotional and highly intuitive.

Western Astrology—The form of astrology most commonly used in the Western World, including the U.S. It is based on the Solar cycle.

End of Chapter Exercise Review Key

Chapter 3: End of Chapter Exercise Review

Aries and Taurus

What follows is my analysis of the chart we looked at in our end of chapter exercise. Read it through and compare your own analysis to it. If your analysis differs here and there, that is fine. It probably shows that you're thinking. But if it differs a very much, you should re-read the chapter to make sure you understand it.

a) Since his sun is in Taurus, things and money are likely to be very important to him. In fact, he will identify with them since Taurus is an earth sign. Taurus is also a fixed sign, so he will tend toward stubbornness and tenacity, but he will be good at following through on things. Taurus' negative polarity ensures that his mother had a very strong influence on him; he will enjoy the companionship of women more than men. He probably has a nice voice, since Taurus rules the throat, and he will have a gentle solidness that makes you feel secure with him.

b) Since his Sun is in the 2nd house and Venus rules both the 2nd house and Taurus, this intensifies the action of his Taurus Sun. It's almost like saying the Sun is in Taurus twice. It emphasizes his attachment to things and it is good for his natural talents, which he probably has plenty of. Making money will be important to him and he will probably be good at it, too! He will either be very talented, very materialistic, or both.

c) With Aries on his ascendant, he is going to come across to the world with a bang. He will be assertive, aggressive, and dynamic. And since he is really not an Aries, but rather a Taurus, he may often find himself wondering just why he did volunteer for that project or make that offer without thinking first. His Taurus sun is definitely not going to be very comfortable acting like an Aries whenever he meets someone, or begins something new.

d) Mars is action oriented, energizing, and aggressive.

e) Mars in Aries so near the ascendant energizes it, makes its action even more dynamic. I am beginning to think this fellow might come on so strong when he meets people that he will turn them right off. He will be sexually aggressive, competitive, and compulsive.

f) Mars in his 1st house affects him much the way it being so close to the ascendant does. If it was deeper in the house, further away from the ascendant, it would exhibit the same characteristics but they would not be so obvious.

With his Aries rising, and his Mars in the 1st house and in Aries, too, we also know that Dad was important in this particular Taurus's early life, too, not just Mom. You see, he was encouraged as a child to aggressively pursue whatever he wanted in a manly fashion. But underneath this very Arian exterior, remember we still have a Taurus.

g) Venus' position in the 1st house, in Aries will have the affect of softening the action of Mars. It will take his aggressiveness and give it a cultured edge; it will help him to be a bit of a diplomat in his dealings with others. It will be a big help to him.

h) Venus in Aries in the 1st house will make him nice to look at, pleasant to be around, but also somewhat selfish; that is, he will tend to see things so much from his own point of view that he may never know that yours exists at all. This self-oriented point of view may cause him to take action (Mars) to put himself in the forefront at every opportunity.

A great deal more could be said about each of the above but at this point we will keep it simple. As you gain experience you will have more and more to say, and your ideas will be uniquely your own, based upon the concepts you are learning here. This is what makes astrology such a personal science.

Chapter 4: End of Chapter Exercise Review

Gemini and Cancer

The following is a review of the chart analysis you have just completed. Once again, if your analysis doesn't match this exactly, that is fine. Astrology is a personal science, and as such, every astrologer has a slightly different approach. However, if your analysis was entirely different, I suggest you re-read the chapter before going on.

The following answers are to question 6, a) thru e).

a) The 3rd house deals with thought processes, communication, beginning education, short-distance travel, learning ability, socialization, teaching ability, and siblings. Gemini is very mental, quick moving and thinking, talkative, and flexible. All of these qualities blend very well together and will make the subject of our chart a quick student with an active and curious mind who communicates freely, especially with brothers and sisters. He will be a quick mover, fond of around-town jaunts. He might make a good teacher, if he can stick to it.

b) With Cancer on his Nadir, the nurturing parent was almost assuredly his mother. He comes into life with well-developed Cancerian traits, such as the ability to nurture, and sensitivity to the needs of others.

c) Cancer is on his Nadir, but it also is the sign all through the 4th house. This indicates an early home life that was perhaps somewhat underprivileged—financial security may have been minimal. Certainly it was an emotional childhood, producing insecurities connected to home and family that will persist into adulthood. In adulthood, his home will be very important to him. He will create a nest that is cozy, warm, and safe. It will be a place where he can receive and give the nurturance he craves.

d) Since the Moon rules both Cancer and the 4th house, its placement here intensifies the action of the sign and the house. Home is going to be very, very important to him. His mother will also be very, very important to him. If he marries, his wife may have competition in the form of his mother. If not, he may simply relate to his wife as his mother. One thing is certain: He will always have the need for an emotional attachment to a female in his home. At some time in his adult life, his mother may live with him. At the end of life, it is likely that he will receive care from a female who is a mother figure.

e) In Taurus, the planet Mercury is on solid ground. Mercury in Taurus seeks to give form (Taurus) to thought (Mercury). It does so slowly, methodically, and thoroughly, leaving no stone unturned. Mercury in Taurus in the 2nd house brings natural talent in the form of thinking skills and communication. He may be able to earn his living in the communications field, including anything from sales to computer technician. Since one of the ideas we associate the 2nd house with is self-concept, his self-concept will be strongly routed in his ability to communicate.

Chapter 5: End of Chapter Exercise Review

Leo and Virgo

The following is a brief review of the chart analysis you have just completed. Use it as a guide to check your own analysis against. If yours differs significantly, re-read the chapter before going on.

The following answers are to question 3, a) thru e).

a) With Leo on the 5th house, he will deal with 5th house affairs (his childhood, his oldest child and attitude toward raising children, creativity, gambling, recreation, and romance) in a Leo sort of way. That is, he will approach all of these areas with pride, devotion, and idealism, and will generally follow the traditions of his family and culture. He will have high expectations of his oldest child and may approach his romantic involvements with a Prince Charming flair.

b) The 5th house, as noted above, rules his childhood, his oldest child, and attitude toward raising children, creativity, gambling, recreation, and romance. The 2nd rules earning ability, things you like, natural talent and ability, self-concept, and attitude and values concerning money and things. When the ruler of the 5th (the Sun) appears in the 2nd, it bridges the two houses, causing them to work together. In this case, he may have been an unusually talented child or he may have children of his own, especially his oldest, who are very talented and whom he has high expectations of. He may be able to earn his living or make money by gambling or through fun and recreational things. He may have a natural talent for drama. He may base his self-concept on his romantic entanglements or on his children's successes. His earning ability and his creativity will be closely intertwined.

c) Virgo on the 6th house tells us that he will deal with the affairs of the 6th house in a Virgo fashion. That means that he will be an extremist about health matters—either fastidious or lackadaisical. The 6th house rules everyday life—he will either be a whiz at handling all of those everyday issues or he will be totally bogged down in them. He will either be a slob or a neat nick, or both at different times. He may be a workaholic or he may shun work. He will shine in service-oriented activities since the 6th house rules service, and so does Virgo.

You should by now have realized, that when the sign that naturally corresponds to the house appears on its cusp, it strengthens the qualities of both the sign and the house.

d) The 6th house rules everyday life, matters of health, work, service, and pets. The 2nd, rules earning ability, natural talents, self-concept, and attitudes and values toward things and money. The bridge created by Mercury (ruler of the 6th) being located in the 2nd, assists these two houses in working together. He may earn his living in a health or service field. He may, in fact, have natural healing abilities. These two houses, remember, are both earth houses, which further enhances their ability to work well together. He should be quite good at earning a respectable income. And perhaps the fixed quality of the 2nd house will even help him to keep some of his extremist tendencies in check

e) Mercury's primary focus is communication and mentalism. It will affect the Sun by speeding up the usual slow and methodical Taurean way of thinking, and may even contribute some natural talents involving communication skills.

When considering the above interrelationship between the 2nd house and the 5th, the 2nd house and the 6th, and the Sun and Mercury, you could easily establish this gentleman as a salesman of health care or related products, as a school teacher, or even as an actor!

Chapter 6: End of Chapter Exercise Review

Libra and Scorpio

The following is a brief review of the chart analysis you have just completed. Use it as a guide to check your own analysis against. If yours differs very much, re-read the chapter before going on.

The following answers are to question 5, a) thru g):

a) With Libra on the 7th house cusp, relationships will be very important to this person. He will behave like a Libra in his relationships—that is, he will go out of his way to satisfy all of his partner's needs almost before the partner even knows she's got them, even neglecting his own needs in the process. But he will be resentful of his partner if, as is likely, the partner takes him for granted and does not do the same in return. He will probably marry a person who also relates like a Libra— that is, she will be social, mental, a good mediator, and, like him, try to fulfill all of his needs, but neglect her own. In this relationship, if neither person is self-responsible, a lot of resentment can build up. If neither person lets the other know what their needs really are, they are in big trouble because the road to you-know-where is paved with assumptions.

b) Venus, ruler of the 7th, is in the 1st, thereby tying together these two houses. This insures that relationships will be a focus in this man's life. Since his Venus in the 1st makes him rather self-concerned, he is likely to have trouble perceiving the real needs of anyone else beside himself, even though his

Libra on the 7th makes him think that he puts everyone else first. And indeed, he does go out of his way to do for you and give to you exactly what he knows you need. Never mind that you did not ask for it, do not want it, and it is really something he wants so much he just knew you would love it, too.

Since Venus rules women in general, and it is in his 1st house, he expects his wife to put him first, and stand behind him in everything he does. But remember that Venus in the first has an Arian quality, so she is likely to be a go-getter herself, and may even compete with him. Sounds like a fun relationship, doesn't it?

c) Scorpio on the 8th house gives the 8th house a sort of double dose of Scorpio energy. Therefore all of the affairs of the 8th house will be enhanced and magnified.

d) Mars, ruler of Scorpio, is in the 1st. This placement ties together the 1st and the 8th houses. Since the 1st house, the *I Am* house, is the way you reach out to the world, this will bring his 8th house (as well as his 7th through Venus) to the forefront in the way he deals with the world outside of himself. He may present himself as a businessman and a wheeler-dealer. Or he may come across in a very secretive manner. Since the 8th house rules sex, he may use his sexuality as a controlling force, a power-tool. But the idealism of the Aries 1st house will help him to overcome obstacles in his personal growth and transformation.

e) With Pluto in his 4th house, in Cancer, we can expect him to be obsessive and controlling in his home, and especially to be involved in power struggles with his mother. On the other hand, both his mother and his home situation will ultimately lead him toward the transformation (Pluto) of his own emotional insecurities (Cancer).

f) With Pluto in the same sign and house as the Moon, we can expect an intensification of the emotional (Moon) side of Pluto's obsessive-manipulative behavior. Both his mother and any woman he is closely associated with at home can be the focus of this need to manipulate women. His mother probably was very manipulative and controlling. At home, he may be moody and behave in a very Scorpioic (because of Pluto's natural co-rulership of Scorpio) manner, but the world outside of the home will never see this side of him.

g) Pluto being in the 4th but co-ruler of the 8th ties these two houses together. He may use sex to control his mate, or vice-versa. He might do a lot of financial work at home. He might be receiving money in a will from his mother. He might be very interested in occult or metaphysical things but will only pursue these within the privacy of his own home. In tying together these two houses, we end up with all of the affairs of the 8th house being done at home.

Chapter 7: End of Chapter Exercise Review

Sagittarius and Capricorn

The following is a brief review of the chart analysis you have just completed. Use it as a guide to check your own analysis against. If yours differs significantly, re-read the chapter before going on.

The following answers are to question 5, a) thru f):

a) Sagittarius on the 9th house shows this person will be an idealist in his philosophical and religious outlook. His view on these things will probably be traditional, since they are idealized forms.

b) Jupiter in the 7th house in Libra expands the things of this house. This person will attract a good partner. The mate may be overweight or big in some way, or have money, or have connections to other cultures, religions, and ways of thinking. This mate will be a person who encourages friendship in the relationship, as well as generosity. Other relationships also will be healthy and fruitful ones with this Jupiter placement. This person themselves might be gregarious and friendly and form close one-on-one partnerships easily.

c) Jupiter is in the 7th house, but rules the 9th house. This will combine the affairs of the two houses. This person will seek honesty and have high ideals in his relationships and in dealing with others, especially in marriage. Religion and philosophy may be an important unifying factor in marriage, and this person might either take classes with their mate or enjoy doing some long-distance traveling with them.

d) Capricorn on the Midheaven tells us that this person has very high career aspirations, and wants the world to view them with respect and to see them as highly successful and responsible. He will want to be at the top of his profession. The 10th house with Capricorn in it says that he wants a career that will generate respect for his achievements. He will do best in a career that puts him in a position of authority and prominence, and one that requires slow and steady effort.

e) Saturn, ruler of the 10th house in the natural zodiac, is in the 1st house in this chart. This draws the 1st and 10th houses together. Both of these houses deal with how the world sees us. From this, you can easily see how important it will be for this person to achieve his career recognition. Saturn's placement in the 1st will probably help him in this endeavor, generating, as it does, an aura of authority that will aid in his upwardly mobile career path.

f) Saturn in the 1st house causes this person trouble, even though it may aid his career aspirations. Saturn is not comfortable in the 1st house because the 1st house has an initiatory energy, moving us quickly into things; Saturn's energy progresses slowly and cautiously. Saturn, in the young person's astrology chart, shows what he tends to approach with fear and what his weak points are. This person will be fearful of new beginnings of all kinds. The Aries ascendant is an intellectual achiever, yet Saturn in Aries undermines this person's confidence in his ability to achieve. Capricorn, which Saturn rules, being on the Midheaven heightens this dilemma. It will make him fearful of attaining the success he so desires, until later in life when he has overcome some of Saturn's lessons, making his weakness his strength. Saturn also indicates the way this person's father related to him as a child. Saturn in the 1st house shows restriction of his ability to reach out to the world, so we know that sometime during the childhood years, his father undermined his ego by rejecting or restricting the personality and capabilities indicated by the other planets in the 1st house.

Chapter 8: End of Chapter Exercise

Aquarius and Pisces

The following is a review of the chart analysis you have just completed. Once again, if your analysis doesn't match this exactly, that's fine. But if there is a major difference between your analysis and mine, I suggest you review the chapter once again.

The following answers are the question 5, a) thru e).

a) Aquarius on the 11th is strong due to the natural correspondence of the 11th house and Aquarius. This person will have many friends, many of them of an unusual nature. His friends will come from all walks of life. He will relate to his friends in a very intellectual manner. This person's hopes and dreams will be rather impersonal, possibly universal in scope, as with the sign Aquarius. He will be so gregarious and have so many different types of friends that some friends will tend to be there with what is needed when any need arises. The best way he knows to give his love is by accepting others as they are.

b) Pisces on the 12th house again is strong due to the fact that Pisces is on the 12th in the natural zodiac. This person will have many unconscious habit patterns and unconscious fears, both from past lives and this one. As there are no planets in this house, these fears and unconscious patterns of behavior may not be dealt with easily and some problems may be caused by them. This person will be highly intuitive and creative and will have an active dream life.

c) Uranus, ruler of the 11th house and Aquarius, is in the 2nd house in Taurus. Uranus is not comfortable in Taurus, since Taurus is fixed, orthodox, and materialistic, while Uranus' true nature is unusual and changeable. However, Mercury also is in Taurus. As Uranus is the higher octave of Mercury, this placement will enhance the communication ability of this individual. He might be capable of receiving higher abstract thought and translating it into form. He might be an artist or musician and also might do very well with computers or in the communications field. Uranus' placement in the 2nd house ties the 2nd house to the 11th. In practice, this means he would work well with friends, that business dealings and money-making schemes might involve friends and organizations he belongs to, and that he might develop his natural talents through his friends.

d) Neptune, ruler of the 12th house and Pisces, is in the 6th house in Virgo. Neptune is not comfortable in the sign opposing the one it naturally rules. Here Neptune, the planet of both inspiration and delusion, is subjected to the critical analysis of Virgo. Those Neptunian dreams will be earthed and there will be very few delusions, also. However, Neptune in the 6th house could cause an unrealistic attitude toward employment, or the employment could be in an imaginative and creative area. Neptune here might make this person unrealistic about health matters or cause him to be attracted to spiritualist healing. Since Neptune's natural rulership is the 12th, this automatically ties the 12th house to the 6th. This causes this person's unconscious 12th-house patterns to appear quite readily in his 6th house of everyday life. He will either be very psychic or very troubled. Also, any issues he is suppressing could erupt quickly into health problems.

e) Jupiter's placement in the 7th house also ties the 12th house to the 7th house because Jupiter naturally rules the 12th. This could create a very strong unconscious link between this person and his mate. He might share dreams or they may know one another's thoughts easily. This person might also see his mate acting out his or her own unconscious patterns.